(EXTRA)ORDINARY

365

ORDINARY
MOMENTS
WITH AN

Anything but Ordinary

GOD

BY STEPHEN INGRAM

Published by: YM360

**(Extra)Ordinary: 365 Ordinary Moments
With An Anything But Ordinary God**

STOP!

This awesome little (OK, big) book works differently than any book you've ever seen. Before you start reading this book, make sure you turn the page to read what makes it so unique.

HOW TO USE

WHAT MAKES THIS BOOK SO DIFFERENT?

What makes this book so different? And how to do you use it? Great questions . . . Here's what makes *(Extra)Ordinary* unlike any other year-long devotional book you might have seen.

(Extra)Ordinary isn't a book that starts at the beginning and ends at the end.

You don't begin reading with Day 1 and end with Day 365. This book is one that you read according to how you feel, or what's going on in your life. That's right. It's a book that is as unique as you are. Let's take a closer look at how this works.

(Extra)Ordinary has three sections. And each section is for you to engage with depending on what's going on with your life.

SECTION 1: ORDINARY TIMES
There are a little over 100 daily devotions in the Ordinary Times section. These are devotions you can pick up and read when life is feeling, well, ordinary. You'll notice each one of the Ordinary Times devotions has an image associated with the title. That's because this is kind of how Jesus taught, using simple, everyday images to make powerful points about your faith.

SECTION 2: CRAZY TIMES
The devotions in the Crazy Times section are organized by themes. And these themes are all about stuff you're dealing with in your life. Is life feeling awesome? Then you may want to turn to the FLOOD section and spend a few days reading those devotions. Life beating you up a bit? Spend a few days with God in the WEARY section. Crazy Times are devotions tailored for how you feel.

SECTION 3: HOLIDAY TIMES
Merry Christmas! Happy Easter! Happy Birthday! (That's right. There's even a devotion for your birthday. We think you're that cool.) The devotions in the Holiday section are for, well, holidays. Want to do 40 days of devotions for Lent? We got you covered. Need an Earth Day, or St. Patty's Day devotion? You'll find them in the Holiday section.

Now do you see why this book is unlike any other?

This truly is a book that adapts to your life. Why make such a book? Because it's already hard enough to make time to meet God in the pages of the Bible. *(Extra)Ordinary* is all about helping pave the way for you to engage with God in meaningful times of prayer and worship. So take advantage of it. Don't miss the opportunity to make a daily time of hanging out with God part of your life.

NOW THAT YOU KNOW WHAT A KILLER BOOK IT IS THAT YOU'VE GOT IN YOUR HANDS, DON'T JUST SIT THERE. TURN THE PAGE AND PICK OUT A DEVOTION!

TABLE OF CONTENTS:
ORDINARY TIMES

TABLE OF CONTENTS:
CRAZY TIMES

Sometimes you feel like you're on top of the world. The "Mountain" devotions are for those times. Other times, nothing seems to go right. The "Valley" devotions will help you make it through these times.

Are you inspired by social compassion and giving of yourself to meet other's needs? The "Giving" section of devotions is perfect for you. Ever thought about what it means to be someone who "receives" well? If not, take some time to check out the "Taking" section of devotions. You'll love what you find.

Jesus came so that you could live a full life here on earth. The "Life" devotions will help you go deeper into what this means. The "Death" devotions are for those times when you, like all of us, lose someone you love.

What do you do when it feels like God is just showering you with awesome goodness? You read the devotionals in the "Flood" section, that's what. And in those times where it seems like God is far away from you? Spend a few days in the "Desert" section to find that you're not alone.

Feel like you have it all figured out? Spend 10 days in "Confident" learning how spiritual disciplines can help show you the depths of loving God. Feel lost? Like this whole faith thing is a mystery? Then "Confused" will give you the practices you need to begin growing closer to Christ.

GAIN / LOSS

Sometimes you win. Especially when you come to know Jesus. The "Gain" devotions will help you understand what you actually gain by following Jesus. The "Loss" devotions help you know how Jesus calls you to deal with those times in life when you lose.

GROWING / WEARY

Are you at a point in your faith where you want to push yourself some more? Then spend some time in the "Growing" section of devotions. There are also times in our faith where we are just tired. It happens. If this is where you are, check out the "Weary" section of devotions.

EXCITED / ANXIOUS

Ever feel like your faith needs a little boost of excitement? Then spending 10 days in the "Excitement" section is just the thing. Worried about life? Nervous about something coming up? Take some time to focus on the devotions in the "Anxious" section and meditate on God's faithfulness.

BUSY

Most days are busy. But some days are super busy. Out of time but still want to check in with God? Choose one of these 20 one-word devotions to interact with.

TABLE OF CONTENTS:
HOLIDAY TIMES

ORDINARY TIMES

Ordinary Times are devotions designed for your average, ordinary day. There is no order to go in. Each devotion has a one-word title and an image to go along with it. This is because Jesus used a similar method of teaching. He'd use simple, everyday objects (think mustard seeds, fig trees, salt, and so on) to drive home powerful spiritual truths. Not only do these devotions pattern themselves after the style of Jesus' teachings, they help you focus on one thought, one image, as you go through your day.

Here's how to get started: Simply thumb through the section until an image jumps out at you. Then, read the passage and the devotion. And then respond to the "Go and Do" section. It's that simple.

Enjoy your "ordinary times" with an extraordinary God.

ANCHOR

> *Proverbs 1:5* <

Let the wise listen and add to their learning, and let
the discerning get guidance

You've probably heard the phrase "you should be anchored in your faith" before. You may have heard it in a sermon, Bible study or at youth group. This is a great statement on how we should always trust in God and believe that the faith that God is calling us to is right and true. But there's a problem with this statement, though, or at least a problem with how people interpret it. A lot of times people think of being anchored in their faith as having a rigid faith that does not change and cannot be moved. When we do this we step into a very dangerous place.

Whenever we commit ourselves to this understanding we're saying two things. The first thing we're saying is that the things we know and understand at this time and place are the pinnacle of our knowledge and that we can't learn any more. The second thing we assume is that the things we know in this time and place are all correct. These are two pretty big assumptions to make and can be pretty dangerous.

Throughout Scripture the Bible warns against being prideful in what we think we know and to always be open to learning more and having our ideas and convictions change. Some will say that when our convictions change we don't have enough faith or that we're compromising. The truth is that we have faith, it's just not in our own scope of knowledge. We're essentially saying that yes, we can and hope to learn more than what we know now. My hope is that you'll be anchored in God and let God continually grow and challenge you and your faith for the rest of your life.

Go and Do
This isn't something you can just do today or tomorrow, but hopefully for the rest of your life. I want you to enter into every conversation about faith with an open mind. I want you to seek out God and God's truth and only that. We can learn from everyone. Listen to other's views and ideas and give them real thought. But seek after that which is true. God is all truth, and when I seek Him I believe I will find God. I hope that you'll do the same.

APPLE

> Genesis 3:2-5 <

The woman said to the serpent. "We may eat fruit from the trees in the garden.
but God did say. 'You must not eat fruit from the tree that is in the middle of
the garden. and you must not touch it. or you will die.'" "You will not surely die."
the serpent said to the woman. "For God knows that when you eat of it your
eyes will be opened. and you will be like God. knowing good and evil."

Isn't it amazing how the things we can't have are so often the things we want?
You tell a child to not touch a cord and the first thing they do when you turn
your back is sprint for the nearest corded item in sight! We're the same. You're
the same. I am too. It's crazy how we obsess over those things that we shouldn't
or can't have. Why is that?

I think it goes back to two things. First, we think that the thing we shouldn't have
is mysterious and must be awesome (or else why would people not want us to
have it). Second, most of us don't do a good job telling ourselves no. We want
what we want when we want it, especially if we're not supposed to have it!

Here's the thing, the reason why some things are off limits is because we can't
handle or should not have to handle the consequences that those things bring.
Take the fruit in the Garden for example. God wanted Adam and Eve to live in
a world where they didn't have to worry about what's wrong and what's right.
God wanted them to live where their entire focus was on God. Then they ate.
Their eyes were opened and life became a lot more complicated, for all of us!

The moral of the story is this. There are just some things in life that we either
need to wait on or not do at all. There are also people in your life who want to
help us know which fruit to try and which to leave alone. Find these people (parents are usually a good place to start) and listen, learn, and don't bite off more
than you can chew!

Go and Do
Make a list of those people who will help you look out for the rotten apples in life.

BEACH

> Job 6:2-3 <

"If only my anguish could be weighed and all my misery be placed on the scales! It would surely outweigh the sand of the seas—no wonder my words have been impetuous.

I love the beach. I bet you do too. The breeze, the ocean and all of the billions of grains of sand that sift through your toes as you walk barefoot beside the water. The beach is usually a happy place, a place for vacations, youth trips, and getaways of all sorts. For a guy named Job it reminded him of something far more depressing.

Job had a good life, family, friends, wealth, possessions, and power. Then in a blink of an eye, it was all gone. At one point in chapter 6 he says that if all of his troubles were put on a scale, they would weigh more than all of the sand in the sea. Wow. That is an incredible statement. I bet you have felt like that at some points in your life. I know I have.

I actually found this verse just after my parents divorced, my mom left, I broke my leg, had ankle surgery, had a lung collapse, and watched my girlfriend break up with me! That all happened in just a few months. Needless to say, I was feeling a little Job-like. The amazing thing about the Book of Job is not that all of the bad things happened to him, but that through all of that he remained faithful to God. Through it all he did not blame God, he simply tried to draw closer to him and hold on tightly in the storm. So if you're feeling buried, and like your pain and pressure are weighing down on you in colossal proportions, take heart, lean into God, and know that you're not alone.

Go and Do
One of the best ways to process difficult times is to write out what you're feeling in a journal or note-taking app. Today, take some time and begin a journal. It could be an everyday journal or simply a journal that you use when you're in high and low points in your life. Use these journal entries as prayers and letters to God.

BELL

> *Isaiah 30:21* <

Whether you turn to the right or to the left, your ears will hear a voice behind you, saying, "This is the way; walk in it."

Bells create different emotions in most teenagers, right? It's crazy how the exact same bell can mean you're late for class, going to gym, starting a period with your worst teacher (or your best), and even releases you to go on Summer break! When we're in school, bells mark transitions in our lives. They mark the time during the day when we're supposed to move from one part of our day to the next. And yet, there are times in our lives where bells would be really helpful in letting us know that it's time to move from one thing to the next.

Wouldn't be nice if a bell went off every time we needed to stop hanging out with a friend who is making bad choices, or really commit to a relationship that is in its early stages? Wouldn't it be great if a bell started ringing when we visited the college that is right for us, or when it was time to break up with that boy-friend or girlfriend? As you get older it would be even more helpful, like when to ask someone to marry you, take a new job, move, buy a new car, and even when to start having kids. The tough part is that there are not audible bells that go off to mark transitions.

We have to depend on some less concrete markers like our heads, our hearts, prayers, Scripture and the advice of trusted friends and adults. Listen closely to these bells in your life and together they will help you know when it's time for a change.

Go and Do

It's important to always be in a mode where we're listening for God and making good decisions (this is called discernment) about our lives. One way to make decisions is to take a sheet of paper, turn it sideways, and make five columns marked Head, Heart, Prayers, Scripture, and Friends/Mentors. Then take the decision you have to make and write what each one of those is telling you.

BENCH

>*Matthew 11:28-30*<

Come to me, all you who are weary and burdened, and I will give you rest. Take my yoke upon you and learn from me, for I am gentle and humble in heart, and you will find rest for your souls. For my yoke is easy and my burden is light.

Central Park in New York City is an amazing place. There are always thousands of people running, exercising, playing softball, walking, throwing Frisbee, boating, playing kickball . . . basically if you can name a game or activity it's probably being done in Central Park at any given moment. Your local parks are the same way; maybe not as big but they are places that are meant for action and activity.

Parks also have another component: park benches. Park benches are one of the often-overlooked elements in parks. They are overlooked because you think about going to a park to do something, to be active. But benches are for sitting. They are for taking a breather and seeing the world around you from a different perspective. They are for rest. Too often life is like a park: it is full of people running around, going from one activity to the next without ever stopping. But rest is important.

Recall, God rested. Jesus rested. And so should we. I'm not talking about the "sleeping until lunch" kind of resting. I'm talking about sitting back from all of the action going on around you and breathing, resting, and gaining a different perspective on all that's going on around you. Resting is important because it's something we need and are called to do. Jesus said "come to me and I will give you rest." Find a bench in your life, sit back, breathe and rest.

Go and Do
When do you intentionally rest? Do you have a time each week where you disconnect from your technology? Where do you rest? Is it the same place each week? Figure out a time and a place that is restful for you. Make an appointment on your phone or calendar, set a reminder, and follow through with grabbing some rest this week.

BIRD

>𝓜𝓪𝓽𝓽𝓱𝓮𝔀 6:26<

Look at the birds of the air; they do not sow or reap or store away in barns, and yet your heavenly Father feeds them. Are you not much more valuable than they?

I sit early in the mornings, usually writing, at my kitchen table. As the sun begins to come up they begin flying in. There are blue birds, finches of all sorts, sparrows, pigeons, and cardinals. They come and eat the bird food from one of the feeders that hang on my back deck. I love watching them fly around. I'm thankful for their company in those early hours of the morning.

These birds remind me of Jesus' teaching in the Sermon on the Mount. He uses the image of birds to teach us about not worrying. Jesus explained to the disciples (and us) that God loves those little birds and loves them so much that He takes care of them. Jesus tells us that if God loves them enough to take care of them and for them to not worry, then how much more does God love us and how much less we should worry. This is easy to read, but can be much more difficult to put into practice at school, home, before a big game, on a date, and so on. But when you're tempted to become anxious, think about the birds that gather on my back porch.

God chooses to provide for those little guys through me. Could God provide and take care of all of by Himself? Sure. But the beauty of the gospel is that God chooses to provide for us, many times, through each other. As people of faith we belong to a community of other believers who are called from the beginning to be about the business of taking care of others. Do the birds go hungry? Not the ones in my neighborhood. How about in yours?

Go and Do
Being a part of God's work of taking care of others is a holy and life giving act that, as Christ-followers, we are called to again and again in Scripture. Take a moment and picture those people, things, and places in your world that need taken care of or looked out for. Then as you are envisioning them, ask God to help you know how you can make the lives of those people and things better. Write these down and begin your days by praying for the items on your list each morning.

BLANKET

> *Psalm 73:28* <

But as for me, it is good to be near God. I have made the Sovereign LORD my refuge;
I will tell of all your deeds.

Do you have a blanket? I mean a real blanket. Not something you just bought at the store a year or two ago but an old, worn down, beat up blanket. I do and I have had it since I was born. My great grandmother made it for me and it's been one of the few constants in my life ever since. I used it as a little boy, as a teenager, through college, and we still use it now in my family with my kids today! There's just something about those types of blankets; when you cover up in them you feel pure warmth wrap its arms around you and everything is just perfect.

John Wesley, a minister and founder of the Methodist church felt God in this very same way as he was listening to someone talk about the change that God works in our heart through faith. Wesley said: "I felt my heart strangely warmed." There is something so special when we are strangely warmed by the love and presence of our God.

The psalmist tells us that it's good to be near God, and that God is his refuge. The word refuge literally means a place to take safe cover from storms and danger. So many times in our lives we feel lost, confused, angry, and scared as life storms around us. It's in these moments where we have the opportunity to let God wrap us up in God's love. Surrounding us with His good and unending love, God warms us, protects us, and gives us shelter from the storm.

Go and Do
The next time you find yourself in the midst of hard times, I want to encourage you to find something that brings you great comfort. Maybe it's a blanket or a favorite pair of pajama pants. Whatever it is, wrap yourself up in them and picture the warm loving arms of God holding you close and safe from whatever is happening outside. Remember that God is your refuge and your shelter in the storm.

BOAT

> *Matthew 14:28-29* <

"Lord. if it's you." Peter replied. "tell me to come to you on the water." "Come." he said. Then Peter got down out of the boat. walked on the water and came toward Jesus.

There's this old quote that says, "A boat in port is safe, but that is not what boats were built for." Imagine what the disciples must have felt. The seas were high. The lightning highlighted the whitecaps as they crested over the edges of the boat. The disciples were all alone. In the distance, a shadow, a figure, began to emerge. At first they were scared. Then they recognized that it was Jesus, walking to them on the water.

OK. Time out. This is amazing! Can you even imagine what that would be like, to actually see a person walk on water? I'm not sure about you but I would've just sat and watched, mouth wide open, eyes fixed, and mind racing. But that's not what Peter chose to do. He wanted to be more than an onlooker; he wanted to live, to be fully alive, to walk closely with Jesus even if that meant walking on water. So, instead of staying in the safety of the boat, he called out to Jesus and Jesus responded with the simple invitation: "come."

We are not meant to sit around as bystanders of faith, in the comfort and safety of our boats. We are built to walk closely with our Lord and participate in the miracles of His ministry then and now. Our life with Jesus calls us to adventures, to pushing the boundaries, and to doing things we never thought possible. Want to feed the world? Step out of the boat. Want to help the sick? Step out of the boat. Want to live a passionate, love filled, life full of wonder that makes a difference in the world? Step out of the boat.

Go and Do
Tomorrow go and talk with your youth minister about some ways you can step out of the boat in your church, city, and school. God gives us passions and gifts and when we match those passions and gifts with helping the world in Jesus' name, incredible things can happen. So how can your interests and passions match up with the Kingdom of God? Let the adventure begin!

BOOK

>1 Timothy 4:12<

Don't let anyone look down on you because you are young, but set an example
for the believers in speech, in life, in love, in faith and in purity.

Have you ever heard the saying, "You can't judge a book by its cover"? Yeah, it's not true. Think about it, you can and do judge books by their covers all of the time! It's just like people are judged often by what they say and how they act. The deal is that the cover is a part of the book, but it's not the only part.

Our lives are like books. We have our covers--what comes across about us on the outside. We also have the pages--the content of our lives. Our stories are on the inside and the things we do that no one else sees or knows about. Both are important.

So, what do people read about your life based on your cover? Do your outside actions, your speech and life give a good glimpse of the story that's happening on the inside? The content is also just as important! Have you ever picked up a book because the cover looked so awesome and once you got into the actual story you were really disappointed? When people see you talk and act like Christ-followers on the outside but then, when they get closer and start to read the pages of your life, find something all together different, it's terribly disappointing. It can also make them shy away from others whose covers look similar. Let your life be such that people are not only attracted to Jesus, but when they dig deeply into your pages, they see a story that's better than they could have ever imagined!

Go and Do

Today take each of the ways we are supposed to be an example Speech, Conduct, Love, Faith and Purity and use them to examine your life. Ask yourself, "do I live in such a way in each of these categories so that my 'pages' reflect the cover that people see?" Take a piece of paper and make five columns, one of the words at the top of each. Then write, under each, how you are an example to others in you faith. Then below those, write those pieces of each category that you need continue to work on. Work on making your life's book one that everyone wants to read!

BREAD

> *Matthew 26:26* <

While they were eating. Jesus took bread. gave thanks and broke it. and gave it to his disciples. saying. "Take and eat: this is my body."

Most Christians will agree with each other that God is everywhere, though I'm not sure we really think about the amazing consequences of that belief. When we think this it's not that we believe that God is just in churchy, holy-feeling things, but that we're also saying He is also in the most mundane and normal things as well. Throughout Jesus' entire ministry we see Him going around taking the most simple and common things and people and helping us see God through them. Simple things like fishermen, seeds, birds, and of course, one of the most common elements of the first century life, bread.

When we look at all of these stories we cannot help but think that Jesus wants us to always be looking for God through the normal things in our lives. It might not be fishermen and seeds for us today, but God's Word continues to teach us about who God is and how we should live. It might be a sunset, a tree or a bench in a park, but God is still telling His story today through these simple and common things.

When we are aware of this we get to open our eyes, walk, and think about it a totally different way. We get to go through our days looking for God everywhere, learning, being inspired, and ultimately following Jesus more closely because everywhere we look we are reminded that God is with us.

Go and Do
God is always teaching us something about His Kingdom through our everyday lives. Today, look for one thing in the world around you that reminds you of God in some way. Take a picture of it on your phone and make it your screen saver. Let it remind you that God is always looking to draw us closer to Him.

BREATH

> Genesis 2:7 <

The LORD God formed the man from the dust of the ground and breathed into his nostrils the breath of life, and the man became a living being.

I love this image. We were inanimate, lifeless, a lump of mud, then . . . God breathed life into us. It's pretty awesome that people can go 40+ days without food and four days without water, but only four minutes without air before we die.

Every time you take a breath it's an involuntary action. You do it without thinking. It's the thing that keeps you alive, thinking, walking, and functioning. Every time a new breath of air comes through your nostrils it's both a remembrance of your own mortality and an act of defiance of that mortality. Every time you draw in a breath of air your body is saying to the world that you'll live for another moment. Every time you draw in a breath you are also saying that this is something you depend on; without it you will cease to exist. Every time you breathe it's an admission that you can't do this on your own.

God gave us this tension to live in. We have the most amazing abilities to do so much, but we're still completely dependent on this one simple thing: breathing. Something that we think so little about means so very much to us all. How many other things in our lives do we take for granted? How many other things do we do each day and never realize their importance? God breathed life into us at creation and continues to breathe life into us today. Take a moment to breathe in deeply and thank God for this gift.

Go and Do
Stop what you're doing. Take a deep breath. Exhale slowly. Now another. Deep. Exhale. Deep breathing, especially during times of stress can be so very helpful. When we breathe shallow breaths, we deprive our brain of oxygen and that can hinder our ability to think, and usually compounds the problem that we're facing. Next time you're stressed, slow down, breathe, and thank God for the gift of life.

BRICK

> *Jude 1:21-22* <

Keep yourselves in God's love as you wait for the mercy of our Lord Jesus Christ to bring you to eternal life. Be merciful to those who doubt.

Bricks have been around forever. From some of the earliest known civilizations men and women have been making bricks. Some were hewn from rock. Others were made with clay and straw. Bricks have been used to make one-room dwellings all the way to the greatest of human structures, like the pyramids of Giza.

I saw a brick the other day and it was all by itself. It was being used to prop open a door between two rooms. It was a brick that was used in the original construction of the house and was a left over. As I passed by it, I thought just how different its use is as opposed to how other bricks were being used in the house. It is a lot like humans. By ourselves we can do good things and be very good and useful in our world. However, when we join together for a greater purpose and commit to working together we can achieve great and amazing things.

Just as the bricks that make up a house don't work alone, we too are called to work together and build off of one another for the good of our world. Unlike bricks, we're not all uniform, fitting perfectly together. This means we have to work harder, each of us figuring out our individual roles in the greater scheme of life. Our calling as Christ-followers is to be graceful with others as they find their places and work through doubts and questions. Each person has a place. Each one of us has a role. And together we can build great and wonderful things in our world for our God.

Go and Do

Unlike bricks we're all unique. What are your unique qualities that you can add to what God is calling us to do in the world? What are the things that you've been given to help advance God's mission in the world? Take sometime and list some of the things that you love and are good at and then begin to think about how those things can be used to bring about God's goodness, grace, and love to those around you.

BRIDGE

> *Matthew 28:19* <

Therefore go and make disciples of all nations, baptizing them in the name of the Father and of the Son and of the Holy Spirit.

There is this bridge in New Orleans that I love. It's called the Lake Pontchartrain Causeway Bridge and it's the longest overwater bridge in the entire world! This bridge is 28 miles long and runs the entire length of Lake Pontchartrain. Bridges are such interesting and amazingly helpful pieces of our society. They help people get from one side of land to another over an otherwise impassable gap. As Christians we have the opportunity to be bridges as well.

Thousands of years ago, Jesus called us to be bridges. Jesus commanded us to be bridges for people all around the world, helping them become His followers. We get to be bridges because we're called to help people bridge the gap from their world to Jesus' world. In Jesus' final words in the Gospel of Matthew, He tells us to go into the entire world, and help lead others to become followers of Jesus' way. What we have to remember is that some bridges are very long like the Lake Pontchartrain Bridge, while others are relatively short. Some take a while to cross and others are fairly easy. Either way we're called to act as those connectors helping others come across to following the way and life of Jesus.

So how do we become bridges of faith? We bridge the gaps through service, love, telling the story of Jesus, knowing and following the way of Christ, seeking justice, and worshipping God with our lives. These actions and attitudes lead others closer to God.

Go and Do
This week go around your community or city and find the bridges that connect the places where you live. Notice the differences. Using your phone's camera, or another type of camera, take some artistic pictures of the bridges and print them out. Hang them in your room and use them as reminders to pray for those who you are intentionally trying to be a bridge to Jesus for.

CACTUS

> *Matthew 5:45b* <

He causes his sun to rise on the evil and the good, and sends rain on the righteous and the unrighteous.

Some days are going to be good, others, not so much. Life and even our spirituality are not constants. Sometimes there is abundance and other times there is drought. When I was a teenager, I would feel like God was very far from me in these desert times. I remember feeling like my faith was all dried up and I wondered at points whether God was still active in my life. A mentor once told me during one of these times that it's important to keep doing what you've been doing spiritually and to not worry, that God was still there. He told me that I just have to be prepared for times in my life like this. It was good advice then, and it's good advice now.

The cactus is always prepared for tough times. It has an incredible ability to live in some of the most arid places in the world. The cactus, during the dry times, knows what to do to conserve water and take advantage of the abundance of sun. It adapts itself to the dry times. We have to do the same. We have to know what things feed us and keep us going. We have to know not to forget them when things get difficult.

For everyone these habits are a little different. For some it's prayer practices and for others it's Scripture reading. For some they continue their faith in tough times through meditation and fasting. Even others work through these times through conversations with friends and mentors. Find your constants and flourish in the dry times!

Go and Do

There are tons of different spiritual practices that have grown the faith throughout the history of Christianity and the church. Most of us don't know the majority of these practices and are missing out on a wealth of ways to connect with God. There are a few books that are wonderful at explaining these practices and how they connect to your life today. This week order one of these books and begin exploring ways to sustain your faith in the dry places. "The Way of Life," "The Sacred Way" and "Celebration of Discipline."

CAMERA

>Genesis 12:7<

The LORD appeared to Abram and said. "To your offspring I will give this land." So he built an altar there to the LORD. who had appeared to him.

Some people are great at capturing moments. You know them: they're always the one at the parties, on trips, and when you're just hanging out, who get their phone out and get those awesome candid shots of people. They put them on social media and your night, party, youth group trip or whatever is immortalized by all who come across your Facebook or Instagram. I love those people, because they help me remember experiences in a way that last long after the event.

Cameras help us mark special moments in our lives. In the Old Testament they didn't have cameras so they did something a little different to mark special moments where they encountered God. In the Old Testament they would make altars when they would have an encounter with God. These altars would usually be a large pile of stones that were stacked and named for how God interacted with them in that time and place. They would usually leave these altars there and anyone who passed would be able to see the place where God had done something amazing in the life of the builder.

It's important to have markers in our lives, ways to remember the time and place when we have special experiences with God. These markers are like snapshots from a camera. They capture the moment and help remind us of that unique experience. How do you mark times in your life where God was most evident and doing incredible things? These markers are important as places of celebration, witness to what God has done, and reminders of a very real moment where God seemed very close. So, what snapshots or altars would you include from your life so far?

Go and Do
Begin collecting little mementoes of the times where God was most real in your life. Pick up a stone or something from the place you want to remember and carry it home. Take pictures or write about that moment. Whatever you do, begin to collect these small pieces of your spiritual history, keep them in a place where you can see them, and be reminded of the times and places where God came close.

CANVAS

> Genesis 2:19-20 <

Now the LORD God had formed out of the ground all the beasts of the field and all the birds of the air. He brought them to the man to see what he would name them; and whatever the man called each living creature, that was its name. So the man gave names to all the livestock, the birds of the air and all the beasts of the field. But for Adam no suitable helper was found.

My wife is an artist. It's incredible the stories she can tell and the places she can take you to with some simple colors and a blank canvas. She has the ability to imagine whole worlds and literally brush them into existence in just a few short hours. She has a gift, and it's incredible to watch her use it. Most people are not professional artists like my wife. Most of us have a difficult time imagining non-existent people and places, yet alone create them with such vivid detail, personality, and life. It's a unique skill.

One of the many names for God is the name Creator. When I hear that name I don't think of an old, white-bearded man sitting up in the cosmos speaking things into existence through out the vast nothingness. I think of an artist. I see God creating on an empty canvas all that we see around us. In Genesis 2 we see God doing something extraordinary, God calls Adam to be a co-creator. It's incredible to think that the great Creator wanted Adam, and in a way, us, to create alongside Him.

One of the most extraordinary tasks that God calls each of us to is to be co-creators of our own life and story. We have a blank canvas that we get to begin a co-created masterpiece on. Each of us come to the canvas with different tools and materials but each of us are called to, with God, create something that's worthy of the great Creator's name. We often look at life as something we do. How different your life would be if you began to understand yourself as an artist who was commissioned with co-creating your life's masterpiece. I bet things might get a little more colorful!

Go and Do
Art is an amazing tool in our spirituality. Over the next few days begin a search for a piece of art that describes where you are in your life and your spirituality.

CAR

>2 Samuel 11:2-4<

One evening David got up from his bed and walked around on the roof of the palace. From the roof he saw a woman bathing. The woman was very beautiful, and David sent someone to find out about her. The man said, "Isn't this Bathsheba, the daughter of Eliam and the wife of Uriah the Hittite?" Then David sent messengers to get her. She came to him, and he slept with her. (She had purified herself from her uncleanness.) Then she went back home.

Do you drive? If not I bet you will some day. There are few things teenagers look forward to more than getting their license. It's a big deal, as you know. For the first time in your life you have this incredible sense of independence. So many opportunities open up socially, as well as the freedom to make a lot more decisions on your own.

David was a man of great power. He was the king of a people and a strong nation. He could literally do anything he wanted. And sometimes, like in the verses above, he did. It's incredible just how quickly the story escalated isn't it? He went from not knowing her in verse 2 to sleeping with her in verse 4! The problem is that David had forgotten that the power he had was given to him, not to be abused, but to be used for the good of the world and to further God's message. David chose to abuse the great power and responsibility he had, and he and others paid for that choice dearly.

We each have great power. For some it's our words. For others it's our influence. When you turn 16 one of your main power sources is your ability to drive. The question is not whether you have the power, about how you will use it. I think it was best stated in Spiderman, "with great power comes great responsibility." How will you use the power that you've been given?

Go and Do
It would be easy to think that this devotion only applies to those who are driving or are about to drive a car. It's not. We each have varying degrees of power in our lives that we can choose to use for good or bad. Today think about the power each word carries in it and how strong each action really is. Each time you think of it ask yourself, "Am I using responsibly the power that I've been given"?

CATHEDRAL

> *Isaiah 6:1-3* <

In the year that King Uzziah died, I saw the Lord seated on a throne, high and exalted, and the train of his robe filled the temple. Above him were seraphs, each with six wings: With two wings they covered their faces, with two they covered their feet, and with two they were flying. And they were calling to one another: "Holy, holy, holy is the LORD Almighty: the whole earth is full of his glory."

One of my favorite things to do when I travel abroad is to visit cathedrals. I love the art, architecture, and history of the ancient places of worship. I love to study them, and to learn the stories they tell. But the real thrill comes when I walk into the main naive of the cathedral. When I step in, I'm usually overcome with a sense of awe. Between the amazing stained glass, the beautiful altar pieces, and the vaulted ceilings you feel like you've crossed over into another world.

Two of my favorite cathedrals are the Church of the Gesu' in Rome, Italy and Sainte-Chapelle in Paris, France. The Gesu' is especially unique in that its ceiling is painted so that it looks like you're looking up directly into the heavens. It really is amazing, primarily because when you're in these places you feel like you've stepped across a portal into a holy, God-infused place.

Most of us, including me, can't simply jump on a plane to Paris or Rome when we need to be in an inspirational place. Fortunately, I have other "cathedrals" closer to home that inspire the same amount of awe in my life. I love to go into the woods by waterfalls and rivers and stand underneath great trees and feel the awe of creation as they draw my gaze up into the heavens. I also love to find myself in valleys surrounded by great mountains. These things inspire worship in me. Where are your places of awe and worship?

Go and Do
Take a page in your journal and make a line straight down the middle. On the top of one side write "My Places of Awe" and on the second side write "The World's Places of Awe." In the first column list the places you can visit regularly or within a certain distance that inspire you and allow you to worship God. In the second column, begin a "bucket list" of places around the country or world that you hope to visit someday.

CHAIN

> *Acts 12:7* <

Suddenly an angel of the Lord appeared and a light shone in the cell. He struck Peter on the side and woke him up. "Quick, get up!" he said, and the chains fell off Peter's wrists.

The early church leaders, like Paul and Peter, were no strangers to chains. From the earliest days of the first church they found themselves locked away because of their faith. This something that, if you're in a country that has laws against religious persecution, you're not as familiar with. I would bet that most of you reading this devotion live in a place where you can practice your faith openly and free of any legal ramifications. And so while we're not in immediate danger of being locked up for our faith, most of us find ourselves in chains everyday. These are not chains you or others can see or feel but they exist nonetheless. These are chains that hold us back and cause us to not be able to live and do what all we're called to.

These chains look different for each of us. For some it's pride; they care more about being right than they care about learning from others. For others it's a sense of failure and loneliness that hangs around their necks. Even others find themselves weighed down by people's expectations, believing that they must be whatever it is that everyone else wants them to be. Have you ever felt similar chains? This is why I love this passage in the Book of Acts. Peter is imprisoned. He is bound and chained. Then, out of nowhere, an angel appears, tells him to get up, and the chains are gone!

God is calling you and me to get up! We have too much to do in this life to be bound by the chains that are holding us back. God does not want you to be chained up and kept from living as He made you to be. "Get up quickly" and watch your chains fall off!

Go and Do
Over the next day or two, have some conversations with close friends and mentors. Ask them what they think are your greatest strengths and weaknesses. Use these conversations to help you know what chains are holding you back as well as what strengths you can build upon.

CHAIR

>Proverbs 3:5-6<

Trust in the LORD with all your heart and lean not on your own understanding; in all your ways acknowledge him, and he will make your paths straight.

I will never forget when it happened. It was Christmas. We were at my grandparent's house. I was sitting down at the table next to my grandfather. Just as I began to lean back into the seat it happened. There was no warning, no cracking, no wobbling . . . just CRASH! The entire chair crumbled under me and I was laying on my back wondering if a bomb had just gone off! I was really embarrassed, stunned and a little sore for a few days. Up until that point I had always just sat down in chairs without another thought. A chair was always something I could depend on. I never assumed anything other than the fact that it would do what I trusted it to do. From that point until now, I am still uneasy.

There comes a point in most of our lives where we feel like we have a similar experience with God. We live our lives trusting God and never questioning His faithfulness. Then something happens. Someone dies. Parents get a divorce. A friend leaves. And the bottom completely falls out. We find ourselves on the floor wondering what in the world just happened and why God let it happen. What we have to remember is that God never promised us that it would be easy and that we wouldn't have struggles. Jesus actually told us that if we followed Him just the opposite would happen.

When life's struggles come, and they will, we have to remember that it was not God who let us down. It's just the nature of the life we live. We can lean on passages like the one in Proverbs 3. Lean into God, relax, and know that He can always be trusted.

Go and Do
This week spend some time reading the Book of Job. Notice how Job continued to trust God even when his friends and family told him to turn his back on God. Notice how Job responds to them with faith and trust in God.

CHURCH

>1 Corinthians 12:12-13<

The body is a unit. though it is made up of many parts; and though all its parts
are many. they form one body. So it is with Christ. For we were all baptized by
one Spirit into one body—whether Jews or Greeks. slave or free—and we were all
given the one Spirit to drink.

Do you go to church? If so what does it look like? What do other churches
around your town look like? Are they brick, wooden, tall, or short? Do they have
giant sanctuaries or small chapels? Do you have stone, carpet or wood on your
sanctuary floor? Does your church have video screens or a pipe organ? Do you
have stain glass windows or no windows at all? Are you a church that is in the city
or country? Or does your church look different than anything I have described
above? I love to visit churches all over the world. I've been in the largest church
in the world and I've been in some of the oldest chapels in the world. They are all
so different and yet they are all still the same. They are church buildings.

Church buildings aren't the only thing that comes in many different shapes, sizes, and colors. So are the people who actually make up the church. Just as there
are loads of different kinds of churches there are also loads of different kinds of
beliefs that make up the church. You have Baptists, Catholics, Methodists, Lu-
therans, UCC, Pentecostals, Presbyterians, Episcopalians, Quakers, and so many
more! These different denominations are all VERY different in many of their beliefs, but they all still make up the church. The church is also worldwide so there
are all different kinds of languages, cultures, skin colors, and traditions that add
to this great mixing pot called the church.

So when you think of church, don't just think about your church that sits on the
corner of that street in your town. Think about the wide variety of people, languages, beliefs, traditions, and places that make up Jesus' church!

Go and Do
This week, be aware of the different churches in your area. Look at their buildings. Then, pick some of these churches and add them to a prayer list, praying
for your brothers and sisters in Christ.

CLAY

>*Isaiah 64:8*<

Yet, O LORD, you are our Father. We are the clay, you are the potter; we are all the work of your hand.

Have you ever worked with clay? You may have molded it with your hand or maybe used a wheel to spin it into bowls and vases. Clay has been used for thousands of years to create beautiful art, as well as the tools and vessels that have given people all over the world the ability to live. In the hands of a master potter it can be made into almost anything.

There is a fairly common theme throughout the Bible where we are referred to as clay and God as the potter. This passage from Isaiah is a beautiful image of God working with us, taking who we are and molding us into beautiful pieces. If you've ever worked with clay, you know it can sometimes be a frustrating experience. When I do it I just can't seem to always get the clay to the beautiful creation that I imagine it to be. I keep working it and re-working it until it comes out into something that I'm proud of.

In our lives we are a lot like clay. We're often tough to work with and mold, even for God! But, God does not become fed up with us and throw us to the scrap pile. God continues to work and re-work us into something beautiful. It's a process. The masterpiece that God is working to create in our lives doesn't happen instantaneously, it happens over time, with hard work and a lot of care. Remember, you are always being molded, always being shaped. What beautiful thing is God working you into today?

Go and Do
Get a piece of clay. Take it and imagine something beautiful. Then with your hands, begin to mold it into what you imagined. Think about your life as that piece of material. Think about the pushing and prodding that goes into shaping that clay. What are you doing in your life that is making it more difficult for God to mold and shape you?

CLOSET

> *Genesis 3:8* <

Then the man and his wife heard the sound of the LORD God as he was walking in the garden in the cool of the day, and they hid from the LORD God among the trees of the garden.

Do you remember being a little kid and being told to clean up your room? You started on it but after a while you gave up and just started throwing things into the closet. You hid your mess in there, and were ashamed when mom or dad found it. This same concept happens in your youth group, too. It happens every year. It breaks my heart every time I see it begin and I feel helpless when it starts. It usually happens in 9th and 10th grade.

What am I talking about? The youth group kids who have been really involved, growing in their faith, and then they disappear. It usually starts with a new boyfriend or girlfriend or a new friend group. They begin to do some things that they know they shouldn't do; it could be that they start drinking or doing stuff with their significant other beyond what they feel is acceptable. Then they disappear. I think they stop coming because they start hiding. They feel ashamed and they hide from the church. I think they sometimes are trying to hide from God.

It makes me so sad because I want to grab them and scream at the top of my lungs, "Come out of hiding! You are loved!" It's hard though because we've been hiding since Adam and Eve. It's who we are. So, listen closely: if you're doing something you shouldn't, I beg you on behalf of your youth minister, church, and family: Do Not Hide. You don't have to. You're loved, no matter what you're doing. This is your family, the people who love you. There is no need to hide.

Go and Do
Get with your youth minister and write down a list of all of the youth who have not been around in the past 6-12 months. Now, you, your youth minister, and some other friends begin relentlessly pursuing these other youth with no other message than "you are missed and loved." Watch your youth group change dramatically!

COAT

> *Luke 3:10-11* <

"What should we do then?" the crowd asked. John answered. "The man with two tunics should share with him who has none. and the one who has food should do the same."

We are a people of multiples. Right? Stop reading this right now, go to your closet, and count how many pairs of shoes, coats, hats, and scarves you have. Count the number of shirts and pants you have. Were you surprised? It's always surprising to me when I go through my closet. It's also a little embarrassing.

Now, I want to take a time out before we go any farther. This exercise isn't supposed to make you feel guilty. The goal is to make you feel grateful and to be aware of all of the things you have, and what you can do with those resources. The point of the teaching of John the Baptist was not to create a world of guilt-ridden followers of Christ. He taught us this to help each of us realize that the place where the abundance of our resources intersects with the abundance of need in the world we will find the Kingdom of God.

Now that we realize how much we have and how little we really need, what are we to do? Should we go and throw away all of our extra clothes? No, that would be wasteful and would probably get you into a lot of trouble. The goal is to change how you think about what you have. Gradual changes will add up to major differences in your life. You can bring about great change in our world by simply starting with the things you have in your own closet.

Go and Do

Look at all of the things you have and how you spend your time and money. Think about what you waste, what you have that you don't need, and what can be done with those things. Begin conversations with your parents about places where you want to make a difference.

COCOON

>2 Corinthians 5:17<

Therefore. if anyone is in Christ. he is a new creation:
the old has gone. the new has come!

Metamorphosis. It's a biological process by which an animal physically develops after birth or hatching, involving a conspicuous and relatively abrupt change. Paul was familiar with metamorphosis, not in a scientific way but through a spiritual change. In fact most of Christianity's major figures throughout history had some type of spiritual metamorphosis happen in their lives. Some of these like Paul, St. Augustine and C.S. Lewis had dramatic conversion experiences to the faith. Others like the disciple Peter, Martin Luther, and Billy Graham had much more subtle conversions.

When we decide to follow the way of Christ, there's a metamorphosis that occurs in our life. It's like a caterpillar that forms a cocoon and emerges as a butterfly. The amazing part of the story is that our metamorphosis isn't a surprise to God. We're just living into the promise of who God made us to be from the beginning. Remember the caterpillar? He was supposed to be a butterfly the entire time. He just had to grow into what God intended for him.

We're the same. God wants each of us to grow closer to Him. We will look, talk, act, and think differently than we once did. At the end of the day we're not genetically becoming a completely different person, we're simply growing into the full incarnation of who God made us to become all along. How is God renewing and recreating faith in you?

Go and Do
In school you have probably spent time drawing or at least studying the metamorphosis of a butterfly. Today begin a chart of your faith metamorphosis. On a sheet of paper or in your journal draw a timeline that begins with your first memories of your faith. Maybe VBS, Sunday school, or a prayer at dinner. Then begin to track each significant faith experience you've had. Leave plenty of blank pages after your last point on the timeline, as God continues to work in you.

COMPASS

>*Philippians 4:8*<

Finally, brothers, whatever is true, whatever is noble, whatever is right, whatever is pure, whatever is lovely, whatever is admirable—if anything is excellent or praiseworthy—think about such things.

Decisions are tough, especially the ones where the right way isn't really clear. A lot of times people will point to the Bible and tell us that it's the "answer book," and that we should look up our questions, find the answers, and move on it. The problem is that the Bible doesn't always work that way. While the Bible is the inspired word of God, and a wonderful collection of knowledge that help us understand the ways of God and what He's calling us to do, it doesn't have a literal answer for each of our specific questions. (The Bible won't provide the literal answer to what college you should choose.)

The Bible is more like a compass. See, a compass won't answer the question, "which is the right way to go"? It's a tool that tells us what direction we're going. But it won't tell us that camp is 5.3 miles behind us. The Bible is often the same. While there's a ton of direct, specific knowledge in it that provides clear direction for decisions you'll make, it doesn't have any specific verses about what to say when talking with a friend who's dealing with anorexia, or whose parents are going through a divorce. But here is where it functions like a compass . . .

In this passage from Philippians, Paul gives us some things to focus on, some general guidance that will point us in the right direction. Making a tough decision? Focus on things that are true, respectable, fair, pure, what is good and worthy of God. Overlay these criteria on your decisions and follow them like a compass into the ways of God.

Go and Do
When you're faced with a tough decision write your question at the top of a sheet of paper. Then make two columns. In the left column write the things Paul mentions above. In the right, answer your question with each of compasses that Paul gives us. What is true? What is good, respectable etc. After you go through this process your direction should be much clearer.

COMPOST

> *John 11:39* <

"Take away the stone." he said. "But. Lord." said Martha. the sister of the dead man. "by this time there is a bad odor. for he has been there four days."

This isn't a pretty picture. Not only is there a family who is in deep mourning, but the one who they believed could save their brother came too late. Then the unthinkable happened. Jesus told them to remove the stone. The dead man's sister begged Him not to; the stench from the rotting corpse would be overwhelming. Pretty gruesome story right? Sounds like the beginning of one of those zombie shows everyone seems to like. (Not me, by the way. I'm terrified of zombies and aliens, FYI.)

My wife and I like to compost. We take old or discarded fruits and vegetables and take them outside to our compost bin. Compost is an amazing medium for things to grow in. We use it in our gardens and it helps our plants grow. Beautiful things grow from the rotting and decaying fruit and vegetables. While it may sound sort of gross, this story of Lazarus is a little like compost. Jesus took a 4-day dead corpse and transformed it into something beautiful and miraculous.

I'm convinced that as people who follow Jesus, we can never count anything for loss. We can always believe that something beautiful can come from tragedy. That doesn't mean that God causes these bad things to happen; even Jesus wept when He heard the news. But God can transform tragedy into hope and death into life. There may be things in your life that seem dead and hopeless. But know that beautiful life can come from our worst moments and situations.

Go and Do
A lot of times our experiences with this sort of growth can't be seen immediately (like a man walking out of a tomb who has been dead for 4 days). Oftentimes it can only be seen when we look backward after those experiences and see how beautiful things have since become. This week, I want you to look back. Look back at some experiences that were bad in your life and see how God has worked though those experiences and what beautiful things have grown from them.

CONCERT

>*Acts 2:44-47*<

All the believers were together and had everything in common. Selling their possessions and goods, they gave to anyone as he had need. Every day they continued to meet together in the temple courts. They broke bread in their homes and ate together with glad and sincere hearts, praising God and enjoying the favor of all the people. And the Lord added to their number daily those who were being saved.

Some of the most inspiring experience of my life have been at concerts. Have you ever been to a concert? They're amazing. I am not talking about the type of concert where only a few people know the band or their songs. I'm talking about the type of concert where thousands of people love the band and know all of their songs. I was recently at a Mumford and Sons concert and it was one of those experiences. It was an outdoors concert and I was on the third row of the amphitheater. From the first word of the first song to the last there were thousands of us singing together, loud and passionately. There were several times where I would look back over the crowd and everyone was in unison. Everyone was focused and in one spirit. It was amazing.

Sadly, this is not the image that we usually think of when we talk about church. Usually there are lots of divisions. The first church, the one immediately after Jesus ascended, started off with a lot more unity. They developed a community where they were all equal and shared together. They ate together and worked for each other not against each other. It was a beautiful thing. I wonder, now and as you get older, if we all could commit to that kind of church? One where there is less fighting and more working together. One where we focus on the things we have in common and not on the things that separates us.

The concert was incredible. That kind of church could be world changing.

Go and Do
Go and be that kind of church. Today, tomorrow and forever. Refuse to let our differences force us against each other. Find what we can do together and do it well. If we can do this we can do amazing things in our God's name.

CROSS

> Matthew 16:24 <

Then Jesus said to his disciples. "If anyone would come after me. he must deny himself and take up his cross and follow me.

The way we use the cross is kind of strange if you really think about it. For us the cross is a symbol of Christianity, of our faith, and salvation. But if we think about what a cross meant to those of Jesus' time, we might not print it on quite as many shirts and bumper stickers. In Jesus' time, wearing a cross on a necklace or shirt would be comparable to wearing an electric chair or a noose as a fashion statement. See what I mean? Kind of strange.

Jesus told His followers that if they were going to be His disciples they would have to carry their own cross. Not too appealing is it? "Hey guys, if you want to really follow me I am going to need you to carry around the thing that is going to kill you." But Jesus wanted us to know that if we really followed Him, and followed Him closely, it would most likely be a costly venture. I'm not sure that we think about it that way when we wear a cross on a shirt or on our Bible.

So what does the cross mean to you? What does it mean to carry your cross? I think it might look a little like this: if we're not doing some things that ruffle the feathers of those around us, or if our priorities and goals look exactly like those of the world around us, we might want to check ourselves. Carrying a cross might look different now, but I feel certain that it carries the same weight and makes the same difference in our world.

Go and Do
Take an inventory of the things that you do for your faith. Are they costly or are they easy? It's not that all of them should be difficult, but it is that they should not all be culturally acceptable. Remember Jesus was put on that cross because He made the political and religious leaders very uncomfortable. He didn't fly under the radar and neither should we.

CUP

>Matthew 10:42<

And if anyone gives even a cup of cold water to one of these little ones because he is my disciple. I tell you the truth. he will certainly not lose his reward.

A cup of water isn't a big deal, right? It's just a small container, usually 6-12 ounces, full of the most abundant resource on the planet: water. But, when you think about it as a person of faith, you'll see that it means so much more. When you think about it normally, it's nothing more than giving someone something that will give him or her temporary relief from thirst. When you think about it as a person of faith, it's a gesture that you're recognizing his or her humanity. You're showing that you care enough to stop and help.

While it's simple it's also profound. It's profound because it's so much more than a simple cup. When you do this you open up a world of possibilities. Possibilities to get to know people and their story. Possibilities to find out how they can come into relationship with you, and you with them. When you give a person something he or she needs, it also tells him or her that someone cares and that he or she matters. So many people in our world live life every day without their basic needs being met, and they suffer needlessly. By giving, you not only make it one less person who suffers needlessly, you also become a part of the solution to those problems.

It doesn't just have to be a cup of water. It can also be a hug, friendly smile, a handshake, dinner, a blanket on a cold night, a meaningful conversation, a listening ear, or any number of other things. So what simple thing will you do today to change someone's life for the good?

Go and Do
Go and do something simple for someone today.

DIAMOND

>*Romans 12:2*<

Do not conform any longer to the pattern of this world. but be transformed by the renewing of your mind. Then you will be able to test and approve what God's will is—his good. pleasing and perfect will.

If you're a teenager and you're reading this devotional, please know that I have prayed for you. I probably don't know you personally but I understand some of what you're going through. I know that it's tough. I know that everyday is like a pressure cooker, and that you're constantly pulled in a million different directions. I know that you're trying to do what is right but oftentimes find yourself doing the opposite of what you believe. I know that you feel loads of pressure to do what everyone else is doing, and that you feel it every day.

Hold on. While the pressure is strong and the choices are difficult I want to encourage you to hold steady. It will turn you into something beautiful. The process of how a piece of coal becomes a diamond is very similar. Thousands of years of pressure and heat take a piece of coal and turn it into a beautiful diamond. When you find yourself receiving pressure from all angles, do not crack and do not falter. Hold strong and true to what you know is good and acceptable. Just as Paul tells us, "do not be conformed to this world, but be transformed."

A diamond becomes a diamond, not by conforming to the pressure, but by being transformed through it. Be patient, beautiful things are happening through the pressure and difficulty.

Go and Do

A prayer for times of pressure:

God of goodness and light, I know that you are not the author of confusion and anxiety. I also know that you calmed the storm and the raging sea. When my life is chaotic, and full of pressure help me trust in you. Help me remember that you are the one who creates beauty and peace in the middle of pain and pressure. God, give me patience and strength, as you take the pain and pressure in my life and transform it into goodness and hope in you. Amen.

DITCHES

> *Psalm 7:15-16* <

He who digs a hole and scoops it out falls into the pit he has made. The trouble he causes recoils on himself; his violence comes down on his own head.

We all do it. You have. I have. And we both will again! We have this incredible ability to get ourselves into trouble. Then instead of doing what is right, we cover it up and dig our pit deeper and deeper. We continue to do this until we have dug a whole so deep that we can't get out. We are stuck in our lies and the mess we made.

See, we're really good at digging ditches. But we're really bad at getting out of them. The problem is that we often believe that it would be better to try to get out of something and cover it up than actually own up to what we've done and face whatever consequences may come with our decision. Neither you nor I like consequences. So we cover up, thus, digging a deeper and deeper ditch.

Every time that I've ever done this, the lies get too confusing, the stories become muddled, and ultimately I get caught. I've realized that instead of digging deeper and deeper, it would have been a lot better to have just come clean and faced the much less severe consequences. Instead I've found myself stuck in a deep mess.

We need to stop digging! Look around you and know that the truth is always better than lies. If it's deep trouble that you've gotten yourself into, talk to someone whom you trust and ask them to help you figure out the best plan. Whatever you do, don't keep up the lying and the covering up. Put down the shovel and reach out for some help. Climb out of that ditch.

Go and Do

There might be areas in your life that you've covered up for so long that the consequences have past. I'd encourage you to think about those times and spend time talking to God about those areas. If there is guilt or other repercussions that you can't handle alone, talk with your parents, a teacher, or your youth minister. Seek out help. We're not meant to deal with these things alone. Find someone you can trust and ask for help.

DOOR

> *Revelation 3:20* <

Here I am! I stand at the door and knock. If anyone hears my voice and opens the door. I will come in and eat with him. and he with me.

Did your parents ever tell you to make sure to look out the window or through the peep hole before you ever opened the door for someone? If they didn't, they should have! You never know who is on the other side of the door. And because of that you have to check them out before you let them into your home.

We have to do the exact same thing in our lives. There are plenty of people, ideas, voices, and influences that are knocking at our doors. Some are good, some are bad. Who and what we let into our lives is a an important thing that we have to make good decisions about. The things we let into our lives will influence who we are, what we do, and what we value. In the very same way these good and negative influences try to gain entrance into our lives, Jesus also stands at the door and knocks. I love this image, because it shows us that Jesus is pursuing entrance into our lives. He wants to come in and spend time with us and through the story of His life in the gospels, inspire us to follow Him.

Just remember: Jesus isn't the only one who stands at the door and knocks. There are many influences and voices that are crying out for our time and attention. Good voices, and voices that lead us down some very dark paths. Which will you let in and which will you keep out?

Go and Do
Do you have ways that you test out voices and influences in your life? How do you know which ones to let in and which ones to keep out? Today think about what voices in your life are beneficial. Think about which ones have taken you down roads you wish you wouldn't have traveled. What can you learn about these voices and which ones to let in and keep out?

DOVE

> *Matthew 5:9* <

Blessed are the peacemakers, for they will be called sons of God.

The Beatitudes are one of the most profound set of teachings in the Bible, especially this verse. I don't think we think about making peace quite as much as we need to. What if every Christ-follower were to set out every day with one of their expressed goals being to make peace? I think it would revolutionize the world. I think that it would be something that would make people look at Christianity and think, "wow, they're really doing some amazing things in the world. I want to know more about them, because they care about making the world we live in a better place." I believe we would live in a completely different world, one that reflects the goodness of God.

One of the ways we live this out in our family is that I try to remind my kids everyday as I drop them off for school. I will tell them "Mary Clare, Patrick, go and make peace today. I love you." When they come home from school I ask them how they made peace that day. Sometimes it's playing with a kid who was alone, other times it's helping friends stop arguing. But each time they are intentionally thinking about how they can make peace. This is a step for my family, what are some steps for you?

Your attempt at making peace might start with looking inward and seeing what things are in you that cause you to act in ways that promote the opposite of peace. Then it might look like finding out what systems around you promote violence or exclusion. Other steps could be looking for individuals who've been hurt-mentally, physically, or emotionally-and bringing about reconciliation with them. Peace always begins in small ways. Begin making peace today, in the situations that surround you and watch it grow and spread.

Go and Do
Just do it. In every situation you find yourself in think, "how can I create peace here"? Then find creative and innovative ways of doing just that, making peace.

DUST

>Genesis 3:19<

By the sweat of your brow you will eat your food until you return to the ground, since from it you were taken: for dust you are and to dust you will return."

Sometimes we feel down, like we can't do anything right. And then there are other times where everything goes great. We're on top of the world and all we do turns out perfectly. This is a devotional for those times. Because oftentimes when we're successful, on top of the world, and everything is going our way we forget who we are. We lose track of where we came from and where we're going.

The verse above is usually used at funerals and because of that a lot of people look at it as a morbid verse about death. I see it very differently. I see this verse as a way to keep us grounded and understand our lives in context. The context of our lives tells us that we came from God and will return to God. Sometimes in life we begin to believe that we are immortal. We drive too fast, do too many risky things, and oftentimes, especially teenagers, live like there is no tomorrow. This verse helps me remember that I'm human and that one day I'll die. And knowing that I will not live forever helps me make decisions that matter. It helps me make decisions that will make a difference and an impact. It helps me not waste a moment. It's important to remember that we have a beginning and we will have an end here on earth. So make every moment count. Make decisions that you'll be proud of today, tomorrow, and when you're dust again.

Go and Do
On one of my bookshelves I have a small jar of dirt from my grandfather's grave. He was a giant to me and I thought the world of him. I thought he would live forever. He died 8 years ago and as I stood by his graveside, I reached down and took a handful of dirt and put it into a jar. I keep it to remind me that I too will die one day, so today I will live. Go outside, find some dirt put it in a jar, and put it on your shelf, not as a reminder that you will one day die, but as a reminder to live today.

EAR PHONES

> *Luke 5:16* <

But Jesus often withdrew to lonely places and prayed.

If Jesus needed to take a timeout, so do we. Throughout the gospels you will see Jesus, in some of His most busy times in ministry spend some time alone. It seemed to be important to Him. He not only did it Himself, He talked about the value of it.

So my question for you is how and when do you get away? How do you sep-arate yourself from the world and find an alone place? I see a lot of teenagers do this through their earphones. When they want to block out the world, or their parents for that matter, they'll put on earphones. I bet you do this too. A lot of time "getting away" is done as a rejection of someone's presence. But I'd encourage you to think about it in another way.

We need to have alone time. We need to have time to be by ourselves. It's good to escape to a place where we're at rest and at peace. It's great if it's earphones that help you do this. If it's going for a walk alone, go for it. It if's sitting in your room with absolutely no noise, then make that your holy place. Whatever it is, do it and do it regularly. We all need this sort of time. All of us. It gives us time to reflect, think, pray, and to listen. When is the last time you did this? Do you do it regularly? If not how can you?

Go and Do
Stop. Put this book down and spend some time alone, quiet and listening, praying and breathing. Enjoy.

FACE

>2 Corinthians 3:18<

And we. who with unveiled faces all reflect the Lord's glory. are being transformed into his likeness with ever-increasing glory. which comes from the Lord. who is the Spirit.

What does your face reflect? For some of us, it might depend on whether it's early in the morning or at the end of a long, tiring day. Many of us walk around with joy on our faces. Some of us walk around with solemn or sad faces. Others walk around looking indifferent, like they don't care about anyone in the room. Our faces are like a window into our lives. Think about it: usually the way you know if someone is down, happy, sad, scared, excited, or confused comes first from looking at his or her face.

We have the opportunity to, through our faces, share God's love, grace, and compassion with the world. It's amazing the amount of cool things that can happen through a kind smile. It's such a simple act that can make a major difference in someone else's day. Paul, in 2 Corinthians, talks about living our lives with unveiled faces. When Paul talks about this he's talking about having our faces reflect God as an act of worship. What if we understood what we said with faces as an act of worship in the same way as we think of singing, prayer, and Scripture reading as worship? What if our faces told the story of God's warmth and care to those we met?

Unveil your face and reflect the goodness of your God.

Go and Do

For the next few days, spend time thinking about what you project with your face. Be intentional with how you look at others, remembering what messages they see coming from your expressions. One way to think about this is to take a bunch of selfies. Literally take pictures of your face being sad, mad, silly, warm, angry, confused, scared, and loving. Notice how they differ and think about what each of them says about you and your God.

FIELD

> *John 4:35* <

Do you not say, 'Four months more and then the harvest'? I tell you, open your eyes and look at the fields! They are ripe for harvest.

I grew up in the rural South. In the rural South you always know when it's time for the cotton to be harvested. There are these fields everywhere that are covered in these dry brown bushes, then suddenly almost out of nowhere they turn into a sea of cloudy white blossoms. It's incredible the transformation. Then you know, without a doubt, that it's time for the plants to be harvested.

Have you seen fields ready to be harvested? Our lives are much like a field. There are times in our lives where we have rich soil that's ready for something to grow. Other times our lives are in a time of growing; we need nurture, care, and attention. Still there are other times where we just need rest; in farming terms this is called letting the fields lay fallow, or unplanted. Our lives, just like fields, go in cycles. Sometimes we are very productive, other times in a sort of drought. Sometimes we are bursting with possibility, and other times, we just need to rest.

It's helpful to think about your life and the cycles you go through. What cycle are you in now? Are you comfortable with that place in life? It's important to remember that we have to have cycles in our lives. Our brains, souls, and bodies need the variation and change of pace. God did not make you to be in one mode all of the time. Sometimes it's Spring and other times it's Winter. Where are you today?

Go and Do
Over the next year, find a tree or a field and every month on the first of that month take a picture of that tree or field. As the months go past, notice the changes in the pictures. Print them out and put them somewhere you can see them as a reminder of the changing nature of all of creation. Also, use them as a guide to help you understand where you are in your life. Try to identify your place in life with a different month in the cycle.

FIRE

> *Jeremiah 20:9* <

But if I say. "I will not mention him or speak any more in his name." his word is in my heart like a fire. a fire shut up in my bones. I am weary of holding it in: indeed. I cannot.

If you're reading this you're probably living in a place where it's OK to be a Christian. You're probably in a city or a community where your faith isn't going to get you killed, beaten, or put in jail. Because of this, it's often difficult for us to relate to people who experience great persecution, whether in the Bible or in our world today.

Jeremiah was in a bind. He was stuck in the very difficult place between being called by God to be a prophet to the Israelites and being faced with the penalty of being persecuted if he were to open his mouth. For Jeremiah, this wasn't even a real option. He says that if he were to be quiet and not tell about the God who called him, then it would be like the insides of his bones were on fire. There's no way he could keep something that powerful inside him. Is God's presence that strong in your life? Are there things that you've experienced with God that are so powerful there's no way that you can keep it in? Many of us, if we were truthful, would answer no. I don't think this is because God isn't active in your life. I think it's because you haven't really spent time thinking about things like God's grace, mercy and love.

Jeremiah is describing passion, a passion that can't be contained. This passion is a gift from God. Seek it out.

Go and Do
This week go and ask five people who are close to you to name a few things they see you being passionate about. Ask them to try to be as specific as possible. Take these lists and compare them to each other. Do you see some common answers emerging? God instills in us natural passions for certain things. As you discover them, spend time fostering that passion, thinking about why God created that in you.

FISH

>*Matthew 13:47*<

Once again, the kingdom of heaven is like a net that was let down into the lake and caught all kinds of fish.

A lot of times when we read the Bible we can understand the stories that are being told without much translating. Other times we have to think about it a little more. The stories in the Bible about fishing are ones that we have to give a little more thought to. We have to think about these a little deeper because most of us, if we've fished, have done so in a much different way than the disciples.

When we fish, we try to catch a certain kind of fish. Certain lures are made for certain fish, like a plastic worm for bass, or like chicken livers for catfish. (I know, I know . . . super gross.) Jesus' understanding of fishing is much different than that. In His time and place, He and His friends used nets that were weaved together and thrown over the side of the boat. These nets were indiscriminate. They didn't work for just one kind of fish. They weren't made to bring in certain ones and keep out certain others.

Jesus tells that the Kingdom of God is like this. God's love seeks out people of every kind, every race, language, social status, nationality, income level, gender, and orientation. God loves and wants to catch us ALL up in His love. When you show God in your world, what kind of fishing are you doing? Are you fishing with a lure for certain kinds of people? Or are you casting out a wide net, sharing God's good news with everyone through your life, words, and actions?

Go and Do
Get out your journal or a sheet of paper and begin to write down all of the different groups of people in your school that you interact with. These might be friends, acquaintances, or even enemies. Write down each of these groups and the people you can think about who are in them. Now take a different group each day and pray for them. Ask God how you can show your love and God's love to them.

FLOWER

> Matthew 6:28-29 <

And why do you worry about clothes? See how the lilies of the field grow. They do not labor or spin. Yet I tell you that not even Solomon in all his splendor was dressed like one of these.

Sometimes when we read the Bible we have to work hard to understand how this applies to our lives. That's not the case in these verses! It's amazing how much we worry about what we look like and the clothes we wear. I know that many of us will spend a very long time in the morning trying to pick out the perfect outfit. Others will spend loads of money each year trying to make sure we're caught up with all of the new fashions. Our culture reflects this.

And yet, Jesus tells us very clearly in these verses that it really doesn't matter what all we put on. What we wear doesn't make us better or more beautiful. Jesus wants each of us to know that we are our best self not because of what we have on the outside, but because of what God has done on the inside.

Our beauty and value are based on the fact that God made us. When we look at flowers we never try to enhance them by adding things. We want to bring out their natural beauty, and to display them just how they were made. God wants us to understand that there's nothing external we can add that will make us any more pleasing to Him. Know that you are beautiful and good just how you are. You don't have to try to impress anyone, I promise.

Go and Do
How much time do you spend getting ready everyday? Do you find yourself obsessing about what people see when they look at you? Time yourself over the next few days. See what things you work the hardest on and what things cause you the most anxiety when you get ready each morning. Work on ways to not worry about these pieces of your appearance.

FLY

> *Proverbs 12:16* <

Fools show their annoyance at once, but the prudent ignore an insult.

Everyone has them. You always will. It is simply a part of life. No matter where you go or what you do you're going to have people who just simply annoy you. Sometimes it's a personality difference. Other times it's that they are clingy. It can even be something like someone else's voice! An annoyance is sort of like a fly or gnat that you just can't get to leave you alone.

It's important to not let annoyances or annoying people get under your skin. At the end of the day the people who annoy you are just people, like you who are trying to figure life out. In the verse from Proverbs, it tells us that we're the fools when we let others make us upset or annoyed. I think this is for two reasons. The first is that we should be in control of our own emotions and not let others affect us so dramatically. The second, I believe, is even more important. The second is that we have to remember that the people who annoy us are people too. They are people with talents and abilities. They are people with hopes and heartaches. They are people, just like us.

Sometimes we dehumanize the people who annoy us and act like they are flies that we just want to swat away. Remember, they are not some annoying insects that just buzz around, they are beautiful creations of God. Who are more like you than you realize.

Go and Do
The next time someone annoys you try these three things:
1. Look at them and remember they have people who love them and care for them.
2. Find something that you find good about them. It might be small but focus on that instead of what annoys you.
3. Remember that you're not perfect and that you're probably annoying to someone too!

GASOLINE

> *Genesis 2:2-3* <

By the seventh day God had finished the work he had been doing; so on the seventh day he rested from all his work. And God blessed the seventh day and made it holy, because on it he rested from all the work of creating that he had done.

Do you drive a car? Have you ever been in a car that has run out of gas? It's a terrible feeling. The couple of times I've done that I always ask myself, "Alright, so now what?" Usually some kind passerby will stop and help. One time I was in the middle of nowhere and had to walk several miles to get the gas I needed. It wasn't fun. But all that is beside the point. When we run out of gas it's because we've neglected what our car needs: fuel.

God made us in a similar way. We need some things in order to keep going. The three primary things are food, water and rest. Two of these can be very utilitarian. Food and water can be much like fuel and we can use them like fuel to keep us going. Rest is a little different. Granted, if you don't rest you won't be able to keep going. But there's something more to it than that. Rest is a holy thing. It's something that was not only commanded in the Ten Commandments but was also modeled by God. So, while rest is something that's needed to help us do what we want to do, it's also an act of following God's will in our lives.

Resting is a holy practice. It's especially holy in a world that encourages us to do more all of the time. Resting is actually an incredibly countercultural act, an act of worship. So, remember to rest. But don't do it so that you can go more and do more. Do it because God did it. It's a holy and good thing to do.

Go and Do
When do you rest? Do you have a set time each week or do you just try to squeeze it in between sports and school and everything else you do? Begin the practice of intentionally resting this week.

GLASSES

>1 Corinthians 13:12<

Now we see but a poor reflection as in a mirror; then we shall see face to face. Now I know in part; then I shall know fully, even as I am fully known.

I had a friend growing up. She was kind and well liked by most of the school. She and I went to church and youth group together and she would often cry and become very emotional during youth services. Many of us would judge her for this because we knew that the night before she had been out drinking, and worse. We looked at her and we judged her. We had names for her and talked about how she was a hypocrite. We thought we had her figured out. But, sadly, we only partially knew her. If we really knew her we would've known that things at home were very bad. We only knew part of her life. We saw her like looking in a mirror dimly.

Oftentimes we see the world with blurred vision. If you wear glasses or contacts you know exactly what I'm talking about. If you don't you should put on someone else's glasses and experience it for yourself. When you see the world with blurred vision you have a very difficult time with details and what's actually going on in people's lives. I saw this girl and her life in this way, only thinking I knew what was going on. If I could really see her I would've known there was so much more going on in her life. Instead of judging her, I hope I would've helped her. We all need glasses. We all need corrective lenses that help us see the world the way God sees the world, knowing the whole picture, through love and grace.

Go and Do
How do you view people? Do you make judgments about others? Do you find yourself condemning them in your mind? Think about those people who you find yourself judging. Decide to take just one of those people this week and try to get to know him or her better and understand who he or she is. Work to see him or her as God does.

GLOBE

> *Psalm 103:12* <

As far as the east is from the west, so far has he removed
our transgressions from us.

The first time I heard this verse was when I was a kid at my home church. We
had an interim worship leader and, for some reason, that morning when we
arrived for worship there was a globe sitting on the altar of the church. You've
seen one of these globes. It's just like the one that you find in classrooms at
school. We started worship, had the welcome, and sang a few songs. Then
just before the third song he pointed to the globe, which my attention had
been completely fixated on the entire time. He began to talk about the verse
in Psalm 103.

He asked the congregation to point to the east on the globe so we all pointed
right and then he asked for us to point to the West, so we all pointed left.
Then he spun the globe and he said, "If I start going East on this globe, when
is it that I reach the West?" Everyone looked at him. Then he said, "If I start
going West, when will reach the East?" As the globe spun everyone realized
that you can never reach West if you're going East; you'll always be going
East. The same is true if you're going West. He then told us that the East and
West can never reach each other, and that they're separated by infinity. "Our
sin," he said, "is that far away from us when God forgives us."

I know that some of you who are reading this feel very badly about something that you've done and you might feel like you can never be forgiven.
Trust in God's forgiveness. You don't have to earn it. God just wants you to
accept it and know that those sins are completely gone from your life.

Go and Do
Go and live life knowing that you are forgiven.

GOGGLES

>Acts 9:8, 17-18<

Saul got up from the ground, but when he opened his eyes he could see nothing. So they led him by the hand into Damascus ... Then Ananias went to the house and entered it. Placing his hands on Saul, he said, "Brother Saul, the Lord—Jesus, who appeared to you on the road as you were coming here—has sent me so that you may see again and be filled with the Holy Spirit." Immediately, something like scales fell from Saul's eyes, and he could see again. He got up and was baptized.

One of my favorite things about going to the beach is snorkeling. I absolutely love to put on my goggles and snorkel and discover the hidden world under the water. Although it's in plain sight, I call it hidden because you have to have goggles in order to see all of it clearly. Goggles open up an entirely new world to those who wear them in the ocean.

Paul was not always the man who traveled the world, starting churches, being persecuted for his faith, and ultimately dying for that faith. He started out seeing the world in a very different way. Paul saw and understood the world as a place that needed to be purged of Christians. Then, on his way traveling to do what he did so well, namely throw Christ-followers in jail, he saw the world in a way he'd never imagined.

Sometimes we think we know how the world really is. What we don't realize is that we're missing so much. The passage ends with "something like scales fell from his eyes, and his sight was restored." Paul's sight wasn't just restored; it was completely changed. His view of the world was completely different. He put on his God goggles and for the first time, he saw the world as God sees the world, and the world has not been the same since.

Go and Do
What sets of goggles do you see the world through? More importantly do you think you are seeing the world as God sees the world? Try this experiment. Today, go through your day as you would any other day, except each situation you find yourself in, ask yourself "how would God see this situation?" Practice this today and write down how your God Goggles changed how you saw your world.

GOLD

> Matthew 6:19-21 <

"Do not store up for yourselves treasures on earth, where moth and rust destroy, and where thieves break in and steal. But store up for yourselves treasures in heaven, where moth and rust do not destroy, and where thieves do not break in and steal. For where your treasure is, there your heart will be also.

There are a TON of verses in the Bible about gold and treasure. It's incredible just how much the text has to say about these incredibly coveted and valuable things. It's also very interesting that the majority of the verses about gold, unless being used in a religious ceremony, are pretty condemning. Over and over again the Bible tells us of the pitfalls of wealth. If we're not careful, we might fall accidentally into the belief that the Bible is actually condemning the precious medal gold. But it isn't.

In the same way the Bible also talks a lot about treasure, almost synonymously with gold. It's interesting because the focus of the verses is rarely about the actual metal and a lot more on the intention and motives of the person who is holding or desiring the gold. It's really easy for us as a society to focus on materials and act like they are the problem. People will talk about really expensive jeans, technology, shoes, flashy cars, and so on like they're bad. When we do this we're focusing on the wrong thing. The verses in the Bible don't focus on the objects but on how much we long for these objects. The shoes or the car isn't the problem. They are just objects. The problem is that we often want them more than anything else. We let objects become our obsession and we put all of our hopes and focus on them. That's when we miss the point. That's when our priorities become confused. That's when we begin to invest in treasures that mold and rust instead of the ones that last (beyond) a lifetime.

Go and Do
Over the next few weeks do an inventory of your investments. Not only where you spend money, but also where you spend time. What are the things you invest your life, time, money (or parent's money) and emotions in? If you don't like how it looks, what are some ways you can balance it and reinvest in other places?

GUARDRAILS

>Luke 6:39<

He also told them this parable: "Can a blind man lead a blind man?
Will they not both fall into a pit?

Have you ever been on a beautiful scenic drive through the mountains? As a kid my grandparents would often take me to the Smoky Mountains in Tennessee. To be honest, I didn't like it too much at the time. It seemed to last forever and after a while I really got tired of looking at trees. It was boring, that is, until we got to the "Scenic Overlook" part of the trip. Then it got really interesting, and a little scary.

The reason these places were called scenic overlooks is because they were on top of a giant mountain. We were winding up this giant mountain and with every curve and turn my stomach tightened a little more. I was always a little nervous because if we didn't make that turn just right, we would plummet down a deep ravine. It was nerve-racking. The only thing that made me feel better were these little metal bars that bordered the road: guardrails. Guardrails helped keep us from going off the side of the road.

We all need guardrails in our lives, people who help keep us from accidentally making a wrong turn. These are people whom we trust and listen to. Jesus' words in Luke help show us that we don't need someone who isn't stable and ready to help keep us on the path. They must be wise, seasoned, and have hopefully traveled down some of these paths before. No matter how old we are or how much we know, we all need people in our lives who act as guardrails, giving us a little nudge this way or that, helping us head in the direction we need to go.

Go and Do
Who are your guardrails? How do you know? Do they know that they are guardrails for you? Why do you trust them to be this? Who might you be a guardrail for?

HAND

> *Mark 8:34* <

Then he called the crowd to him along with his disciples and said: "If anyone would come after me. he must deny himself and take up his cross and follow me."

They are amazing things. They created the Mona Lisa, built the Golden Gate Bridge, composed and played Beethoven's fifth symphony, and have colored countless pictures that hang on refrigerators. They sign peace treaties and they press launch buttons to fire missiles. They deliver babies, write on chalkboards, wave goodbye, and say hello. They knit clothing and they hammer nails. It's amazing what "hands" have done in our world. Of course we know that hands aren't that unique; it's what we choose to do with them that makes the difference.

What do you do with your hands? Do you help or hurt? Do you hug or push away? Do you build up or tear down? Do you use them to comfort and embrace? Or do you use them to intimidate and bring fear? Are they the hands of Christ or the hands of selfishness? If we're honest we can probably answer "yes" on each of these at different times. The real question now is not how we could answer these questions today, but how we will be able to answer them tomorrow and the next day after that.

What will you use your hands for? They can be used to create beauty or they can be used to hurt and destroy. Even worse, sometimes, they may be used to do nothing at all. What beauty will you create with your hands today?

Go and Do
Look at your hands. Go ahead. Do it. Now think about what all you have done with them. Where all they have been? Some memories might make you laugh, and others might make you sad. Some might even make you cringe with embarrassment. Now think about the things those hands can do that could make a difference in this world in the name of Jesus. What's keeping you from making a difference? What are you waiting for?

HEART

> *Luke 10:27* <

He answered: "Love the Lord your God with all your heart and with all your soul and with all your strength and with all your mind"; and, "Love your neighbor as yourself."

The word love is a word that's used in so many different ways that its meaning and effectiveness are often diluted. Jesus talks a lot about love but He didn't talk about love the way we often do. We say we love that movie we saw. We say we love our new outfit. Jesus doesn't talk about love this way. He's not talking about the emotion (if you can call it that) reflected on those shirts that proclaim "I (heart) NY." No, Jesus is most concerned with a love that involves our entire selves.

When Jesus talked about love in this verse from Luke, He gave the specifics: love involves our heart, soul, strength, and mind. Jesus is telling us to love God in all that we do, and through all of the ways we can. When Jesus talked about this kind of love He was talking about a whole body, whole life, whole everything kind of love. The most amazing part of Jesus' teaching is that He includes how we love the people around us. Jesus equates the importance of loving our neighbors with the importance of loving God. That's a powerful truth.

When you say that you love something, think about what that means. We only have one word for all of the different kinds of love that we're capable of, so make sure to use the word carefully. Make sure to use it when you really mean it. But more importantly, make sure you're showing the word to others. How do you show love? Do you love God and others with everything you have?

Go and Do
Think about the word love and how many times a day you use it. Set a mental note in your brain so that every time you use the word "love" it will trigger you to ask yourself what you mean when you say it. Begin to think about the way you use the word in your life. Then think about how you show God and the world your love.

HOUSE

>2 Corinthians 1:3-4<

Praise be to the God and Father of our Lord Jesus Christ. the Father of compassion and the God of all comfort. who comforts us in all our troubles. so that we can comfort those in any trouble with the comfort we ourselves have received from God.

Home is a place where we should be able to be comfortable, relax in our pajamas, and just be ourselves. Home should be a place of peace, warmth, and happiness. When we're home, we shouldn't have to worry about the world around us. We're able to rest knowing that we're safe. But when we're honest, we can admit that many of our homes are not like this, at least not all of the way.

St. Augustine, in one of his most famous works said, "Our hearts are restless, until they find rest in [God]." Home is a place where we find rest, comfort, joy, peace, and safety. God is kind of the same way. Our truest home is in the presence of our God. When we understand that our home is with the one who created us, we can see everywhere else with a different perspective. Instead of trying to fit in everywhere else, we can rest knowing that we already have acceptance with God.

Stop searching. Find rest knowing that you're home safely in the love of God.

Go and Do
Spend time today thinking about all of the ways you try to find love, peace, and acceptance. Look around you at others who are trying to find the same things. How can you rest deeper in the knowledge that home is where God is? How can you help others know where their home is as well?

INSTAFACETWIT

> *Galatians 3:26-27* <

You are all sons of God through faith in Christ Jesus, for all of you who were baptized into Christ have clothed yourselves with Christ.

Instagram, Facebook, Twitter, Snapchat . . . The list can go on and on and has probably changed a lot from the time I'm writing these words until the moment you're reading them. Social media and these apps have blown up in our culture. It's unbelievable just how many people use these and are connected to them daily, for many even hourly. There are so many awesome things you can do with them and so many ways that they can be used to connect with people.

There are some drawbacks that come with these as well. One of them is that we are able to create whatever reality we want with these sites. Far fewer people will put pictures on Instagram of them eating cereal in the morning, hair messed up, wearing baggy clothes. People are much more likely to put pics of them smiling and jumping at the beach. The same goes with Facebook. We create these profile pages that make us look like amazing people who are always in the right lighting and are always with tons of friends in cool places. We feel like we need to paint these pictures of ourselves and create these images in order to be accepted. We don't have to do this.

Let God be the thing that defines your life. Let the image that others see be God's image reflected in you. You don't have to compete with everyone else to have the most interesting life. It's OK to just be you. :)

Go and Do
The next time you are on one of your apps, really look at the pictures of people. Don't judge them but think about how this is a small glimpse into their lives, just like your pictures are only a small glimpse into your life. Remember, most people only put their best of times and best of pictures out there. What you see isn't the standard, it's the exception.

KEY

> *Galatians 5:1* <

It is for freedom that Christ has set us free. Stand firm, then, and do not let yourselves be burdened again by a yoke of slavery.

Have you ever done something that you weren't proud of? Something that would just kill you if anyone ever knew? All of us have had these things in our lives, things that haunt us for months and even years. When we do something really bad, it's natural to feel guilt and regret. However, sometimes this guilt and regret can go past helpful and into hurtful.

Sometimes our guilt and regret become so strong that they begin to overwhelm us. These emotions can consume our every thought and take away our happiness. Eventually this guilt can take over our entire lives. The book of Galatians tells us that God's grace through Christ sets us free from the heavy weight of our failures. It helps lift the heavy weight, or yoke, of our wrongs off our backs and gives us freedom. Galatians talks about how we let this guilt and our sin enslave us. The key that unlocks the chains of this guilt is to understand and embrace the freedom that we have been given.

We have the key that unlocks our chains, namely God's grace and love offered freely through Jesus Christ. But so often we choose to sit as slaves to our guilt. Take the gift of grace and let it unlock these chains. Live in the freedom from guilt and shame!

Go and Do
Go to a hardware store and find a cool looking key. Not one that looks like your home key or car key. A cool one. Buy this key. And with a permanent marker, write the word GRACE on it. Put this key on your key chain. And each time you notice it, remember the grace that has set you free.

LAKE

> *Luke 5:1* <

One day as Jesus was standing by the Lake of Gennesaret, with the people crowding around him and listening to the word of God.

Oftentimes when I see a lake, I can't help but think of the lake that Jesus began His ministry around. The Sea of Galilee is actually a giant lake in what is present day Israel and Jordan. It was on and around this lake that Jesus began His ministry, walked on water, cast out demons, healed people, fed 5,000, miraculously caught loads of fish, and so much more. I think about how normal of a place that lake was before Jesus came. After Jesus came and started His ministry, people never looked at the lake the same again.

If don't live in the Middle East, you don't have those physical places that Jesus walked that serve to remind us of His ministry. And yet each of us has experienced Jesus and God's love at different points in our lives. Some of us have experienced these times at church, in our room, a forest, and even on a lake.

There's nothing special the Sea of Galilee, except that God did amazing works on and around it. It's just a normal lake where some very incredible God moments happened.

What are the "normal" places in your life where God has done some abnormal things?

Go and Do
Think about those places where you've experienced God in very special ways. Go to these places and take pictures on your phone. Get the pictures developed and take a marker and write Holy on each picture. Keep these pictures in your Bible to remember the holy places where you've encountered God.

LAMP

>2 Samuel 22:29<

You are my lamp, O LORD; the LORD turns my darkness into light.

Have you ever been in your house when the power goes out? It's not so bad during the day. But at night it can be pretty scary and dangerous. All of the sudden a place that's familiar to you, a place you call home, is now a treacherous mine field of things to trip over and doorframes to stub your toe on. Then, someone finds your savior: a flashlight.

In this verse from 2 Samuel, David is praising God for keeping him from the dangers of his enemies. He thanks God for being a lamp in a very dark place in his life, a place that was treacherous and scary. Lamps or flashlights help us see our way around danger in dark places. I've been in some dark places in my life and I bet you have too. It's in these times where we're left confused, afraid, and often not knowing which way we should go. A lamp in these times is a way of gaining clarity and better vision as to what we should do next.

I can promise you, you will go through dark and confusing times in your life. It's inevitable. During these times in our lives we have to have a way to see the path and walk down it without fear and anxiety. God will provide a lamp for you in these dark times, just like He did for David. God may not make the darkness immediately go away. But God will give us the ability to navigate it better. God wants to light your way in the darkness. Give Him the chance to do so and see what happens.

Go and Do
What are some of the dark places you've gone through in your life? What have been the times when you've stumbled? When have been times when you've been able to navigate through some pretty rough situations? What made the difference between the two? What allowed you to make it through the dark times?

LEAF

>*Ecclesiastes 3:1-2*<

There is a time for everything, and a season for every activity under heaven: a time to be born and a time to die, a time to plant and a time to uproot.

Death is hard. There is no getting around it. The death of a loved one or friend can be one of the most difficult things a person will ever have to go through. There are other kinds of death that affect us deeply as well. The death of a friendship, the death of a relationship, or the death of a time period of our lives can all impact us greatly.

I love this passage in Ecclesiastes where it reminds us that nothing lasts forever. We live in a world that changes. People change and situations change. I love the Fall. I love to see the beautiful colors that the trees turn in that amazing time of year. The bright yellow golds, deep reds, and the glowing oranges. It's an amazing time of year. The leaves change just like change comes in our lives. Sometimes they're green and full of life. Other times they're beautiful and frail. And even other times they die and fall off the branches. Everything in life is like the leaves on a tree. Our lives change.

This passage in Ecclesiastes and the verses after it remind us that our lives are dynamic. There is great change. This is both exciting and sometimes scary. It's not something to fear. It's something to embrace. When something changes, be grateful for what it was and look forward to what is ahead. Go through life knowing that change will always happen. Be excited for Spring blossoms, grateful for Summer growth, admire the beauty of the Fall, and thankful for the life that was in the Winter.

Go and Do
Take a sheet of paper and draw a line down the center and across the middle to make 4 even squares. Starting at the top left write Spring, Summer, Fall, and Winter at the top of each square. Now underneath each write things in your life that are beginning (Spring), growing (Summer), changing (Fall) and closing (Winter). Write a few words that describe the emotions involved with each of these.

LIGHTHOUSE

> *Genesis 1:2* <

Now the earth was formless and empty, darkness was over the surface of the deep, and the Spirit of God was hovering over the waters.

Throughout the Bible the sea represents chaos. Notice most times when you read the Bible and it mentions the sea, it's often pictured as chaotic and in disarray and confusion. Even in the first couple of verses of the Bible we see this imagery being used. Formless. Dark. Void. How many times do these words describe places in our lives?

Usually when we see a painting, picture, or postcard of a lighthouse we get a warm and fuzzy feeling. The truth is that lighthouses were a matter of life and death for sailors. These lighthouses marked treacherous outcroppings and rocky shores that the ships would otherwise run into. In other words, if there was a lighthouse around, things were rough.

Life can toss us around like the sea, and if we're not careful we can run into some pretty dangerous places. For me lighthouses are a lot like rules. They help keep me from running into more trouble than I can handle. Rules, like lighthouses, give me warning when I'm getting too close to something dangerous. They help me to know to back off. While rules aren't always a lot of fun, they're usually pretty good at helping us navigate the more dangerous parts of life without doing too much damage to others or ourselves. What are some lighthouses in your life that have kept you from running ashore? What are some that you've seen keep others out or trouble, or that others have ignored?

Go and Do
Many Christians have rules for their life that they follow that they believe will help them live a life that more closely resembles the life of Jesus. What are some of the rules you see Jesus model that you can adopt in your life? Are there some that you can begin to practice today? Go and research some rules that Christians have lived by and passed down throughout the years.

LIST

>*Colossians 3:17*<

And whatever you do, whether in word or deed, do it all in the name of the Lord Jesus, giving thanks to God the Father through him.

If you're anything like me, I bet your reading of this book isn't by chance. I bet you're reading this devotion because you planned to read it. You put it either on a physical or mental to do list. I'm guessing you blocked out time to spend reading this book.

We live in a world where there's no lack of great things we can do. There's always something bidding for our attention. The older you get you'll have to be more and more intentional about what things you say "yes" and "no" to. Each of us has a list of things we believe are important. It might not be a physical list and for many it might not even be something that we have planned out in our heads. But at the end of each day, you can look back at how you spent your time and see the things you believe are important by the amount of time you spent doing them, and the priority they took over other things.

This passage from Paul's letter to the Colossians tells us that no matter what we do we should do everything in the name of Jesus. I hope as a teenager, who doesn't have complete control over what you do each day, you find some comfort in this verse. I hope that when you read it you understand that there are things that each of us have to do each day. For you it's school. For most adults it's a job. Whatever is on your list today, make sure you're doing it in the name of Jesus. Do it well and do it faithfully.

Go and Do
For the next week make a list each day of how you spent your time that day. Determine what on the list you chose to do and what you had to do. Then ask yourself if this is how you wanted to spend your day, and how you did those things for Jesus that day.

MAILBOX

> *Proverbs 11:24-25* <

One man gives freely, yet gains even more; another withholds unduly, but comes to poverty. A generous man will prosper; he who refreshes others will himself be refreshed.

What if a mailbox worked like this: Every time you put something in it you get something in return. So when you put something good in the box, you get something good out of the mailbox. Likewise, when you put something not so good in the mailbox, you'd get something not so good out of it. Beyond the miraculous nature of the mailbox, I bet we would think about the things we put into it a little more. If we knew what we'd get in return was what we put in, we'd probably be a little more intentional about our contribution.

This passage in Proverbs calls us to think about our lives in this way. Now don't get me wrong, I'm not talking about some magic trick where when we do something good that something good magically happens to us. That's not what the Bible is talking about. Proverbs does tell us that when the primary output of our lives is good, then we will experience more good in the world. I don't think this means that God is keeping some sort of checklist for everything we give so that it can be returned to us. I think this verse is more about our attitude. When we have a giving and generous heart the world looks and feels a little different to us.

Have you ever been on a mission trip, served at a food pantry, or given a friend something that he or she needs? It feels good, right? I saw an elderly lady stuck on a hill the other day. She was afraid to walk down because she thought she'd fall. I helped her and was reminded of the richness of my health and my youth. In turn I felt blessed. See how it works? It wasn't that I helped her down the hill and I received a check for $100. It was that my life was enriched by doing good in our world. How will you invest today?

Go and Do
Find five good things you can do today. Not so that you can be rewarded, but so that you can invest goodness into our world.

MEAT

> Hebrews 5:12-14 <

In fact. though by this time you ought to be teachers. you need someone to teach you the elementary truths of God's word all over again. You need milk. not solid food! Anyone who lives on milk. being still an infant. is not acquainted with the teaching about righteousness. But solid food is for the mature. who by constant use have trained themselves to distinguish good from evil.

There may come a point in your faith journey where you may find yourself lacking. It's OK. Do not panic. This sort of thing happens for a lot of people as they grow in their faith.

Consider an infant moving from an all-liquid diet to a more robust assortment of food. If the infant were to continue on just milk, that infant would have a very difficult time developoing. Our theology and spirituality are just the same. When we're beginning on our spiritual journey we need milk, we need to take it slowly and take little bits at a time. But, as we grow we need something a little more robust. That doesn't mean that we abandon the milk, it just stops being the main part of our nutritional plan.

I want to give you hope that what you experience in youth group is not the full plate of what Christianity has to offer. The bad news is that you will have to go deeper and oftentimes develop ways to replenish your soul and put yourself in front of challenging material. This is not always easy but is always worth the effort. So, when you get bored and want more, dig deeper, search farther, and know that God is calling you into a more robust faith.

Go and Do
Where are you now? Wherever you are, be grateful you are there. Remember, you are on a journey. If youth group inspires and excites you, Awesome. If this book challenges you, Awesome. If you need to read big theological books to push you, Awesome. If you do not know where you are on that journey, talk to your youth minister or pastor and see what sorts of ideas they have that will continue to challenge your faith.

MILK

>1 Corinthians 3:1-2<

Brothers. I could not address you as spiritual but as worldly—mere infants in Christ. I gave you milk. not solid food. for you were not yet ready for it. Indeed. you are still not ready.

Are you new to church, the faith, or maybe in your first year of youth group? If so, this one is for you! Do you know someone who fits into one of the categories above? Great. This devotion is for you too. We all start somewhere. We all begin by "drinking milk." When Paul talks about drinking milk he means that we all have to start off theologically and spiritually at a level that we can handle. When a baby is born you don't put a big T-bone steak in front of it. You have to start it off with what it can handle at that point in its life, which is milk.

When we begin in the faith we have to start off with basics, with things that we can digest. This is good. So if this is you, don't look at others who have been in the faith for years and wonder why they think about the faith differently and know a lot about the Bible. They have simply spent more time being formed in their faith. In a few years you will too! In some of the early churches, people had to be taught for a year or more before they were even allowed to be baptized and take communion.

Our growth in the faith is a process and we have to take it slow. If you're reading this and you've been in the faith for a while, make sure that you remember this with your younger brothers and sisters in the faith. Help them, and show them what it means to live as a Christ-follower. We all start somewhere. Just know that wherever you start is exactly where you should be.

Go and Do

Today write yourself a letter about where you are on your spiritual journey. Talk about your favorite verses, the most inspiring things you've read or heard lately and what your most pressing theological questions are. Then seal it up and open it up a year from now.

MOUNTAIN

>*Exodus 19:18-20*<

Mount Sinai was covered with smoke, because the LORD descended on it in fire. The smoke billowed up from it like smoke from a furnace, the whole mountain trembled violently, and the sound of the trumpet grew louder and louder. Then Moses spoke and the voice of God answered him. The LORD descended to the top of Mount Sinai and called Moses to the top of the mountain. So Moses went up.

Have you ever had the kind of moment where you just knew God was there? Those moments don't happen all the time. But when they do it's amazing. In the Old Testament, we see this sort of encounter happen often and many of those times it is on top of a mountain. One of the most famous of those encounters is in Exodus 19. Moses is summoned up to the mountain, and God is there waiting for him.

I love retreats. I love retreats because it feels a lot like the story in Exodus. It feels like God is summoning or calling us to a different place and that God is waiting for us there. God calls us out of our normal lives sometimes to do extraordinary things, so that when we return we're changed. We can bring about God's change in our world.

If you keep reading this story you will find that God does not call Moses to the mountain for no reason. When Moses climbed down he carried God's law for the people, the 10 Commandments. When God calls us to the mountain, we can expect to be changed, but we can also expect that God's going to do change in our world through us as well. Ready to go on a hike?

Go and Do
In this devotional the mountain is a metaphor for a place that God calls us to outside of our normal routine. But sometimes it's really helpful to actually go to a mountain. When you get to the top or to an overlook there's a sense that God is there and that our God is a very big God. Sometime soon, go for a hike, climb a mountain, and look over the inspiring wonders that God created. Go and be inspired.

OCEAN

> Job 11:7-9 <

Can you fathom the mysteries of God? Can you probe the limits of the Almighty? They are higher than the heavens—what can you do? They are deeper than the depths of the grave—what can you know? Their measure is longer than the earth and wider than the sea.

Space exploration is a big deal these days. We've spent the last 50 years exploring outer space. And the results have been awesome. But many scientists have recently turned their attention to another place of exploration: the ocean. While there's still so much to explore in space, we're realizing that the ocean still holds more mysteries than we could've ever imagined. We're constantly discovering new kinds of organisms, plant life, and fish on the bottom of the ocean floor. We're realizing that we've only scratched the surface of what we know about the ocean.

God is much like the ocean. We can observe some things about Him, but there are still mysteries beyond anything we could ever imagine. Someone once told me, "When you think you have God figured out, that's when you need to begin searching even harder, because what you've figured out is not God. God is too big for us to be able to put in a box." While that made me pretty nervous, it did help me to understand that I'll never fully grasp who God is and what God wants me to do. And that's OK.

It's OK because I know that I, like everyone else, am on a journey toward a God who is knowable in a personal way, but still so very deep and mysterious. Don't be discouraged when you can't figure God out. You were never meant to. You and I are both called to keep exploring, discovering, and being amazed by the beauty and wonder that we discover in God's character and His ways.

Go and Do
As you grow in your faith and learn more about who God is, I encourage you to write down your thoughts. Don't be afraid if your thoughts and ideas about God change over time. That's good and natural. It just means that you're still searching and that God is still being discovered in your life.

OSTRICH

> Job 39:13-16 <

"The wings of the ostrich flap joyfully, but they cannot compare with the pinions and feathers of the stork. She lays her eggs on the ground and lets them warm in the sand, unmindful that a foot may crush them, that some wild animal may trample them. She treats her young harshly, as if they were not hers; she cares not that her labor was in vain.

I bet you didn't know the Bible talked about ostriches did you? Yeah, it doesn't speak too highly of the ostrich. Essentially the Book of Job says that the ostrich is a dumb animal. One of the main reasons it talks poorly about the ostrich is how the bird treats its eggs and its young. The ostrich is apparently really careless with its eggs and doesn't protect them very well. So, yeah . . . not a pretty picture.

I've been in youth ministry for 16 years and every time I read this story I can't help but think about how some youth groups treat the young kids who are moving up into the youth ministry. High school kids will talk about not wanting to be with the "little kids" or will put them through a form of youth group hazing. This isn't good at all. Young teenagers are already nervous about coming. The last thing they need is a group who feel it's up to them to make this transition harder.

Those new kids are like the babies of the youth group. They need to be welcomed like a family member. They need to be protected and shown the ways of the group. If you're reading this, I'm assuming that you're in some sort of youth group (if not get in one; they can be pretty awesome). I'm calling on you to help the new kids come into the group and feel welcomed. Don't leave them out to fend for themselves or treat them like you don't like them. Don't be an ostrich.

Go and Do
Think about how you were welcomed or not welcomed into the group. Take some time and talk with your youth minister about how your youth group can more intentionally welcome kids and don't be an ostrich.

PATH

>2 Kings 2:13-14<

He picked up the cloak that had fallen from Elijah and went back and stood on the bank of the Jordan. Then he took the cloak that had fallen from him and struck the water with it. "Where now is the LORD, the God of Elijah?" he asked. When he struck the water, it divided to the right and to the left, and he crossed over.

Do you know the story of Elijah and Elisha? If not, here it is in a nutshell. Elijah was a great man who did loads of incredible things in the name of God. Elisha traveled with him throughout most of these journeys. Elijah was Elisha's mentor and friend. Elijah showed him the way and warned him of the pitfalls. They walked side by side until Elijah was taken up to heaven in whirlwind on a fiery chariot. (Yup, you read that correctly.) Suddenly Elisha was alone.

When I read this it makes me think less of the two men and more of what it looks like growing up in youth group. Usually, in youth group, you're either an Elisha or Elijah. If you are an Elisha you're learning the ropes, coming on the retreats, and playing the games. You usually have some Elijah's that you look up to. Then it happens. You've been hanging out with these older kids and growing up in youth group with them and suddenly they're gone. They graduate and now you feel all alone.

I want remind you that if you have some Elijah's in your life, they will one day leave and you'll be left. Don't let this discourage you, but take courage knowing that you are now an Elijah for someone else. I love in the passage above where Elijah has just gone away. Immediately Elisha picks up where he left off in his ministry. If you're an Elijah, know that there are people looking up to you in the youth group. You can play a role in helping them become leaders when you move on.

Go and Do
Are you an Elijah or an Elisha right now? If you're an Elijah, who are your Elisha's? If you're an Elisha who is your Elijah? How are you preparing for that fiery chariot experience?

PHONE

>Hebrews 10:24-25<

And let us consider how we may spur one another on toward love and good deeds. Let us not give up meeting together, as some are in the habit of doing, but let us encourage one another—and all the more as you see the Day approaching.

A long time ago, like when I was a kid, there was a telephone commercial whose tagline was, "reach out and touch someone." It was a commercial about long distance calling and how you were never more than a phone call away, no matter where you were.

A lot has changed since that commercial. With the invention of cell phones, texting, social media, and the Internet we have the entire world at our fingertips. It's interesting, however, when polled more people than ever feel disconnected and alone. So how can that be? With more ways to communicate than ever, how can we as a people feel so lonely? Just because we have technology that allows to communicate doesn't mean that we should stop spending face-to-face time together. It also means that when we are together we need to really "be" together and not focused somewhere else by being on our devices.

In Hebrews it commends us to not give up meeting together. Now when that verse was written, there were no phones or technology. But the truth is still the same: there is something deeply spiritual and Christian about being together intentionally. When we're together and focus on one another, we gain so much and begin to really know one another. Our social media and technology is no substitute for sharing the same space together. These things aren't bad; they're just not a replacement for real personal contact with friends and family.

Go and Do
This is going to be tough. When you're in a room with family or friends I want you to put your phone somewhere else. Seriously. It might be one of the most difficult things you do this week. It will be interesting to see what you think and how you feel. Try this experiment a couple of times and see how it changes how you talk to people and the kinds of conversations you have with them.

PICTURE

> *Romans 5:8* <

But God demonstrates his own love for us in this: While we were still sinners, Christ died for us.

I bet that most of you who are reading this don't remember at time before there were digital cameras. Many of you might not even remember a time before camera phones. Photography was very different before we had digital cameras. It used to be that you would buy a roll of film, take all of the pictures on it, usually 24 or 32, and you would send the roll of film off to be developed. A week or so later you could come and pick your film up and for the first time since you took the pictures, you would actually get to see them. When you picked them up you also had to buy the whole roll, the good, the bad, and the ugly.

Fast forward to today. You can take 1,000 selfies on your camera phone and choose your absolute favorite and erase the others. Then you can put the pic on social media. We do this because we want the world to see us in a certain way, smiling with our eyes wide open, perfect lighting and doing something awesome all of the time. I think sometimes we believe that we have to present out lives the same way.

We all pretend to have perfect lives, where we're always doing something fun and interesting. That's exhausting. It's exhausting because that's not our lives. We are messy, flawed, sometimes happy, sometimes depressed, and a good bit of the time, uninteresting. And that's OK! You don't have to pretend that you're perfect. You are wonderfully flawed. You don't have it all together. You mess up. But you are deeply loved by God exactly how you are.

Go and Do
Get with some friends and take some "real" pictures of yourselves. Take pictures of yourselves not smiling. Take pics of yourselves looking angry, sad, scared, confused, and silly. Make sure you laugh at yourselves when you do this but then keep them, print them even, and remember that God loves you exactly as you are.

PUPPY

>Ecclesiastes 3:1<

There is a time for everything, and a season for every activity under heaven:

Puppies are amazing. Seriously. They are cute, soft, cuddly, and they smell awesome. They're funny, clumsy, and so darn lovable you just want to hold them all of the time. I'm not kidding. Puppies are one of God's most adorable creations. But, they don't stay puppies forever. I have a Lab/ St Bernard mix named Ruby. She was probably the cutest puppy I've ever laid eyes on. But she's not a puppy anymore. She changed. Do I still love her? Yes. But she's different.

When God designed the earth, God didn't plan for things to be created and stay the same. God made it where all of creation changes over time. From the clouds in the sky, to the rocks that make up the continents, it all changes. So do we. As you grow up, you'll do just that: grow up. You'll change. Your relationships will change. Your thoughts, motivations, actions, passions, and interests will change.

One of the saddest things I see in youth ministry is when people become stuck in one place. This usually happens when they find a place where they feel comfortable. This happens in high school and college a lot. There will be people who are in their 30's who are still trying to live like they are in high school. They live each day trying to recreate those glory days, and it's sad. We change, life changes, the world changes, and that change is good. Don't fear change or reject it. Welcome it as a part of what God created. There is a time for everything and every season.

Go and Do
One of the things that help us with change is to have milestones in our lives that mark change. Some of these are built in, like confirmation, graduation, your first job, engagement, marriage, and so on. I think we should make other milestones where we can look back and see the closing of one chapter and the beginning of another. As you close a chapter of your life, make sure to take some time and reflect on what was and what is to come. Maybe you could do that now?

RADAR

>*Luke 24:30-32*<

When he was at the table with them, he took bread, gave thanks, broke it and began to give it to them. Then their eyes were opened and they recognized him, and he disappeared from their sight. They asked each other, "Were not our hearts burning within us while he talked with us on the road and opened the Scriptures to us?"

Radar devices are used in millions of ways everyday. From keeping planes from bumping into each other, to scanning the bottoms of the ocean, these are amazing machines. You're probable like me when you hear "radar" you think of a round green screen and a line that spins like a clock's seconds hand. When something comes close, within the radars sight, there a blip on the screen that alerts the viewer. I like to think that we as Christ-followers should have a radar of sorts as well. We should always have our radar going for places where God is already working and is calling us to work as well.

It's so easy to walk through our lives with our radar turned off. We miss so many opportunities to join in the work that God's doing. We also miss so many opportunities to do ministry with friends, family, and those we encounter each day. The only way we will be able to know about these chances to join with God is to keep our radar up and looking for where people need God. We have to be intentional or else we will walk through life missing these times.

It can be so easy to miss the presence of God. Just look at these two travelers. They were walking directly beside the resurrected Jesus and they missed Him completely. Don't walk right past an opportunity to show others God and miss your chance to be a light in the world.

Go and Do
Walk today with eyes wide open.

RADIO

>*Isaiah 55:8*<

"For my thoughts are not your thoughts, neither are your ways my ways," declares the LORD.

I try to understand it but I just can't. Every time I do it there's still a tiny bit of amazement that runs through my mind. How in the world does this happen? It makes no sense. I know that theory, I know the science, I know the technology. But how anyone figured it out and made devices to make it works still amazes me. I'm not talking about the creation of the world, or nanophysics. I'm talking about the radio. How in the world does that work???

Again, I know technically how it works. But it makes no sense to me as to how these waves are created that have voices on them, and are shot through the air to a receiver of some sort, that "catches" it and then translates it again through a speaker. WHAT?!?! The other crazy thing is that this all happens in a split second! There are all sorts of things like this that I can't wrap my mind around but I accept it and depend on it every day. Things like the radio, Internet, wireless, cell phones, planes, television, and a million other things. Although I don't understand these things, there are people who do. Not only do they understand it, but they understood it enough that they created it and continue to create other amazing new technologies.

Here's the cool thing: there are things that not even the world's amazingly smart people understand. God is one of them. Now, we can know God. And we can pursue growing our knowledge of God. But, at the end of the day there will just be some things about God and His character that we will never fully understand. God is simply too vast for us to comprehend fully. And that's actually a pretty cool thing.

Go and Do
What are those issues of faith that you can't grasp no matter how hard you try? Keep trying, keep seeking, and keep thinking. But know that there are times when it's ok to look to the heavens and know that God's ways are just higher than ours. And that's OK.

RAIN

> *Matthew 3:16-17* <

As soon as Jesus was baptized, he went up out of the water. At that moment heaven was opened, and he saw the Spirit of God descending like a dove and lighting on him. And a voice from heaven said, "This is my Son, whom I love; with him I am well pleased."

It was March of 2010. I was in Port au Prince, Haiti and you could smell death everywhere. I went to a team just a couple of months after the earthquake in Haiti which killed close to 160,000 people. It was horrible. The streets were filled with debris, buildings had crumbled in on themselves, and there were still thousands of bodies under them. The city was hot and dusty and everywhere you looked was filled with death and destruction. It was overwhelming.

We were working to rebuild a wall just outside of the school for boys. It was a massive stone wall that had fallen during the earthquake and had to come down the rest of the way and be removed. It was hard work and the heat was incredible. We worked a few days in these conditions when it happened. At the end of our third day onsite it began to sprinkle, and in very little time that trickle became a downpour. It was amazing. Everything cooled off, the dust was washed away, and for the first time since we'd been there, the smell of death was not on the air. Everything had been cleansed. Death was seemingly washed away.

This story of renewal reminds me a lot of baptism. It's a beautiful symbol of the washing away of death and the new life that follows. When we're baptized we're symbolically united with Christ through Jesus' death, burial, and resurrection. When that water goes over someone's head it symbolizes that washing away of death and the beginning of a life in Christ.

Go and Do
Have you ever been baptized? You may have been young or it may have been recent. Go this week and see if you can find pictures of your baptism. Talk with friends and family about what that day was like if you can't remember it. Take some time and talk with your pastor about Baptism what it means to them.

RAINBOW

> *Genesis 9:16* <

Whenever the rainbow appears in the clouds. I will see it and remember the ever-lasting covenant between God and all living creatures of every kind on the earth.

Rainbows are always sort of magical and surprising. I've probably seen hundreds of them, but every time I see a new one I find myself in just as much awe and wonder. They really are beautiful and inspiring handiworks of God. This passage in Genesis tells us that rainbows are supposed to remind us of God's covenant with all living creatures on earth. A covenant is a binding promise between two or more people.

When I think of a rainbow, I often think of hope. Noah and his family had been adrift on an endless sea for 40 days when they finally found land. Can you imagine? I'm sure that must have been an incredibly scary and lonely time. After they found land the Bible says that a rainbow appeared in the sky. It was a symbol of God's promise to the earth.

When you're sad, confused, drifting, and scared, what do you find hope in? Oftentimes we believe that we're alone in this world and that there's no hope. As people of faith we never have to feel alone. God really is with us at all times. We never have to feel hopeless either. God never leaves us and has given us a way to live. We can go through this life knowing that we're loved and that God has called us to go and live goodness in our world. You have a purpose and a mission. You are never floating adrift in this life. Experience hope, knowing that the God who created this universe cares individually about you.

Go and Do
What brings you hope? Is it a hug? Helping someone in need? Reading the Bible? What are those things, like the rainbow, that remind you that God is there and will never leave your side?

RAKE

> Micah 4:3 <

He will judge between many peoples and will settle disputes for strong nations far and wide. They will beat their swords into plowshares and their spears into pruning hooks. Nation will not take up sword against nation, nor will they train for war anymore.

Do you know the story of Alfred Noble and dynamite? It's a pretty cool story. Alfred Nobel, they guy who the Nobel peace prize is named after, is the one who invented dynamite. It might seem strange that someone who invented explosives has a peace prize named after him. But it makes sense when you know why he invented it. He invented dynamite to help blast through mountains to create tunnels, bridges, and other important engineering feats. He invented explosives for the good of humanity. Unfortunately, they haven't always been used as such. As you know, explosives have been used to take millions of lives and to do great harm in our world.

In book of Micah, the prophet Micah called us to live into a world where we take things that were made to wage war and cause death and turn them into things that garner peace and produce goodness for the world. He imagines a world where we choose to take the resources afforded to us and create good from them. Think about it: things like the Internet, social media, our words, our hands, laws, power, and a million other things can be used for either great good or terrible evils. We have loads of choices everyday to decide how we will use these things, and what good or harm will be done with them.

Micah chooses to take tools of war and turn them into tools of agriculture so that everyone can eat and have enough. What will we choose to do with the tools we're given?

Go and Do

A resource is neither good nor evil. It's all about how we use it. How do you use your words, influence, and resources for great good or terrible harm? Is God honored or is God's name run through the mud with what you do? How will you use what you have to do the greatest of good?

REARVIEW

> *Philippians 3:13* <

Brothers. I do not consider myself yet to have taken hold of it. But one thing
I do: Forgetting what is behind and straining toward what is ahead.

We knew her as "Crazy Dot." Dot was this wild-haired, short woman who lived in our hometown. You would always see her by herself walking around a grocery store, the post office, or driving her old beat up grey Oldsmobile. This thing would barely run and didn't even have a rearview mirror. She always had a crazy look in her eye, and sometimes it seemed like she was muttering to herself. None of us really knew her but we knew that something wasn't right.

One day after we'd seen her driving around town in that beat up car, we were talking about her and an adult at the church overheard us. That adult then told us Dot's story. Dot used to be married, have kids, a nice house, and was well liked in the community. She was far from crazy. Then she lost everything. Her husband, child, and home were all taken away from her. That was when everything changed in her life. She was never able to get over that loss and she spent the rest of her life living in that moment. First, I felt really bad for making fun of her. Second, I started thinking about that car she would drive around. What if Dot's life were more like her car? What if Dot's life didn't have a rearview mirror? What if she had to stop looking backwards and had to begin looking forward?

Sometimes we live life where we're constantly looking in the rearview mirror and forget to look forward to where we're going. Paul encourages us in these verses to strive forward to what God is calling us to. Don't live a life looking into your rearview. You'll miss the world that's waiting on you ahead.

Go and Do
What are the rearview mirrors in your life? What are those things that you keep you from moving forward? Spend some time figuring out what these are and what are the ways you can stop living in "what was" and look forward to "what is."

RING

>*Matthew 3:14-15*<

Then Jesus came from Galilee to the Jordan to be baptized by John. 14 But John tried to deter him, saying, "I need to be baptized by you, and do you come to me?" Jesus replied, "Let it be so now; it is proper for us to do this to fulfill all righteousness." Then John consented.

I'm a big fan of wedding rings. I love mine. I see it everyday and if I ever take it off (which is usually only when I work with clay or play baseball), I miss it. I like it also because it's a sign to the rest of the world that there's someone to whom I am deeply committed. Someone whom I love beyond anything else. It says something to those who see me. It's an outward symbol of something that's much deeper.

The cool thing about symbols is that they mean something beyond what they are. A stop sign doesn't physically make you stop, but it's a symbol that we all know signifies something. There are things in our life as a people of faith that are outward symbols of something much deeper as well. Things like communion and baptism. There's nothing magical about these two things. They are symbols, deep and meaningful symbols of something much deeper. These are symbols and practices that reflect that we're people of God and that we're aligning ourselves with God. Just like my wedding ring, it's not magical, but it does tell the world something about me.

What are things and practices in your life that tell the world about who you are? What are things you do that symbolize to the rest of the world and yourself who you are and whose you are?

Go and Do
Symbols are really important things. Again, think about the stop sign. Take a look at your life and look at what symbols you carry or promote. What do your symbols say about your life? What deeper truth about you are they reflecting?

RIVER

> John 7:38 <

Whoever believes in me, as the Scripture has said, streams of living water will flow from within him."

If you go to the Jordan Valley between modern day Israel and Jordan, you'll see something absolutely amazing. You will see a literal river of life. Once you get south of the Sea of Galilee the land turns to very dry and dusty desert. There's almost nothing around except for dust and rocks. It's an incredibly desolate place, except for one thin vein of life that runs through the middle. In the middle of this dry and sparse desert there's a green plush strip of life. It's full of vegetation. It's really an amazing site to see. The Jordan River is a literal river of life.

We're called to have these rivers of life flowing out of us. We live in a dry and desolate world a lot of the time. It can be a place that's harsh and very difficult for people to survive in. We have the opportunity to bring life into this often-tough environment. Think about it: at your school, who's the one who brings laughter and joy? Who in your home brings peace and happiness? Who, when he or she sees people sad and alone, steps in to be a friend and helps them out of darkness and into light? I hope you answered those questions with your own name. If not let that be your goal.

Let your faith be contagious. Let your light shine and bring life into all of those you come in contact with. When people meet you, live in such a way so that they know something is very good and very different about you. Let a river of goodness and life flow from your heart, and let that river bring life to all you meet.

Go and Do
Who are people in your life who bring life to you? Who are those people who inspire you and cause you to want to be a closer follower of God? This week go and tell those people how they bring light into your life, and let them know how much you appreciate it.

ROAD

> *Luke 24:32* <

They asked each other, "Were not our hearts burning within us while he talked with us on the road and opened the Scriptures to us?"

One way to understand our life is as if it were a journey. In this journey we travel down many roads. Some roads are paved and easy, others are rocky and difficult. Some roads we travel alone, and others with company. On this journey we meet fellow companions. Some of them are easy to get along with, and others are . . . well let's say not quite as easy to get along with!

I love this story of the road to Emmaus. It's a beautiful story of two companions who meet a stranger. They ask the stranger to join them. They are kind to him, even inviting him to eat dinner with them and stay for the night. Through this hospitality and kindness they realize that the stranger they had been walking with was actually the resurrected Jesus! Pretty cool, right?

You're going to meet so many different people in your life, so many that you won't be able to remember them all. When you do meet someone, no matter who they seem to be, treat them with kindness. We owe that to each other. In this story, because the two friends chose to treat this stranger with kindness, they were able to be in the presence of the living Christ in a way that would forever change them. So when you meet someone, treat them as a friend, take care of them, and show them goodness and love. You never know just how important you can be to him or her. You also never know just how important he or she can be to you.

Go and Do

Do you have a plan for when you meet new people? Most of us don't. We just randomly meet these people and whatever happens, just happens. I want to encourage you to have a plan when you meet new people on your journey. Make sure to introduce yourself, ask about who they are, and show real interest in their answers. Make sure they feel welcome and loved by you.

SCREEN

> John 10:10 <

The thief comes only to steal and kill and destroy; I have come that they may have life, and have it to the full.

Do you like movies? I love them. I love to watch a good drama, action, suspense, comedies, and even the occasional rom-com. Movies are incredible, not just because of the special effects and the awesome plot twists, but because they tell powerful stories that shape our lives and how we understand the world. They give us insight into ways of thinking and of viewing other people's lives like nothing else can.

I love to watch movies about things that really happened. Usually after I watch them I'm left in awe of that person's life and the way they changed the world for good (or for bad). I often leave wondering to myself, "What would it look like if someone were to put my life on film and project it on a giant screen?" Would my story inspire people? Would it make them laugh? Would it be embarrassing? What would my story look like?

John tells us to live a life that's full and abundant. Jesus even goes as far as to say that's one of the reasons He came. Life is a gift. One of my old professors and friends Dr. John Claypool used to say that being born is our only right, and that every breath after that is a gift. So what will you with the gift of your life? Will you waste it away? Will you use it selfishly? Will you bless others with it? What will you choose to do with each of your days? Start writing the story you want your life to tell today.

Go and Do
Buy or find one of those old paper calendars. From this day forward keep that paper calendar by your bed. Each night before you go to bed, in the little box for that day, write what you're proud that you did that day. Let your goal be to put something you are proud of in the box every day. Start writing your story.

SEED

> *Luke 19:7-10* <

All the people saw this and began to mutter. "He has gone to be the guest of a 'sinner.'" But Zacchaeus stood up and said to the Lord. "Look. Lord! Here and now I give half of my possessions to the poor. and if I have cheated anybody out of anything. I will pay back four times the amount." Jesus said to him. "Today salvation has come to this house. because this man. too. is a son of Abraham. For the Son of Man came to seek and to save what was lost."

Read Luke 19:1-10. If someone looked at an acorn they would not be terribly impressed. I mean it looks sort of cool. But it's nothing special. That is unless you know the potential it holds. When people looked at Zacchaeus, they saw a short guy who lied, cheated, and stole from them. That was who he was, plain and simple. Except, not really. When Jesus looked at Zacchaeus He wasn't hung up with what He saw before Him. He was motivated by what He knew was possible.

One of the amazing things we see constantly throughout Jesus' ministry is how He would refuse to accept what everyone saw on the outside of people. Most people saw a woman caught in adultery; He saw a person hurt and needing love. Most people saw a Samaritan; He saw someone who had been abused and without friends. Jesus did this constantly.

When we look at people, do we accept what's on the outside or do we go deeper? Jesus saw potential. He saw deeper truth. Can we? The acorn starts as one thing now. But with some love and time it will grow into something beautiful.

Go and Do
Have you ever grown anything from a seed? If not you should. It's pretty incredible to see something so small grow into something hundreds of times its original size. Over the next few months, plant some seeds, water them, put them in the sun, and monitor them. Watch how they grow. As this happens remember how we're all like that seed; what you see today is not what you get tomorrow.

SHOE

> *Joshua 1:3* <

I will give you every place where you set your foot, as I promised Moses.

I think it's so interesting to look at an old tattered pair of shoes and think about where all they've been. It's fun to wonder how many miles they have traveled, how many puddles they've stepped in, and all of the places they've seen during their life. It's also fun when you get a new pair of shoes to think of where all they'll go.

This verse in Joshua 1:3 is a promise to Joshua that all of the land that was Moses' will also be Joshua's now that Moses had died. It's a verse where God is telling Joshua that he is now the leader of the people. I think we can also read it with that understanding that everywhere our shoe touches, everywhere we walk, is a place God has given to us. Not literally, of course. Please don't walk into someone's house and claim it in the name of God as your own! I do think, however, that every place we walk is given to us as an opportunity to do something for God's Kingdom. We have opportunities to learn, help, reflect, rest, encourage, love, support, change, be helped, and be amazed in every place our shoe walks.

Unfortunately we walk through most of our lives not thinking about the places we find ourselves in this way. We most often don't think about each situation we walk into as an opportunity. In fact we don't consciously think about most of what we do at all. What if we really understood God as telling us that every place we walk is a place that He has given us? Would it change what you do and how you think about the places your shoe touches? I hope so.

Go and Do

Take a moment to write down all of the places your shoes have taken you. Then, beside each place you list, write what you did in that place. How did you take advantage of opportunities? How did you do good in those places? Let this exercise help you go through life more intentional about what you do in the places you go.

SIGN

>2 Timothy 3:16-17<

All Scripture is God-breathed and is useful for teaching, rebuking, correcting and training in righteousness. so that the man of God may be thoroughly equipped for every good work.

Have you have ever been to Disney World? It's a pretty incredible place. There are castles, princesses, roller coasters, and some of your favorite cartoon characters all in one pretty amazing place in central Florida. When you drive down to Orlando and you approach the theme park, there's this massive sign that stretches above the entire road that says, "Welcome to Walt Disney World." That sign is unmistakably pointing you to the Magic Kingdom!

I took my youth group to Disney a few years. When we arrived at the big sign, I pulled the bus over, everyone got out, and we all lined up in front of that massive sign and took a great group shot. We stood there and believed for sure that the big "Welcome to Walt Disney World" sign was surely pointing us in the direction of the "happiest place on earth." Then, after a few minutes, we all got back in the bus and drove home.

Why do you look so confused? Isn't that what you're supposed to do when you're on a trip? Aren't you supposed to plan for months and months, drive for 11 hours, arrive at the sign, get out, take your pics, admire it, talk about it, and go home? Of course not! It was just the sign, and the sign is not Disney World. The sign points us to Disney World. Beyond that sign is an incredible place that will blow your mind. It's the real reason you drive all that way.

Sometimes we treat the Bible like that Disney sign. Many of us stop at it, focusing our time and energy on it alone. But the Bible is only a sign, an incredibly important sign. But one that still only points us to God. The Bible is not God. God is much bigger. Don't stop at the sign. It points to a whole other world that is waiting for you.

Go and Do
Do you stop at the sign or do you go beyond?

SKYSCRAPER

> *Psalm 72:18* <

Praise be to the LORD God, the God of Israel, who alone does marvelous deeds.

Skyscrapers never cease to amaze me. I remember the first time I saw a real skyscraper, I just couldn't stop staring at it. Its enormity was dizzying. After I became used to the sheer size and mass of a building like that, I began to think about how incredible it is that we, as humans, could build something that huge. It's incredible to think about all the parts that have to be just right to make that sort of building stand on its own. It's also amazing to think of all the innumerous tons of steel and other materials that had to be made to make that building. Finally, to think about all of the hands that worked on those materials to put them into place and build this incredible structure.

But what if we went even further. What if we thought about those hands a little more, about how there are in that hand, 27 tiny intricate bones, with 35 muscles that move and connect those bones? What if we thought about the body that hand is connected to, how it has 350 bones that make it up? Or about how there are around 650 muscles that control those bones and allow them to do amazing things? Or what about the almost 100,000 miles of veins that provide blood to the body to make it work? We have skin that sheds and renews itself constantly. We have a heart that pumps blood through veins that connects to our lungs which take in oxygen that will then be put back into that blood. We can see, eat, talk, and write, each of which are processes that originate from our brain. We are amazing beings.

Those skyscrapers are incredible. We can truly make amazing things. But I think it may be even more powerful to think of how God's incredible creation, humans, trumps anything we can create.

Go and Do
Look into a mirror today and be in awe at what God created when He created you.

SMILE

> *Proverbs 15:30* <

A cheerful look brings joy to the heart, and good news gives health to the bones.

It's incredible the amount of influence we have in people's lives without ever saying a word. Our faces tell the story of our emotions and moods and often send those emotions to others. There are actually scientific studies that tell us that when we smile we cause ourselves to be happier and cause others around us to be happier as well!

The verse in Proverbs 15 reflects this. When we enter into a room with our shoulders slumped and a frown on our face, we automatically tell the room that we're down. We can cause the rest of the room to come down as well. On the other hand, when we show happy emotions on our face, smile at others, and reflect joy, we can bring the entire room's mood to a whole new level. Now, don't get me wrong; I don't think we should fake being happy. No one wants you to fake happiness when you're feeling down. However, a lot of our happiness depends on our perspective.

I'm sure you've heard the question asked before, "Do you see the glass as half full, or half empty?" I hope you look at your own life as a life that's "half full." We have so much to be grateful and thankful for. I hope that you spend your life being grateful for what you have and helping to bring joy to others you meet. I hope you smile. Smile because you're alive! Smile because you have others who love you. Smile because you have a reason to live. Smile because you have no clue how much joy you can bring to those around you with such a simple action. Just smile.

Go and Do
Today, constantly ask yourself, "what am I telling others about my life with my facial expression"? Also think about how you're helping others feel with how you express your emotions. Go and make the world a little brighter today.

SONG

>1 Chronicles 15:22<

Kenaniah the head Levite was in charge of the singing: that was his responsibility because he was skillful at it.

Do you understand the power of songs? Songs are incredible. They can often express things that words alone don't have the ability to grasp. We can sing when we are joyful; we can sing when we are sad; we can sing when we do not know what else to do.

I remember in January of 2011 watching the earthquake in Port au Prince, Haiti. Death, destruction, chaos, and fear. Piles of rubble three stories high were covering what were once stores and homes. Disaster in the midst of poverty eclipsed every frame of every picture taken in those days and months after the earthquake. But, a few days after the main earthquake, with the ground still shaking with tremors and aftershocks, in the middle of those frames of chaos, they sang. It started as a small group but before long there were hundreds. It was mainly women, women who had lost sons and daughters, husbands, and parents, friends and neighbors. And they sang. They walked through the streets between the towers of rubble lifting their voices. They sang out of fear and they sang out of hope. It was powerful.

Songs have the ability to take us to a different place. Especially songs of praise to God. They allow us to overcome where we are and see something different than what's in front of us. Songs are entertaining, yes, but they're so much more. Let your voice lift in song to God. When you're happy. When you're sad. And when you don't even know what you are. Don't worry about how you sound. Just sing.

Go and Do
Make a list of songs. Not necessarily the most popular songs or even your favorite songs, but a list of songs that move you. Make a list of songs that take you to another place and transform you from the inside out. Then beside each song, write why it moves you. Be aware of these songs and how others affect you. Find God in these and let them be an offering to God.

STARS

> *Psalm 8:3-4* <

When I consider your heavens. the work of your fingers. the moon and the stars. which you have set in place. what is man that you are mindful of him. the son of man that you care for him?

Have you ever just sat and looked at the sky late on a dark night? It's overwhelming. There are just so many stars, they're all so very far away, and are so bright. You can't count them. There are simply too many. For me it's humbling to look at them. When I look at them and know that they're light years away, well, it's difficult to look at that masterpiece and not feel so incredibly small and insignificant.

David did this. I imagine him lying on his back looking up at the wonder that is the night sky. Then it hits him: wow we're small! And David was right: we are so very, very small. But our God loves us and knows us just the same.

This gives me hope. It gives me hope that I matter, that I am loved, and that I am known. It's truly amazing that a God who busies Himself with creating massive balls of intergalactic fire traveling at thousands of miles per hour chooses to call me His own, and to know every hair on my head. It's humbling and it's challenging. It makes me want to matter, to do something to honor the one who loves me. More than that, though, I find myself just marveling at the power and creative genius of God. What a mighty God we serve.

Go and Do
Find a clear night sky, sit under it, and let the enormity of it all consume you.

STATUE

> *Proverbs 22:1* <

A good name is more desirable than great riches; to be esteemed is better than silver or gold.

One of my favorite things to do is to look at statues. They are incredible works of art that last for hundreds even thousands of years. In some museums you can even touch ancient statues. Sometimes statues are made purely for the purposes of art, but most of the time they're made to honor someone. Many times it's to honor someone who has contributed to our world in positive ways.

I think about the statues of Abraham Lincoln and Martin Luther King Jr. in Washington DC, and the statues of leaders and martyrs throughout the world. The statues that seem to matter the most are ones that are created based on people who did great things, not who had great riches. Sure, you can commission a statue of yourself if you have enough money, but these aren't the ones that stand out. The ones that we celebrate are the ones that represent people that changed our world for good.

Often when I see statues I will think of those people in my life who I would have a statue made of. Those people who have done good in my life and have inspired me to be better. I also hope that I've been that for people; that I've inspired them changed their lives for the better. In downtown Birmingham there's a statue of a man kneeling down looking up toward God in prayer. It's called the Brother Bryan statue named after a Presbyterian minister who loved the city and worked to make it better. He was a forerunner to the Civil Rights movement in the city in the 30's and 40's. He's a man who deserved a statue. Who in your life deserves one too?

Go and Do
While most of us don't have the money or the artistic ability to make statues for those in our lives who deserve them, we can do something else to honor them. I would encourage you, this week, to write a list of each person in your life who are your "statue people." Then every week after write one letter to each of them to tell them that they are statue people to you and why.

STEPS

>1 Corinthians 6:12<

"Everything is permissible for me"—but not everything is beneficial. "Everything is permissible for me"—but I will not be mastered by anything.

When I was a kid there was this saying that kids would say to each other when they didn't want to be bossed around. When they felt that someone was overstepping their bounds in telling them what to do the kid would respond, "its a free country I can do what I want!" I often remember thinking to myself, "Well I guess they're right, they can do what they want." But there are benefits and consequences to everything we do. It really goes back to making good choices; not just doing what we want, but doing what's best.

It's like if you're interested in losing weight you have choices every day that will either send you in the right direction, or in the wrong one. You can choose a salad over a burger, or grilled over fried. Or it's like being at the mall and choosing to take the stairs instead of taking the escalator. Sure there is nothing wrong with taking the escalator, but is it really helping you become who you want to be?

In our lives we have loads of choices to make everyday. We must practice making the best choices, even when we don't have to, or when no one is watching. Think about what is beneficial, not just what's acceptable. These types of choices are the things that will make long-term differences in your life and the lives of others. So, is it going to be the escalator (the easier choice) or the stairs (the better choice) today?

Go and Do
Remember these aren't going to always be terribly obvious choices. It's pretty easy to see those major things and know that we're not supposed to do them. The question here is about the small choices that add up to a big difference. Things like: is playing 6 hours of video games the best use of your time today? Should you really leave those comments on that social media site? What are those small changes that over time will make a big difference?

STONE

> *Joshua 4:20-23* <

And Joshua set up at Gilgal the twelve stones they had taken out of the Jordan. He said to the Israelites. "In the future when your descendants ask their fathers. 'What do these stones mean?' tell them. 'Israel crossed the Jordan on dry ground.' For the LORD your God dried up the Jordan before you until you had crossed over. The LORD your God did to the Jordan just what he had done to the Red Sea when he dried it up before us until we had crossed over.

One Summer I was working in Asheville, NC with the Jr. High group at my church. We were supposed to pick vegetables in a large field with all of the going to the poor and needy in that area. At least that's what we were planning on doing until the flood came. The night we arrived it rained five inches. The following day it rained another three inches. When we were finally able to get into the field it looked like someone had come and dumped a million stones all over it. The rain had washed all of the dirt away exposing all of these rocks. The farmer said that unless the stones were removed he wouldn't be able to work the field with his tractor. There was also another problem: all of the rain had washed out the little creek making it impassable for the tractor. So we began . . .

One five-gallon bucket at a time we cleared the field. Not only did we clear the field, we took the buckets and one by one dumped them into the creek. We took the stones that were in the field and built a bridge across the creek for the tractor. We worked hard all day. Finally the field was mostly cleared. It was pretty incredible. What was even more incredible was all of the stones that we could have just discarded had been built into a bridge across that creek. It was amazing seeing stones that were a hindrance turned into a help.

Go and Do
What are the stones in your life that you'll use to build something for God? What are those things you would usually pass by or discard that you can use to honor and remind those around you of who you are and what God you serve?

STOP SIGN

> *John 14:26* <

But the Counselor, the Holy Spirit, whom the Father will send in my name, will teach you all things and will remind you of everything I have said to you.

Jesus was crucified, buried, and rose from the dead on the third day to sit at the right hand of God. In other words, He's not here any longer. So how do we know what He would want us to do? How do we know how He would want us to follow Him? Well one way is the Bible. God's Word is an incredible guide for living as Christ-followers. Still, there are times where even after consulting the Bible, we're still confused. What can we rely upon in these situations? Jesus talked in John 14 about a help that would come lead us through this life, drawing us closer to God. Jesus said that God would send the Holy Spirit to give us direction.

The Holy Spirit works sort of like a stop sign. He gives us instructions about how to proceed. Now the thing about stop signs is that you have to depend on the person driving to actually follow the sign that is given. It's the same with the Holy Spirit. If you don't listen and follow, then it will be of little good.

God speaks to us through a variety of means: situations, circumstances, the voice of trusted friends and mentors, but most importantly, through the Holy Spirit. The Spirit is often that urging inside of us that seems to tell us when something is just not right, or points us to act on certain opportunities. Listen to the Spirit. Obey Him, just like you would a stop sign. And trust that God is calling you, through the Spirit, to live your life on mission for Him.

Go and Do
It can be difficult to determine what signs are from God and what directions are coming from our own wants and desires apart from God. Here's one thing to know: The Spirit never leads us to do anything that conflicts with God's Word or God's character. If you have questions about a specific leading you feel but don't know if it's God or you, always take it to the Bible. If it seems out of line with who God is, it's probably your desires leading you and not God's.

STORM

> Matthew 14:25-30 <

During the fourth watch of the night Jesus went out to them, walking on the lake. When the disciples saw him walking on the lake, they were terrified. "It's a ghost," they said, and cried out in fear. But Jesus immediately said to them: "Take courage! It is I. Don't be afraid." "Lord, if it's you," Peter replied, "tell me to come to you on the water." "Come," he said. Then Peter got down out of the boat, walked on the water and came toward Jesus. But when he saw the wind, he was afraid and, beginning to sink, cried out, "Lord, save me!

Peter always tried his hardest. You can see it over and over again in the gospels. He always wanted to be the one who jumped in and gave 100%. He was also the one who often made a fool of himself a few times. He would sometimes falter, his enthusiasm failing him in the midst of crucial times. The story of Peter walking on water is one of them.

Now, don't get me wrong; I completely understand why he sank. I'm not even sure I would've gotten out of the boat. Peter sank because he bought into the lie that the wind and the waves were more powerful than the one who was calling him to step out of the boat. Peter is often judged harshly because of this. But we all do it everyday. God is calling us out of the boat to do awesome and incredible things. And yet when we start to step out of what is safe, we take our eyes off the one who is calling us and instead focus on the storm that surrounds us.

Do you think that Jesus would have called Peter out onto the water just to have him drown? Me either. Jesus wanted Peter to experience something amazing. He wants to do the same for you, too.

Go and Do
If you know God is calling you to do something, you can trust that God is going to give you the strength and ability to do what He's called you to do. Pray today that God would give you the strength to follow through with obeying His calling.

SUITCASE

>*Isaiah 43:25*<

I, even I, am he who blots out your transgressions, for my own sake,
and remembers your sins no more.

It's incredible how quickly God is to forgive us and how difficult it is to forgive ourselves. I was 17 and I had messed up. I had done something that I wish I hadn't and I was ashamed. The weight of my guilt was heavy. I mean, I could physically feel it holding me down. I knew God had already forgiven me and my wrongdoing had already been taken away. While I knew God had let go of my sin, I could not. I carried it around with me like a suitcase.

I think a lot of us do this. We carry our guilt around with us holding onto it as though our lives depend on it. Many of us have a guilt suitcase and it's completely packed, overflowing even, and we carry it around with us every day. It's so difficult for most of us to understand that God forgives us with no consequence.

God tells us through the prophet Isaiah that He blots out, or erases, our transgressions. God says that He does it for His own sake. It's in the nature of God to forgive us. God finds pleasure in forgiving us and loves to make things right in our life. God also finds joy when we can actually forgive ourselves as well.

So put down the suitcase, unpack it and leave it behind. God has. So should you.

Go and Do

If you're struggling with guilt, find an old shoebox. Take it and let it be your suitcase. Write down the thing that's causing you guilt. Pray, thanking God for forgiving you, and asking Him to help free you from the guilt you feel. Then, put your paper in the shoebox. When you feel that you've come to a place of self-forgiveness, open up the shoebox and take out the paper. Wad or rip the paper up and throw it away. Remember that God has already done this. Let yourself do it as well.

SUN

> *Matthew 5:16* <

In the same way, let your light shine before men, that they may see your good deeds and praise your Father in heaven.

Most of what we see each day is made possible because of the light from the Sun. We can see a tree or the grass because the Sun's light illuminates them, reflecting off of different objects making them visible to us. If it's night time and we're in our house, chances are if we can see anything at all it's because the light from a light bulb is illuminating the things around us. Even the moon is an object that's visible only because light reflects off to it.

Jesus said that if we let our light shine before others, they would worship God as a result. I've always found this verse interesting. There are so many people in the world who do good things, and instead of God being praised because of it, they're the ones who receive all of the praise. I'm not saying that there's anything wrong with celebrating human accomplishments. But so often God is never thought of when goodness happens in our world.

We have to remember that when we do good in the world, we're being good reflectors. Like the Sun, God is shining down on us. We have a choice: do we dampen the light or do we live lives that reflect the light wherever we go? In order to reflect the light of God we have to make sure our lives reflect God's goodness. What are you doing to be a better reflector? How do you live in such a way that it shows others who God is and what He's doing in your life?

Go and Do
Oftentimes the places in our world that are the scariest and most dangerous are the places where there are few people who are there reflecting God's light. God calls us to step into that darkness and begin reflecting the light of God's goodness. Today I want you to think about situations around you or in your community that are full of darkness. Now, figure out how you and others can come into those situations and reflect God's goodness!

SWORD

> *Matthew 26:52* <

"Put your sword back in its place." Jesus said to him. "for all who draw the sword will die by the sword."

Too often we act as though violence creates peace. It doesn't. When you're angry with someone, hitting him or her doesn't make the situation better. When someone has talked about you, chewing him or her out does nothing but make more violence and hurt. When people kill because others have been killed, it only creates more killing. It hardly ever solves the problem. People often think it will make them feel good to hurt someone who hurts them. Though it might feel good for a moment, no good can come from this kind of situation.

God calls us to a different way of conducting ourselves. God has shown us through the life and teachings of Jesus that we don't have to return violence with violence and hate with hate. We have the choice to stop the cycles of violence and hate and not retaliate against those who hurt us.

Jesus was being falsely accused and arrested. In this verse, Peter acted as many of us would. He was ready to fight for his Lord and friend. But Jesus told Peter to put his sword away. Jesus knew that violence would only create more violence. Jesus knew that the way to peace and goodness in the world couldn't happen by harming those we were called to love, even those who we call the enemy. What enemies in your life need to be responded to with love?

Go and Do

When someone harms us, we want to hurt him or her back. It might not be with physical violence, but we want them to feel the pain that we felt. This is isn't the life Jesus called us to. We're called to love and pray for those who harm us. You're goal when someone hurts you should be to take a deep breath and remember Jesus' call. Respond appropriately. Live into the higher standard Jesus has called you to. And watch how God will change the world through your love.

TABLE

> *Acts 2:42* <

They devoted themselves to the apostles' teaching and to the fellowship, to the breaking of bread and to prayer.

Some of the best times I can remember happened around a table. Whether it was playing board games, sitting at lunch with friends growing up, Thanksgiving and Christmas meals, dates with my wife, eating fish and plantains in Panama, or sitting down with my wife and three kids for breakfast every morning, time around the table is special for me. I look forward to making even more memories around tables.

The table, and meals in general, have always held a special place in our Christian faith. The first Christians in the Book of Acts made the table a centerpiece of their ministry to the world and to each other. We even see Jesus, on the night He was to be betrayed, not running around trying to get everything done, but sitting and eating with His friends.

The table forces us to slow down. To take a breath. To look at the person across from us in the eyes and be on the same level as him or her. The table provides a common place where, no matter where we come from, we can share a moment together. The table is important. Do you have a time in your life each day where you sit around the table with the people you love and who love you? Being with people, in an intentional way, in a godly way, is what the table is for. Go. Sit and be with the people whom God has given you.

Go and Do
I know this is probably going to be difficult, but I want you to talk with your parents this week about sitting down to eat dinner together. I know everyone is very busy but this is important. Set a goal as a family and work toward making your schedules fit around this sacred time. See what can happen when you sit and are intentionally with each other.

TONGUE

>*James 3:3-5*<

When we put bits into the mouths of horses to make them obey us, we can turn the whole animal. Or take ships as an example. Although they are so large and are driven by strong winds, they are steered by a very small rudder wherever the pilot wants to go. Likewise the tongue is a small part of the body, but it makes great boasts. Consider what a great forest is set on fire by a small spark.

The tongue is the strongest muscle of the body. I would go as far as to say that it's also the most powerful muscle in the body. You might ask, Aren't those the same? Not really. Strength is measured by the amount of force a muscle can exert. When I say powerful, that's not what I'm talking about. Our tongue's power comes from its potential to cause great harm or great good.

Our tongue is what enables us to speak. And those words have the ability to cut someone down and alienate him or her from a group. Words even have the ability to cause others to go into a depression. Every year words are one of the leading causes of suicide among teenagers. Every year people are bullied and hurt deeply by the words of others. Teenagers your age die every year because someone used the power of their tongue to degrade someone else and make him or her feel much less than a beloved child of God.

Of course there's a flip side to our tongue. It can be used for the greatest of goods. It can be used to build each other up. It can be used to stand up for others, and help them know they are loved. Your words have the power to turn the direction of a conversation, situation, and event the course of a life. What will you use your words for today?

Go and Do
One way we can make our words count is to listen to what we say. We have the opportunity to say things that matter and not just fill the air with our words. I want you start to listen to and take note of the things you say. Is it helpful, hurtful, funny, depressing, or just meaningless? Make those words count.

TOWER

> Genesis 11:4 <

Then they said. "Come. let us build ourselves a city. with a tower that reaches to the heavens. so that we may make a name for ourselves and not be scattered over the face of the whole earth."

Read Genesis 11:1-9. The story of the Tower of Babel is one of those interesting stories that is used to explain how different languages and ethnicities evolved in our world. When I read this story, I often think of something else though. When I read this story I think of how different our understanding of God is now than it was then. Now we believe that God is not high on some mountain in the sky but here with, through, around, and in us. We believe that we're always with God and that God is always with us.

I say that we know this, but we often act in the same way as they did in the city of Babel. A lot of times we construct these towers that we believe will bring us closer to God. For some, these are theological towers, intricately constructed and woven together with all of the right words. For others there are towers of holiness; the more strict their belief and action the closer they feel that they'll be to God. Even for others there are towers of deeds where the more bricks of good works we stack, the higher we will go.

No matter what materials you use, the problem is still the same. As we build these towers, we forget that God isn't a God that calls us to build, but a God that calls us to be faithful. Oftentimes we end up doing these things for ourselves and even sometimes to show others just how religious we are. Remember that no matter how much you do or don't do, no matter how tall your tower grows, God still loves us the exact same.

Go and Do
Think about what sorts of towers you build. Don't hear me wrong: thinking theologically and trying to live a good life are good things. Just remember whatever we do or don't do, God is going to love us exactly the same. Know that no matter what you do, God loves you. So, go and accept God's unconditional love today.

TRASH CAN

>1 Corinthians 15:58b<

Therefore. my dear brothers. stand firm. Let nothing move you. Always give yourselves fully to the work of the Lord. because you know that your labor in the
Lord is not in vain.

I want you to have an empty trashcan. Yep, you heard me right. I want nothing in your life to go to waste. I don't want you to ever have to look back
and think to yourself, "I completely wasted my time and energy on that." I
want you to see the things you spent your time on in your life and know that
those were things that brought goodness to the world and advanced God's
Kingdom.

One of my biggest fears is that I'll be on my deathbed and I'll look back and
not be able to see all of the good because I'm overwhelmed with regret because I could've done more. I don't want to lay there and wish that I would've
loved more, spent more time with my family and friends, given more, or lived
life more. I want to enter into that final place here on earth with a smile on
my face because I lived a life full of love and grace and never took a moment
for granted.

My prayer is that you'll "always give yourself to the work of the Lord, because
you know that your labor in the Lord is not in vain."

Go and Do
Over the next week write down all of the things you're involved in and find
yourself doing each day. Focus on them in big chunks like school, work,
sports church etc. Then divide them up into the things you have to do (like
school and sleep) vs. things you choose to do. Look at the second list and
ask, "are these things I really want to spend my time with?" If it's something
you love doing and find joy in, that's good! But look at the balance of your
life. Look at how you spend your time as a whole and ask the questions, "Is
this the life that I can look back on and be proud of? Or are there some ad-
justments I need to make?"

TREE

> *Jeremiah 17:8* <

He will be like a tree planted by the water that sends out its roots by the stream. It does not fear when heat comes; its leaves are always green. It has no worries in a year of drought and never fails to bear fruit.

A Pine tree has a very shallow room system and they grow to be very tall. When a storm comes, pine trees go down very easily. An Oak tree has a deep, interconnected root system that spreads out, sometimes over hundreds of feet. Oaks are known for their strengths and their long life. Which would you rather be? A Pine or an Oak?

Our faith can only grow up as much as it's grown deep. We have to surround ourselves with the teachings of Jesus and the deep truths we find in Scripture. We have to plant ourselves in the way He showed us and taught the disciples. The way that Jesus says "leads to life eternal."

I love the verse in Jeremiah where it is talking about the tree: It will not fear in the heat and the drought; it doesn't cease to produce fruit. When we're not deeply rooted in the teaching of Jesus, fear and anxiety are common. We often have a hard time weathering a storm or a drought in our lives. The reason why roots go deep is to provide stability and to receive water to nourish the tree. Stability and nourishment. Dive deeply into the words on the pages of the Bible. Let them give you balance and stability. Let them nourish and challenge your soul and your life. Remember, you can't grow bigger than you're willing to grow deep; when you do and adversity comes, you'll topple like a Pine tree. Instead plant deep roots, let them nourish you, and hold you steady during the most difficult of times.

Go and Do
On top of using this book each day, I'd also encourage you to make sure you are in a Bible study group or a small group where you can process your faith within that community. Let others keep you accountable. And you keep them accountable. Track your progress and watch how you'll grow deep as God transforms your life.

UMBRELLA

> Psalm 18:1-2 <

I love you, O LORD, my strength. The LORD is my rock, my fortress and my deliverer; my God is my rock, in whom I take refuge. He is my shield and the horn of my salvation, my stronghold.

There are few things worse than getting caught in a downpour without an umbrella. It can completely ruin your day, especially if you have somewhere to be and you don't want to walk in looking like a wet dog.

Sometimes life can feel like a storm that comes out of nowhere and finds you running for shelter. There are a lot of times when we have conflict or situations come our way and we can handle it. But there are other times where we need serious help and protection. David had some of those times. When he talks about God as being his rock and strength, he is giving us an insight into his life. We can understand that David isn't writing these words as a theory about God, but as someone who has experienced some very difficult times. During these difficult times, David had come to trust and lean on the shelter that God provided. Storms can be very scary things. But they aren't nearly as scary when we have some protection from the wind and the rain.

Next time you pull out an umbrella and are walking in the rain, I want you to think about how God has sheltered you in your life. What has God protected you from in you past and has helped you get through without feeling the force of the storm?

Go and Do
You may have heard the world "shelter" used in other instances in life. We often talk about a place for homeless people as a shelter. We also reference a place where women and children escape violence as a shelter. These are places that give them protection from the storms that they're facing in their lives. If your youth group doesn't already help out with homeless shelters or other kinds of places of refuge, take some time this week and talk with your youth minister about how you and your friends can become involved in helping to provide places of shelter for those in your community.

VALLEY

>*Ezekiel 37:1-3*<

The hand of the LORD was upon me, and he brought me out by the Spirit of the LORD and set me in the middle of a valley; it was full of bones. He led me back and forth among them, and I saw a great many bones on the floor of the valley, bones that were very dry. He asked me, "Son of man, can these bones live?" I said, "O Sovereign LORD, you alone know."

Oftentimes when we think of a valley we think of a place that's between two beautiful mountains, all green grass, and flowers. In the Bible a valley was a much less hospitable place.

In cultures where land wars were prevalent between tribes or ethnic groups, valleys and the cliffs that surrounded them were very strategic in warfare. In these battles those who were in the valley were at a major disadvantage because their opponents could attack them from above, which almost always meant defeat for those in the valley. So to encounter a valley of dry bones was an ominous sign that there had been a lot of death in this valley.

Pause now and read the rest of the story in Ezekiel. I love how in this vision of a valley of absolute death, God chose to bring about life. It reminds me that when we're in our valleys, those places that are ominous and scary, God is there too. When we read the Bible, God doesn't seem to let death have the final say in anything. We must remember that the final say is God's. So when you are in those valley places, remember that not only is God there, the God that is there is one who loves to resurrect things.

Go and Do

Many of you might not be in a valley place now, but I bet some of your friends are. Think about who these people are and what they're going through. Why are they in the valley? What can you do to join them during these troubling times? Have you called them, or talked about it with them?

VASE

>1 Peter 3:3-4<

Your beauty should not come from outward adornment, such as braided hair and the wearing of gold jewelry and fine clothes. Instead, it should be that of your inner self, the unfading beauty of a gentle and quiet spirit, which is of great worth in God's sight.

Have you ever seen someone "ooh" and "ahh" over a vase of flowers? You know how it goes: it's Valentines Day or a birthday and someone gets a vase of flowers. Is he or she surprised and happy because of the vase or what the vase contains? Of course. It would be silly to get a vase of flowers only to take the flowers, cast them aside, and relish the vase. That's not how it works. And yet, as silly as that sounds, we often do that in our lives.

So many times in our society we value a person by what he or she has on the outside (clothes, looks, possessions, etc.) when the most beautiful part is on the inside. Oftentimes we're guilty of throwing out the flowers and only admiring the vase in which they came. When we focus on the outside we miss where the real beauty resides.

Have you ever looked at one of those videos on the Internet of how magazines photoshop and airbrush models and celebrities? It's amazing. They can make anyone look a certain way. What they can't do is photoshop what's on the inside, things like character, honesty, humility, love, and grace. These are things that define true beauty and can't be manipulated or altered superficially. In 1 Peter we see that God's focus is on the beauty within and how that beauty manifests itself out into the world. What are you focusing on: the vase or the flowers?

Go and Do

What do you value as beautiful? What are the things you put priority on when you look at someone or get to know him or her? In your own life, where are you placing your focus? Today, draw two stick figures of your self. On one put all of the things you try to project to people. On the other, write and/or draw all of the things that are inside. Now look at the two and think about which are you more comfortable with, and how you can bring the two "you's" together.

VINE

> *John 15:5* <

I am the vine; you are the branches. If a man remains in me and I in him, he will bear much fruit; apart from me you can do nothing.

This is one of the most famous verses in the Gospel of John. John records Jesus' teaching about our dependence on God by using the metaphor of the vine and the branches. Jesus compares us to the branches that grow off a grape vine. The fruit actually grows on the branches, not the vine. But separate the branches from the vine, and the branches die.

If I'm being honest, I've struggled with this verse some over the years. See, I can look around and see plenty of people, folks who could care less about God, who are doing just fine in the world. So what's Jesus really trying to tell us here? Is He just wrong? Well, if you read all of John 15:1-17, you see that Jesus isn't just talking about being a good person. He's talking about living our lives in such a way that when people see what we do, they see the God that has called and empowered us to do it. Now none of this is to say that people who are doing good in the world don't have their place; our world is a much better place because of these people. We should be grateful for them. The difference is that when we, as Christ-followers, do good in our world we have to constantly point back to God as the source and enabler of the goodness that comes from us.

A vine is the life-source of the branches. We must understand our relationship with God in much of the same way. We grow because God grows us. We're strong because God strengthens us. We produce good fruit because God is good.

Go and Do
Part of understanding how to show God to others through your actions is to know how God has gifted you. Discover the areas that God has equipped you in, and think about how you can use those things to show the world around you the love of God and the difference knowing Him has made in your life.

WATER

> John 4:14 <

But whoever drinks the water I give him will never thirst. Indeed, the water I give him will become in him a spring of water welling up to eternal life.

Water is essential to our lives. A human can only go around three days without water. Thankfully, most of us will never have to even have that as a possibility. Not only do the majority of our houses have running water, we can find clean drinking water almost anywhere in our country. This wasn't the case for people in the first century in Jesus' part of the world. Water was just as important, but was often a scarce necessity. If we want to go on a trip or vacation we don't have to consider how many days we'll be gone and pack enough water to make sure we don't die. In Jesus' day, this was a very real concern. For most people, much of their day was occupied with getting water and cooking food.

I remember being in Panama a few years ago. There was no running water where we were staying. We had to form a bucket brigade every morning where we would haul bucket after bucket of water up a massive hill in order to have what we needed for the day.

Most of us don't spend each day figuring out where our next glass of water is coming from. But many of us are constantly looking for that next way to feel filled spiritually. We often find ourselves thirsty for ways to feel closer to God. Jesus is telling us in this verse, just as He told the woman in this story, that when we join with the mission of God, we don't have to thirst again. We have the opportunity to be filled with God's goodness. It's a permanent fullness that only God can offer.

Go and Do

How does God fill you? How does God quench your thirst and give you the strength to go about His business in the world? It's important to know the ways that God fills you. Make sure that you're constantly renewing yourself with these practices. Identify these practices, learn more about them, and let God fill you on a regular basis for your work in the world.

WEB

>*Ephesians* 4:29<

Do not let any unwholesome talk come out of your mouths, but only what is helpful for building others up according to their needs, that it may benefit those who listen.

Have you ever seen a spider build a web? It's really an amazing thing to watch. Each strand added makes the pattern more and more complex and beautiful. But spider webs aren't meant to be beautiful, they're meant to be deadly. Spider webs aren't works of art the spider creates for you, or me, or a pig named Wilbur. Spider webs are meant to be lethal traps for any bugs or insects that are unfortunate enough to fly or crawl by.

We weave webs ourselves. We weave webs of lies and mean spirited gossip. Some of us do this unintentionally, while others have grown to become masters of these subtle techniques. These webs we weave with our words hurt people. They undermine their personhood. To be blunt, it's not fair. I can't tell you how many times I've seen someone completely crushed because a couple of his or her peers decided that they were going to start some rumors. There's no room for this.

Paul warns us that the only words that should come from our mouth are words that are going to be true and helpful. Every time you speak, you have a choice: will you say words that are helpful and lift others up? Or will you hurt others with lies, rumors, and underhanded comments? Your decision will dramatically help or hurt those around you. Choose wisely what comes from your mouth.

Go and Do
Pause. Before you speak, before a word comes out of your mouth, simply pause for a second. Ask yourself, "is this helpful or harmful? Is this truth or a lie"? Then make your decision. For the next few days practice this. I bet you'll catch yourself more than you realize.

WIND

>1 Peter 1:8<

Though you have not seen him, you love him; and even though you do not see him now, you believe in him and are filled with an inexpressible and glorious joy.

The wind is a powerful thing. I live in Alabama and we know about how powerful wind can be. We get a number of tornadoes each year that devastate our land, homes, and lives. The strange thing about wind is that you can't see it. You can feel it. You can see the effects of it. But you can't actually see the wind.

So here's the thing: I, like a lot of you, try to have a very logical faith. I like to think things out, ask hard questions, and learn as much as I can about God and His ways. But at the end of the day there are just some things that I can't explain. One of these things is how I believe that God is real. I've never seen God, or heard God talk. But I have felt God's presence and I know He exists. This is tough in some ways because I have no proof. But I can point to the effects.

I can point to how God changed my life and continues to change my life inside and out. I can point to how God changes other's lives and how I see God at work in the world. So is God any less real because I can't show you God directly? No. I can't show you the wind, but you can certainly feel it and see the effects of it. As people of faith we can't be frustrated by the fact that we can't "show" God to others. All we need to do is point to all of the places where God's effects are really felt.

Go and Do
This week spend some time looking for the effects of God. Look around you, in your life, and the lives of others. Look and see what God has done and ask others to tell you their stories. Look for beauty, reconciliation, and goodness because they are the things left in the aftermath of God.

WOOD

> *Matthew 7:3-5* <

Why do you look at the speck of sawdust in your brother's eye and pay no attention to the plank in your own eye? How can you say to your brother. 'Let me take the speck out of your eye.' when all the time there is a plank in your own eye? You hypocrite. first take the plank out of your own eye. and then you will see clearly to remove the speck from your brother's eye.

People are peculiar. Some days we can be full of great good, and doing incredible things in the world. Other days we can, well, let's say be a little less than that. No matter whether we're knocking it out of the park, or really messing up, we have to realize this one thing: we will never be perfect and will always have faults of our own.

In the verse above, Jesus helps us think about how we judge others. Using the illustration of a 2x4 sticking out of someone's eye, He helps us see 1) how unaware we often are about our own faults, and 2) how we're not called to be the judges of other people's faults. Notice how He tells us that we need to worry about our own faults first. He also doesn't say that when we deal with them, that we should then start judging others. Instead, He says that we should help remove the piece of sawdust from our brother and sister's eye.

We live in a world that does a lot of judging and very little self-evaluation. There are a lot of people in our world walking around with 2x4's sticking out of their eyes who tell others about the speck in their own eye. As people of faith, we have to be aware of our own sin at all times. We can't ever hold others to a standard we can't meet ourselves.

Go and Do
Self-evaluation is about two things. First, it's about humility. We have to know that we mess up, and will continue to mess up. This helps us be a less judgmental of others. Secondly, it's about grace. We have to have grace toward ourselves, knowing that God forgives us, and extend grace toward others. So what planks are sticking out of your eye?

ZOO

>*Colossians 3:23*<

Whatever you do, work at it with all your heart, as working for the Lord, not for men.

Zoos are interesting. On one hand I love them. It's incredible to go and see these amazing animals from all over the world. It's so fascinating to be close to them and see how they act and play. I love watching the large primates like gorillas and orangutans. I sit there for hours and watch their every move. That leads me to my second point, one that's sort of sad too. While it's cool that we can watch them, the reason we can watch them is because they are behind glass for our viewing pleasure. I bet it's tough to be behind that glass knowing that someone is always watching you.

Have you ever felt like you're behind glass with people watching your every move? I know I have and do often. As someone who works in a church, people are always watching me to see what I do. The temptation could be to become angry or even do things that people see so that they'll be satisfied with how I live my life.

As Christ-followers in a Jr. High or High School, I bet you feel like you're behind glass, with people watching you all the time. This passage in Colossians helps us remember why we do what we do. We're never to follow Jesus closely because someone else expects us to. We're supposed to only serve one master and that's our God, and to do so with great joy. Every task we're called to do should be done as if God Himself were asking us to do it.

Go and Do
One of the reasons we do a lot of the things we do is because others are watching. This can be a positive motivator and help us think about our actions before doing them. But it can also be something that causes us to become bitter and resentful. This week, when you do what you do, ask yourself your motivations. If it's not for God, that doesn't mean you stop. It just means that you work to change who you're trying to please.

CRAZY
TIMES

Crazy Times are devotions that address the specific issues you deal with as a teenage Christ-follower. The idea is that you thumb through the sections (or maybe the table of contents) and find an issue affecting your life. Then, spend ten days working through what God has to say about that issue.

Crazy Times devotions are as unique as you are. Maybe today you're not dealing with any of the issues covered in Crazy Times. But maybe some day you will.

As you encounter these issues, check back in to see what you can learn from God and His Word.

MOUNTAIN *pg. 115–124*

You know the feeling: you're at camp, just got back from that mission trip, or are about to head off on that big retreat where you just know God is going to show up. We usually call these "mountain top" experiences. This whole section is just for those times. These ten devotions not only help you experience the mountain top, they also help you know some of the risks so you don't fall off the cliff!

VALLEY *pg. 125-134*

If the old saying, "when it rains is pours" feels like an understatement, then this group of devotions is for you. There will be times in our lives where we're walking through the valley and everything just seems to go wrong. These ten days of readings will take you through Psalm 23 and help you walk through the valleys in your life.

CALM ON THE MOUNTAIN

> Genesis 8:1-4 <

But God remembered Noah and all the wild animals and the livestock that were with him in the ark, and he sent a wind over the earth, and the waters receded. Now the springs of the deep and the floodgates of the heavens had been closed, and the rain had stopped falling from the sky. The water receded steadily from the earth. At the end of the hundred and fifty days the water had gone down, and on the seventeenth day of the seventh month the ark came to rest on the mountains of Ararat.

The mountain represents those times where we are closer to God. Throughout the Bible we see God encountering people in special ways while on a mountain. For many of us a mountain encounter is on a retreat, mission trip, or other time when we're away form what's normal. Our focus is on God. We experience different things while on the mountain. The first mountain story is Noah on Mount Arafat where the ark came to rest after 40 days of the flood. Can you imagine what an insane 40 days that must have been? Floating aimlessly, death all around, and wondering the entire time if this was the new norm. I bet a lot of us find ourselves feeling the exact same way. Each day wondering if the next day will be the exact same.

One of the most important pieces of a retreat or an "on the mountain experience" is that we're able to get above all of that. When the ark came to rest on the mountain and the waters receded, I can imagine that there was a great calm in Noah's mind. Finally, everything was calming down. Don't doubt the importance and absolute need that we have for retreat and calm. Don't let these times just come randomly. Make sure to plan times to get away form the chaos and confusion of life and spend time in a calm, refreshing place that provides a real change of pace.

SACRIFICE ON THE MOUNTAIN

> *Genesis 22:2* <

Then God said. "Take your son. your only son. Isaac. whom you love. and go to the region of Moriah. Sacrifice him there as a burnt offering on one of the mountains I will tell you about."

This story has always troubled me. It doesn't make sense. Why would God ask Abraham to sacrifice the son that he had wanted for so long, and that God had promised him? It doesn't make sense until we understand that God was setting a new precedent. Abraham and his people believed that the way to please God was to give living sacrifices. This was not an uncommon practice (though sacrificing a child was definitely frowned upon). God was not changing the fact that He wanted Abraham to sacrifice; He was changing what He wanted Abraham to sacrifice.

When we're on the mountain, it's often a time where we have to bring those things that mean the most to us and lay them before God. We lay them before God, not to kill them, but to ask God how we can be better with the things we value. Also, it's a time where we make sure the things we value are what God wants us to value. I remember being at a conference when I was 17. I was actually doing the drama for the conference and was seen as a leader. What no one knew was that I was very, very angry. I was holding on to some deep anger and it was the number one thing in my life at that point. When I went to that conference to lead, I wasn't expecting that I was going to have to sacrifice my anger. But I did.

On the third night of the conference, it was clear to me that in order for God to do what He wanted to do in my life, I was going to have to sacrifice my anger and leave it there. It was an amazing experience and I was changed in some pretty powerful ways that night. I wonder what it is that God is calling you to sacrifice, lay down, and leave? I wonder what you might need to re-prioritize or give-up?

LEARNING ON THE MOUNTAIN

>Exodus 19:20-22<

The LORD descended to the top of Mount Sinai and called Moses to the top of the mountain. So Moses went up and the LORD said to him. "Go down and warn the people so they do not force their way through to see the LORD and many of them perish. Even the priests. who approach the LORD. must consecrate themselves. or the LORD will break out against them."

Read Exodus 19:16-20:12. A lot of time the term "mountaintop experience" is used to describe an emotional moment where we see God in new ways. While that's a part of the mountain top, there are also many other things we can experience that have nothing to do with emotion. One of these is learning. We're called to learn on the mountain top.

One of the most famous moments in the Bible is when God gave Moses the 10 commandments. While this was a mind blowing and miraculous experience, emotion and amazement weren't the point. The point was for the people of Israel (and us) to learn a new way to live. God calls us to learn when we're on the mountain top. God wanted the Israelites to be a people who lived by a different set of standards . . . God's standards. So, God gave them a new set of rules to follow. When we're on the mountain top God calls us to not only learn, but to take what we learn and be set apart when we leave the mountain. We're called to be different. If we can't be defined from our culture by the way we live, then how in the world will our culture see the God that we love?

We have the unique ability to learn in a different way when we're on the mountain. Often, we're able to absorb what God is teaching us there because we're away from everything else and can more fully concentrate on God and His voice. Moses walked down the mountain with two stones that taught us to live in a different way. What are you walking down the mountain with?

PROVING ON THE MOUNTAIN

>1 Kings 18:38-39<

Then the fire of the LORD fell and burned up the sacrifice, the wood, the stones and the soil, and also licked up the water in the trench. When all the people saw this, they fell prostrate and cried, "The LORD—he is God! The LORD—he is God!"

Read 1 Kings 18:30-39. Oftentimes we enter into mountain top situations needing proof. Sometimes it's for us sometimes it's for others. I know many youth who, going on a retreat or conference, had little to no belief in God or what God could do. They went for friends, fun, or because their parents made them. I've seen many of these same youth be blown away from what they experienced on these trips. The mountain top is a place where God proves Himself.

In this story, Elijah, an Old Testament prophet wanted to prove to the prophets of another religion that God was real. Many of us come to mountain top experiences doing the same thing, except we do it believing that God will not show up. We don't believe God can affect that situation at home, bring healing to our friendships, or pull us out of that depression. So we harden ourselves. We go in with a bad attitude. We're soaking the altar, just daring God to do something. God has this incredible way of proving Himself in these situations. It's not always in this big ball of fire like in the story. Sometimes it's through a conversation, a message preached, or a song sung.

God doesn't have to prove Himself through dramatic actions. Sometimes His presence can come in the quietest and most unsuspecting of forms. For some reason though, God seems to prove Himself on those mountain top experiences. So I ask you: are you coming as an Elijah, expecting to see God? Or as a prophet of Baal believing that God won't show up? Either way, get ready. God has a tendency to prove Himself in amazing ways when we least expect it.

SILENCE ON THE MOUNTAIN

>1 Kings 19:11-12<

The LORD said. "Go out and stand on the mountain in the presence of the LORD. for the LORD is about to pass by." Then a great and powerful wind tore the mountains apart and shattered the rocks before the LORD. but the LORD was not in the wind. After the wind there was an earthquake. but the LORD was not in the earthquake. After the earthquake came a fire. but the LORD was not in the fire. And after the fire came a gentle whisper.

It's interesting that in just one chapter of 1 Kings we go from God hurling down this massive, all-consuming fireball to making His presence known in a very small voice. It's a pretty amazing shift in such a small amount of time. Sometimes it's big, other times it's very small.

Sometimes our lives are chaos. When our lives are like this, we don't necessarily need another giant ball of fire to fall to earth and consume all it touches, right? God chooses to speak to us in unique and personal ways. It's beautiful really. Think about this violent raging chaos all around, completely consuming all of your senses, and through it all a still small voice breaks through, calling out to you, whispering goodness and love. Beautiful. While the storm and chaos is raging around you, it slowly becomes muted under the voice of your creator, your loving parent calling you by name, calling you into His presence.

I know some of you are in a raging chaos even as you read these words, but remember that God is there. God is not causing the chaos that surrounds you. God is calling to you in the midst of it and calling you out of it. Listen closely. Listen for that small voice that whispers through the storm. Listen for the God who loves you and wants the best for you. Listen.

MOUNTAIN 6
TEMPTATION ON THE MOUNTAIN

> *Matthew 4:1* <

Then Jesus was led by the Spirit into the desert to be tempted by the devil.

Read Matthew 4:1-10. Usually when we think about having a mountain top experience, we don't think of it as a bad thing. But sometimes it certainly can be. Jesus' first mountain top experience was just that. Jesus was ending a 40-day fast in the Judean wilderness. He was tired, weak, and hungry. Satan came to Jesus and tempted Him three times. On two of the temptations, he took Jesus to a mountain. The second temptation was on the Temple Mount and the third was on a high mountain where Jesus could see for very far distances.

Sometimes when we're on the mountain, we can become full of ourselves and believe that we can do all of this life without God. That's what Satan was trying to get Jesus to do. He wanted Jesus to do things that God wasn't calling Him to do. Many of us can get a certain spiritual high when we have mountain top experiences. That can often be when pride and "I've got this figured out" syndrome creep in. When we have these experiences we must remember that it's God who calls us, and it's God who meets us on the mountain top.

Pride is one of the subtlest, yet strongest temptations. Jesus answered these temptations with grace and strength. Each time Jesus was tempted, He referred to God and His ways as the only way. This admittance from Jesus (and remember, Jesus is pretty awesome) tells us that no one, not even Jesus is above the ways that God calls us to live. So, while you're on the mountain top, don't let your pride become the thing that causes you to stumble on the way down.

CHALLENGE ON THE MOUNTAIN

> *Matthew 5:17-20* <

"Do not think that I have come to abolish the Law or the Prophets; I have not come to abolish them but to fulfill them. I tell you the truth, until heaven and earth disappear, not the smallest letter, not the least stroke of a pen, will by any means disappear from the Law until everything is accomplished. Anyone who breaks one of the least of these commandments and teaches others to do the same will be called least in the kingdom of heaven, but whoever practices and teaches these commands will be called great in the kingdom of heaven. For I tell you that unless your righteousness surpasses that of the Pharisees and the teachers of the law, you will certainly not enter the kingdom of heaven.

We've already talked about how the mountain top is a place where God teaches us. We can't forget that the mountain top is a place where God challenges us, as well. There are many levels of our faith that we experience. When we're new to the faith, we're trying to understand it in order to live it out. As we grow in our faith, we learn more about what God expects of His children. Many of these teachings make sense and are relatively easy to follow (we know that we shouldn't murder, steal, and that we should love God). But along our faith journey there comes a time where Scripture begins to open up in new ways to us. We see that our faith isn't just about following a set of rules, but encompasses an entirely new understanding of our life. For me Matthew chapters 5-7 do just that.

Read some portions of these chapters. Jesus calls us beyond legalism and shows us that our entire lives must reflect God's goodness in the world. These teachings aren't easy. As we mature in our faith, it's these teachings that will challenge us to grow closer to God and in relationship with those around us. God not only comforts on the mountain top, God also challenges beyond anything we could have ever expected.

AWE ON THE MOUNTAIN

> Mark 9:2-4 <

After six days Jesus took Peter, James and John with him and led them up a high mountain, where they were all alone. There he was transfigured before them. His clothes became dazzling white, whiter than anyone in the world could bleach them. And there appeared before them Elijah and Moses, who were talking with Jesus.

Read Mark 9:2-8. A lot of the stories in the gospels are very practical and teach us how to live our lives. This mountain top story is very different. Jesus, with His three original closest disciples, travel to a high mountain and something amazing happens. The Bible says that Jesus transformed, not like in those Transformers movies, but in a way where the disciples saw God in Him. Then out of nowhere Elijah and Moses (two other mountain top guys) appeared with Him.

The disciples were amazed and I would imagine a little shocked by what they saw. Jesus, who was their friend and rabbi (teacher), just revealed Himself in a new and miraculous way. They stood in awe . . . for a moment. Then Peter tried to do something practical. "Hey Jesus, should I make some tents so we can stay here"? Not exactly the right way to take in the moment.

Sometimes God does things on the mountain top that we don't understand. They're beautiful and amazing but not always practical. For many of us, we want to make sense of these experiences. But there are times in our lives where we just need to be in the moment. I'm a very practical and action oriented person, but sometimes I have to let go of that and bask in what God is doing in that moment. We don't need to do anything except let ourselves experience the beauty of what God is doing. We just need to let go and need to take it in.

HOPE ON THE MOUNTAIN

>*Revelation 21:10–11*<

And he carried me away in the Spirit to a mountain great and high. and showed me the Holy City. Jerusalem. coming down out of heaven from God. It shone with the glory of God. and its brilliance was like that of a very precious jewel. like a jasper. clear as crystal.

Revelation is the last book of the Bible. And in the last part of the last book of the Bible we see God back on the mountain. Many people will debate about the intention and meaning of John's revelation, but the best scholars agree that it is a book of hope. In the final passages of the book we see this hope in its highest form. The book was written to the Jewish Christians in the first century, a people who were without much hope. Their temple had been burned to the ground, they'd been kicked out of their synagogues, and the Roman government was persecuting them. They were full of uncertainty about the future. This book was written to and for them.

In these verses their home city of Jerusalem was new and beautiful. The city had been restored and made even better. It wasn't under occupation and it was a place where worship of God could happen without persecution or fear. There were no tears and no crying. Everything was right.

When we go to the mountain we're often lifted out of despair and pain to see the way things could be. We're lifted to the mountain to give us hope of a better tomorrow. When you're on the mountain top let God show you what He wants for you. Take that hope to help you get through what's back in the valley. When you come down from the mountain, come down with a renewed hope, knowing that through God your entire world can look completely different.

GIFT ON THE MOUNTAIN

>*Matthew 15:37*<

With a loud cry. Jesus breathed his last.

Read Mark 15:22-41. The place where Jesus died is known by several names: the place of the skull, Golgotha, and Mount Calvary. It's on this hill where God did something amazing. God taught us, through His son, what love really looks like. I believe that Jesus could've gotten off of the cross and walked away, but He didn't. I also believe that He could've called forth a political revolt against that Roman government, but He didn't. He could've done a number of things. But He sacrificed himself, willingly. He looked over the crowd, the ones who mocked Him, condemned Him, and even nailed nails into His body, and instead of cursing them He forgave them.

Many will discuss all that Jesus did on the cross, but for me, the gift that Jesus gives is both the ability to love and forgive in any situation, and to have courage to respond with love in the face of absolute. Jesus gave us a different way to see and interact with each other that day. He gave us a new way to live.

When we're on the mountain we have to understand that Jesus, in His worst hour, still found the courage and strength to show us a better way. And He calls us to live in this way today. That's the challenge of the mountain. What do we do with what God gives on the mountain? Let these experiences change us so that we can then go and change the world.

RESTING IN THE VALLEY

> *Psalm 23:1-2* <

The LORD is my shepherd. I shall not be in want. He makes me lie down in green pastures. he leads me beside quiet waters.

One of the most famous chapters in the entire Bible is Psalm 23. It provides us good insight into what it looks like to walk through a difficult time in our lives. King David is dealing with a very difficult emotional time and writes this as a song/prayer to God. For this series of devotions on "valley" times in our lives, we will focus on the words of this one particular psalm.

In the first verses David writes that God is his shepherd and that God leads him to rest in places that are safe and nurturing. When we're in these valley places in life, the furthest thing from our minds is the idea of rest. We're usually thinking more along the lines of survival. But God calls us to not become frantic and to make sure to rest in these moments of uncertainty. When we don't rest, we slowly lose our ability to be rational, thoughtful, and make good decisions. Also, when we're lacking rest, especially in stressful situations, we're more likely to drop into depression. I know what you're thinking, "How can I rest when everything is so stressful and uncertain?" Part of the answer is believing that God is with you.

I love how the psalm begins, "The Lord is my shepherd, I shall not be in want." It's almost a confession, or a mantra: "I know who God is and I know He will take care of me." What if we began everyday by praying, "God, I know who you are, and that you're with me. I trust you." When things become crazy don't forget to lie down in some green pastures.

NOURISHMENT IN THE VALLEY

> Psalm 23:2-3 <

He makes me lie down in green pastures. he leads me beside quiet waters. he restores my soul. He guides me in paths of righteousness for his name's sake.

I know this is going to sound crazy, but when you're in a valley time, you can't forget to feed yourself well. I know when I am in stressful times, especially times when I'm extremely worried about a situation with myself or someone else, I lose my appetite. You have to eat, not junk food or fast food, but good healthy food that will nourish your body. Healthy fruits and vegetables not only make your body healthier, but they also make your mind healthier. It's crazy how interlinked our body and mind is. Certain foods will either improve your mood and outlook, or more unhealthy ones can actually cause your mood to take a nosedive.

We also have to remember to nourish our souls. Many times when we're in a valley experience we isolate ourselves and think about the problem all of the time. While it's good to think about our situation, thinking about it too much can cause real harm. Also, we're communal creatures, we need people. Don't isolate yourself and pull away from friends and family during difficult times. Surround yourself with the people who love you and let them nourish your soul. Friends and family can be some of the most important pieces to making it through valley times.

Finally, make sure that you're not pulling away from your faith during valley times. Find some meaningful connection to God and stick with it. It might be prayer, Scripture reading, meditating, or even something like committing to youth group. But make sure that you have a consistent faith element while you're in the valley. This isn't the only way God speaks to us when we're down but it can certainly be an important one. Make sure to take care of yourself, find nourishment and stay strong.

DIRECTION IN THE VALLEY

> *Psalm 23:3* <

He restores my soul. He guides me in paths of righteousness for his name's sake.

Valleys are confusing. When you're in a real valley you oftentimes can't see the landscape around you. You cannot usually see too far ahead of you. Usually you can only see your direct path, and the walls of the valley. It's hard to know what direction you're heading in. Depending on how narrow the valley is, you may not feel as though you have much choice in the direction you have to travel.

When we're in a metaphorical valley time in our lives, we can have the exact same problem. Most of the valleys we find ourselves in are so difficult because we feel as though we have little control over our path. None of our options are very attractive. That's why one of the most important things we can have in our valley times is direction.

In this verse, David tells us that God guides him and directs his paths. When we have no clue where to go or how to go there, we can trust in the direction God gives us. We read in the Bible how to live our lives, treat others, and live out our faith. This knowledge will give us direction and clarity on where we're supposed to go, and who we're supposed to be in the valley. Directions are not always clear but when we continue to live the life that Jesus taught us to live, we can trust that no matter what the valley throws at us, we still have the ability to be a faithful witness to God's goodness and love.

VALLEY 4
COURAGE IN THE VALLEY

> *Psalm 23:4* <

Even though I walk through the valley of the shadow of death. I will fear no evil. for you are with me: your rod and your staff. they comfort me.

The most well known line of this psalm is "Though I walk through the valley of death, I will fear no evil." Wow! That's an incredibly powerful line. It's a courageous line that defines David and his time in the valley. The writer is making a bold statement of courage, not just in a valley, but "in the valley of the shadow of death." I don't know about you but that sounds like an incredible scary time and place to be.

Think about what this means. You're in a deep dark valley and death is so close and so big that its shadow is looming over you. Yet, David proclaims that even though that's the case, he will fear no evil.

I want to encourage you, when you're in these deep, dark, scary times, to not be afraid. God is with you and will never leave you. I know that sounds like something from a sermon but it really is true. In the darkest of nights, God is with you. In the middle of depression, hatred, and loneliness, God is with us. You can take courage because you're not alone and you'll never be alone. I also want you to be courageous because there are others, people of faith, who want to travel through those valleys with you and help you along your way. Be strong and courageous and know that our God is a God that doesn't abandon us whether we're on the mountain top or in the deepest valleys.

DISCIPLINE IN THE VALLEY

> *Psalm 23:4* <

Even though I walk through the valley of the shadow of death, I will fear no evil, for you are with me; your rod and your staff, they comfort me.

For me this is one of the most interesting parts of this verse, "your rod and your staff comfort me." When you think about a shepherd, you often picture them with some sort of staff. This is a pretty common image. Many of us think this is just for walking, but it had several purposes. One was for protection. The staff was used to fend off predators. It was a practical device that provided, at a moments notice, the ability to fight off other animals that might hurt the sheep or even other humans that might want to steal them. When we think of the rod and staff in this way, this definitely comforts us and helps us trust our shepherd.

But, sometimes the staff is also used in another way. A staff can also be used to discipline the sheep. When we think about discipline, it's not about punishment but about guidance. Shepherds would use their staff to bring the sheep back in line and to keep them within bounds of safety. When we're in the valley, we have to be sensitive to the staff of our Shepherd as He moves us and guides us towards the path He has set out for us. It's important that we understand that while we're in the valley, we can't feel sorry for ourselves and give up. We must accept God's guidance and instruction while in the valley.

Who are the people in your life that God uses a staff? Who are the ones that help push you to the middle and keep you safe in the valley? Who are the ones who challenge you to not sink into sadness or bad habits when you're down?

TRUST IN THE VALLEY

>*Psalm 23:5*<

You prepare a table before me in the presence of my enemies.
You anoint my head with oil; my cup overflows.

This is where God begins to call us into some pretty incredible areas of trust. David tells us that God prepares a table for us in the presence of our enemies. I don't know about you, but I can just picture me sitting there at the head of the table and on both sides of a long banquet table. I just picture all of the bad guys from Disney movies licking their chops just waiting to get me. But in many ways this is the image that we're given. We sit down with those people who are against us, and then God throws a banquet for us in their presence.

So what does this mean? I think it means a couple of things. One is that in the presence of our worst enemies, God will be there and celebrate us. There's no need to fear but even beyond it being a safe place, it's a place where we are celebrated. Secondly, I think it's a calling for us to trust God that we can be in the presence of our enemies and be OK. I think too often when we have enemies we villainize them so much so that we totally avoid them and never communicate with them. I don't think this is the way God intended it. I think God wants us to seek reconciliation with our enemies and to show them the love of God.

Remember this isn't just a verse about how we can trust God to protect us from our enemies, it's a verse about sitting with our enemies as well. How are you reconciling with your enemies today, and how are you trusting God to help you in that process?

GOD'S CALLING IN THE VALLEY

> *Psalm 23:5* <

You prepare a table before me in the presence of my enemies.
You anoint my head with oil; my cup overflows.

Sometimes when we're in a bad place we become focused on ourselves. It's very easy to see all that is happening around us and think that the world is against us and get a "poor me" mentality. We can't lose our identity while we're in these valley times. We have to remember that we're defined by something different than our present circumstances. When we get that "poor me" mentality we're choosing to let ourselves be defined by something external, something that we shouldn't let have power over us. As Christ-followers we're defined by something other than what is outside of us. We're defined by the good work of God that goes to the very core of our identity. God isn't external and God's calling on our lives isn't something that comes from outside. It comes from the very core of who we are and who we are made to be.

When David says "you anoint my head with oil," he's recognizing that God not only calls us, but also blesses us with purpose. To be anointed with oil in the ancient world was a very special marker that you were being blessed. And in the terms of Christianity, being blessed for a purpose. God doesn't want us to forget who we are in the midst of the shadow of the valley. We are God's. We're called to God's work no matter where we are; on the mountaintop or in the valley. Don't forget your identity or your purpose. Remember that in the midst of a great struggle God still has a great purpose for you and your life.

GOD'S BLESSING IN THE VALLEY

> *Psalm 23:5* <

You prepare a table before me in the presence of my enemies.
You anoint my head with oil; my cup overflows.

It seems counterintuitive to talk about blessings in the valley, but David does so in a very visual way. David gives us a very beautiful description of God's blessing. It's not that God blesses us with just enough. God blesses us with more than we need. Now some people will misrepresent this verse and turn it into a verse about God giving us everything we want. That's not what this verse is about at all. This section is about God giving us every bit of what we need.

I've heard some theologians and preachers talk about this image and say that when our cup flows over it means that we have enough to make sure that others have what they need as well. This makes a lot of sense with other passages and teachings in the Bible. We see this in the verses that tell us that we're blessed to be a blessing, and where Jesus talks about giving our shirt as well as our cloak and never denying those who need to borrow from you. Again, while in the valley we have to remember that we're not called to focus just on our needs, but to remember that even in these terrible circumstances we're called to live out God's mission.

I had a former student who dealt with anorexia for many years. It was a horrible disease that consumed her. She never found relief from it until she went to college. When she went to college she discovered a calling to the nursing field. When she found herself taking care of others, so much of her anxiety and the urges that drove her anorexia subsided. Instead of worrying only about herself, she began to use the gifts that God gave her to do good in the world. Remember that in the valley God blesses us, not just for ourselves but so that we can be blessings to others as well.

GOD'S LOVE IN THE VALLEY

> *Psalm 23:6* <

Surely goodness and love will follow me all the days of my life, and I will dwell in the house of the LORD forever.

At the end of the day it's called a valley for a reason. It's not fun. It's tough and it often pushes us to our limits. During these moments, it's often that all we need is God's love to wrap around us and tell us that it will be ok. The Beatles said it best, "all you need is love; love is all you need." One of the amazing things about our faith is that we believe that God is love, and wherever God is there's also love. There's an interesting piece of this verse that many people often overlook. It says that God's goodness and love will "follow" us all the days of our lives. This is a very interesting part of the verse that tells us something about God's love but also how God's love should affect those how are around us.

Have you ever seen a boat pushing through a calm still lake? As the boat moves forward you don't see much of its impact in front of it. But you can certainly tell where it's been from the ripples that are created from it moving through the water. I imagine this verse talking about those ripples of God's love that follow us as we push forward. The ripples are evidence that the boat has traveled through that area. They fan out and affect others who are near and behind.

How does God's evident love in our lives live on long after we're gone? How does that love fan out from our path through this life? Live in God's love in such a way that this love is evident long after you're gone.

OUR COMMITMENT IN THE VALLEY

> *Psalm 23:6* <

Surely goodness and love will follow me all the days of my life, and I will dwell in the house of the LORD forever.

No matter where we are, we are God's. No matter what valley, mountain, or desert we find ourselves in we have the opportunity to be with God. We have to believe in our minds and our hearts that this is true and commit ourselves to understanding our lives in this way. This commitment is a two way street. God's already committed to never leaving or giving up on us. We have to commit to our part of that deal as well.

There are times, especially in the valley, where we want to stop believing, or caring. Sometimes when we're in the valley we want to pull away from church, family, and friends. Sometimes this is because the reason we're in the valley is because we put ourselves there though bad choices or actions. We have to, especially in these cases, recommit ourselves to being actively in relationship with God and those who love God. We have to find ways to "dwell in the house of the Lord." We must put ourselves actively in front of God to be shaped and molded by Him. This is different for different people. It can come in the form of Bible study, devotions, worship, prayer, fasting, study, hanging out at youth group, going to counseling, or seeking out a mentor. Whatever the case, there are many ways to dwell in God's house, and the ways that make the most sense will often change as we journey closer to God.

No matter the form, make sure that you're always striving to put yourself intentionally in front of God and what He wants to do in your life, even when you're in the valley.

GIVING *pg. 137-146*

God called us to a life of sacrifice and service.
In these ten devotions you'll be challenged like
never before to join in the good work of God
in this world. You'll spend time going through
some of the passages of the Bible dealing with
social compassion. Hopefully, you'll be stretched
to serve our God in ways like never before.

TAKING *pg. 147-156*

As Christ-followers, there are certain things that we take and have to learn to take well. Things like learning to take "no" or rejection can be just as important as learning to take praise or help. No matter what, we have to learn to "take" well. Dive into this ten-day devotion section on learning to receive like a person of faith.

FEEDING THE HUNGRY

> Matthew 25:37-40 <

"Then the righteous will answer him. 'Lord. when did we see you hungry and feed you. or thirsty and give you something to drink? When did we see you a stranger and invite you in. or needing clothes and clothe you? When did we see you sick or in prison and go to visit you?' "The King will reply. 'I tell you the truth. whatever you did for one of the least of these brothers of mine. you did for me.'

Have you ever been hungry? No, I don't mean that your stomach is growling because you missed a meal or because you went to bed after a light dinner. I mean really hungry, hungry because you go to bed night after night having only eaten a portion of food that day. Hungry is going to bed again without dinner because your family can't afford to buy food and knowing that tomorrow will be more of the same. This is hunger.

Hunger happens all over the world, from Sub-Saharan Africa, to central America, form North Korea to the mountains of Appalachia, right here in our country. Hunger is something that's been around since way before the time of Jesus and will be around long after we're gone. Once I heard someone talk about hunger as the problem that will never go away. Maybe, but that should not determine our actions. I've heard people talk about it as such an overwhelming problem that we should focus on other more "solvable" issues. I couldn't disagree more.

Hunger is a problem that we can solve, but we have to commit that solving it 1 million people at a time or one person at a time is still solving it. Hunger is one of the core issues of our world and it's a solvable problem. Will you be a part of the solution? There are ways in your town or city to do this today. There are also ways to become involved in larger global efforts that you can also research and become involved in as well. How will you feed those who hunger?

GIVING DRINK TO THE THIRSTY

> Matthew 25:37-40 <

"Then the righteous will answer him. 'Lord. when did we see you hungry and feed you. or thirsty and give you something to drink? When did we see you a stranger and invite you in. or needing clothes and clothe you? When did we see you sick or in prison and go to visit you?' "The King will reply. 'I tell you the truth. whatever you did for one of the least of these brothers of mine. you did for me.'

I was in Haiti just after the earthquake in 2010, and experienced one of the most gut wrenching images of my life. Let me set the stage. It was hot. Some of the hottest weather I'd ever experienced in my life. We were clearing a giant stone wall that had fallen. We were working hard, taking water breaks every 15-20 minutes because of the extreme heat. And still we were slowly dehydrating.

While we were working, 50 to 70 kids surrounded us; they had nothing else to do but come watch. We had coolers of water but the children had none. We were told we couldn't give them food or water because if we did it would cause a riot, as others were so desperate that fights would break out. It was a horrifying experience every time I filled my water bottle, knowing that those around us were dehydrating and there was nothing we could do about it. What happened next broke my heart even more.

As we walked to get some lunch we passed by this giant drainage/sewer canal. It was disgusting. The canal ran through the heart of the city and collected sewage and run off. It felt unsafe just to be around much less touch. Then we saw them. 30-40 kids and adult knelt down in the canal, washing clothes, splashing their faces, and drinking this rancid water. It was horrifying.

This isn't an uncommon scene in our world. Pollution, corrupt governments, and poor technology are some of the leading causes of thirst in our world. There are ways to prevent this sort of scene from happening. There are ways that are already being implemented and there are ways that haven't even been thought of yet. Will you be a part of the solution? How will you help the thirsty drink?

VISITING THE PRISONERS

> *Matthew 25:37-40* <

"Then the righteous will answer him. 'Lord. when did we see you hungry and feed you. or thirsty and give you something to drink? When did we see you a stranger and invite you in. or needing clothes and clothe you? When did we see you sick or in prison and go to visit you?' "The King will reply. 'I tell you the truth. whatever you did for one of the least of these brothers of mine. you did for me.'

There are those that our society forgets. They commit crimes, sometimes horrible crimes, and we lock them away and mostly forget them. I befriended two of these people, Jack and Ward, in 2007. They were both on death row convicted of murder. I met them because I read this verse about visiting prisoners. I wondered why Jesus would say this if He didn't mean it. And so I did it.

I was really nervous at first. I went through multiple levels of security, each time another door locking behind me. When I first met with Ward we talked a lot. He introduced me to his best friend, Jack. When I met Jack he was the longest serving prisoner on death row. Over the next year I would visit them once a month. I heard their stories, what led them to prison, and what daily life was like on death row. They were real people. Jack was executed September 16, 2008. He was a friend of mine, and I miss him.

I think Jesus wants us to visit the prisoners because of this very reason: to remember that even though they're guilty of committing crimes, God still loves them. Jesus died for their sins, too. I know that if you're reading this you're probably a teenager and can't run off to your local jail and hang out with an inmate today. But there are others who are in "prisons" all around you. These are people who society has rejected or has written off. Find these people who live in the corners of our society, befriend them, and break through their loneliness. Befriend someone who no one else will. Not only will it change his or her life, it will change yours as well.

WELCOMING THE STRANGER

> *Matthew 25:37-40* <

"Then the righteous will answer him. 'Lord. when did we see you hungry and feed you. or thirsty and give you something to drink? When did we see you a stranger and invite you in. or needing clothes and clothe you? When did we see you sick or in prison and go to visit you?' "The King will reply. 'I tell you the truth. whatever you did for one of the least of these brothers of mine. you did for me.'

The funny thing about strangers is that they're only strangers until we introduce each other. Welcoming the stranger has less to do with them and more to do with you. It depends completely on our attitude and actions towards those who we don't know. When we meet someone we don't know we have two options: to keep the relationship the same, continuing to see him or her as a stranger, or we can invite him or her into our lives.

Hospitality is one of the core principles in both the Old and New Testaments. Throughout the Bible we constantly see God rewarding those who welcome the stranger and give rest to the weary. Biblical hospitality is not about having the house clean and serving teacakes and cookies when someone comes to visit. Biblical hospitality causes us to go out of our way to make sure that those who are strangers are taken care of and made to feel welcome.

One of the best examples of welcoming the stranger is seen in the story of the Good Samaritan. The Samaritan went to extravagant means to see if the Jewish man was OK. This is the hospitality that Jesus calls us to.

You have to look at the world around you and see who the stranger is. It could be the homeless person or the new kid in the neighborhood. It could be someone you just met or someone who you've known of for years. No matter who it is, the burden rests on your shoulders. Take time to turn that stranger into a friend.

GIVING 5
CLOTHING THE NAKED

>Matthew 25:37-40<

"Then the righteous will answer him. 'Lord. when did we see you hungry and feed you. or thirsty and give you something to drink? When did we see you a stranger and invite you in. or needing clothes and clothe you? When did we see you sick or in prison and go to visit you?' "The King will reply. 'I tell you the truth. whatever you did for one of the least of these brothers of mine. you did for me.'

This isn't something we often talk about a lot. Everyone in our country, and the majority of the developed world, has at least some access to clothing. Few people in the entire world walk around naked because they don't have a choice. So do we ignore this part of Jesus' teaching or do we probe deeper into its meaning?

There's a show on the Discovery channel called Naked and Afraid. The concept of the show is to put two complete strangers into a survival situation together, with one catch: they're each naked. The idea is that the contestants are to find out very quickly just how critical clothes are to survival. This is an interesting example to me; we often forget that the purpose of clothes isn't to make a fashion statement. Clothes keep us warm, protect us from the elements, and give us a sense of security. Without them we're exposed.

There are a lot of people in our world who have plenty of clothes but who are left outside in the elements, exposed to all sorts of injury, insecurity, and pain. Every night homeless people live with these realities. They go to sleep cold, not knowing where their next meal will come from, fearful that they'll be mugged in the middle of the night or even worse. These are "naked" people, completely vulnerable to everything around them. So should we clothe the naked? Yes we should. We should work diligently to help people have security, be less vulnerable, and have hope for tomorrow. Remember, in our world, being naked isn't just about a lack of clothes. Let's do all that we can to clothe our brothers and sisters.

HEALING THE SICK

> *Matthew 25:37-40* <

"Then the righteous will answer him. 'Lord. when did we see you hungry and feed you. or thirsty and give you something to drink? When did we see you a stranger and invite you in. or needing clothes and clothe you? When did we see you sick or in prison and go to visit you?' 'The King will reply. 'I tell you the truth. whatever you did for one of the least of these brothers of mine. you did for me.'

Unless you're planning on being a nurse or a doctor, this call from Jesus might seem a little difficult. This call should teach us something not only about how we're supposed to interact with people who are sick, but even more how we have to understand ourselves as a part of a larger community. Like I said, unless you're a doctor or nurse, there isn't a lot that you can do by yourself. However, if you understand yourself as a part of a larger community, one that's bound by our call and our faith, then our possibilities are limitless.

Malaria, AIDS, Cancer . . . by ourselves there's very little we can do. But together we're already helping to bring relief and find a cure for each of these diseases. There's a worldwide effort in churches not only to buy mosquito nets for areas with malaria, but to also push to actually eradicate malaria all together! These churches have pooled resources and are cooperating to make sure that this very solvable problem will be taken care of in just a few years. Have you ever walked in a Relay for Life? I bet some of you have. Each time you do, or each time you raise money for the American Cancer Society you're helping fund research and ultimately cure cancer. Churches throughout the country have in recent years come together to forward the cause of AIDS and HIV research as well.

Alone, there's very little we can do. Alone we're virtually powerless against these diseases. But together we have amazing opportunities to change the world by doing exactly what Jesus called us to do; heal the sick. You are more powerful than you may realize. You have the ability to organize people to work together to help meet the needs of the sick and to make a dent in the eradication of these diseases. What are you waiting for?

GLEANING AND HAVING ENOUGH

> *Leviticus* 23:22 <

When you reap the harvest of your land, do not reap to the very edges of your field or gather the gleanings of your harvest. Leave them for the poor and the alien. I am the LORD your God.

As we talked about in the earlier devotion on hunger, there's enough food in the world. There's more than enough. Part of the problem isn't always about a lack of food. Sometimes it's about a lack of generosity. Sometimes we act like we're doing something extra or bonus when we give of what we have to help others. Others will have a much worse attitude about such giving, saying that people who have nothing should work harder and then they can pull themselves out of their poverty and hunger. Neither of these are the attitude God has called us to take.

It wasn't until much later in my life that I discovered the gleaning laws in the Old Testament. The gleaning laws commanded everyone to harvest the inside of their fields, but to leave the outer rows so that foreigners and the poor would have food to help them out and make sure that they were taken care of. God understands that most of us have enough. Notice that this isn't a suggestion. This is a commandment from God.

Most of us have enough. The problem is that we live in a culture where enough never feels like enough. What we have never feels like what we need. And so we work and work trying to get more and more. This is an endless cycle where we constantly have a feeling that we're lacking. Advertisements are designed to make us feel this way. They create a "want" in us and convince us that their product is what we need. But we don't need it. Not really. We have enough and there are many out there who don't. Just like the gleaning laws, we're called to make sure that those who are in need have their needs met by people of faith, people like you and me. It's not a bonus activity. It's not something we should do when we feel generous. It's a core part of our DNA as followers of Jesus.

MAKING PEACE

> *Matthew 5:9* <

Blessed are the peacemakers, for they will be called sons of God.

A lot of people have the wrong idea about being peacemakers. So many times the image of a peacemaker is of someone who is very passive, maybe a hippie with an "it's all good" attitude. Nothing could be further from the truth. There's nothing passive about being a peacemaker. Even the word peacemaker denotes action and movement. Peacemakers live life in a very intentional way. This intentionality calls us to an active life of searching out places and situations where there is unrest, violence or inequality.

When we make peace there are a few things that are important to remember. The first is that we, as people of faith, can't make peace through violence. We undermine our core mission and principles when we decide to use the tool of violence in order to bring about the semblance of peace. Jesus teaches us that this is not way and if we "live by the sword we will die by the sword." The second thing to remember is that we will not always be seen as a hero. There will be some who won't like the peace we try to make. In many situations there's a lack of peace because one person or group of people are taking advantage of another person or group of people. When we try to level these situations out, those who benefit from other's misfortune won't be very happy with what we've done and will let us know about it.

Lastly, making peace is not about us. It's about God and God's vision for this world. There's a verse in the last book of the Bible, Revelation, that talks about God's vision for the world being like a lion lying down with a lamb. This is an extreme idea of peace, one that's against the natural order of things. God wants a peace that surpasses expectations. Now go and make peace wherever you are and do so in the name of our God.

CARING FOR THOSE WHO CANNOT CARE FOR THEMSELVES

> *Acts 2:45* <

Selling their possessions and goods. they gave to anyone as he had need.

The early church's mission was pretty simple. They worshipped and lived together, told others about what they had experienced of God, and took care of those who couldn't take care of themselves. This was the original church. Does it look like the church now? The church now looks very different. We have done a lot of things for the good, but one thing I'm afraid we've lost from the first church is the idea that the church is to take care of those who can't take care of themselves.

Churches, on average, only spend 1-3 percent of their budgets on missions and helping others. The vast majority of church budgets are used to take care of buildings and property, and to pay staff. None of these things were priorities of the original church. Granted, it's not "apples to apples" due to significant cultural differences. But, the heart and mission of the 1st century church should match ours. And when it comes to this specific area, it often doesn't.

Not only do our budgets not reflect this core call of the church, neither do our time investments. For most, church is something done on Sunday morning. And if they're really committed, they might attend a small group of Bible study at some other point in the week. While service trips and working in the community seem to be making somewhat of a comeback in our church culture, it's nowhere near the percentage of our time for it to be considered a core part of what we do. So how will you work to move your priorities back to the place where taking care of the "least of these" is a core value in your faith? You have the chance to shape the future of the church. Will you shape it to reflect our culture's values? Or will you shape it to look more like an expression of God's heart?

LIVING TO GIVE

> James 1:27 <

Religion that God our Father accepts as pure and faultless is this: to look after orphans and widows in their distress and to keep oneself from being polluted by the world.

Each of the previous nine devotionals are all great ideas. They are all great things to do, and anyone would be proud of you for doing them and helping others to do them as well. While doing each of these things is a great help and will do good in the world, there's a greater calling than just doing. God wants to not just do these things as a way to check off a sort of spiritual checklist so that we can say that we're "good Christians." God calls us not to just make change in our world, but to also be changed inside.

At some point it's not going to be as popular to serve as it is now. What will you do then? At some point it won't be convenient and will actually cost you valuable time and money. What will you do then? At some point giving and serving will be tough, and not nearly as mentally or spiritually rewarding as it might feel right now. What will you do then?

When our understanding of service goes beyond what feels good or rewarding or is even popular then it becomes a heart issue. Unless what we give and how we serve first starts from a conviction in our hearts, then it'll always be something that we do. If, however, we understand that this is our calling, and that we've been given so much more than enough, our actions will begin from our hearts and the core of who we are. This type of generosity grows from a deep place of gratitude. Pray that God will help you experience the joy of giving, and that it will go from being something that you like to do, to something that's so deeply a part of who you are that you can't not do it.

TAKING A CALL

>1 Samuel 3:8-10<

The LORD called Samuel a third time. and Samuel got up and went to Eli and said. "Here I am; you called me." Then Eli realized that the LORD was calling the boy. So Eli told Samuel. "Go and lie down. and if he calls you. say. 'Speak. LORD. for your servant is listening.'" So Samuel went and lay down in his place. The LORD came and stood there. calling as at the other times. "Samuel! Samuel!" Then Samuel said. "Speak. for your servant is listening."

Read 1 Samuel 3:1-10. I'm a firm believer that God calls each of us. Every single one of us is called by God to go and do. Unfortunately a lot of people only think that God calls people when they're going into a ministry position and that everyone else just has to figure out what they're going to do. This is not the case. God has given each of us abilities and gifts that He is then calling us to use and go into the world and worship Him with. Unfortunately we can often mistake God's call as just us doing what we're good at.

We can often mistake the voice of God for the voice of society, friends, or family. This can be an easy thing to do since so many of us have never thought about our vocation or passions as given by God. Samuel did this, too. When he heard God calling him he kept thinking it was his mentor Eli. Fortunately Eli knew what was going on and he told Samuel that the voice he was hearing was the voice of God, and that he should answer Him. I think this advice is good for us even today.

The world around you didn't give you your passions and strengths. God gave them to you and He's calling you to use them for His glory and the goodness He wants to grow in the world through you. The first step in all of this is to make sure that you're taking this call seriously and understand it for what it is. It's a calling from the living God. A call that will not only shape us but will shape our world as well.

TAKING FORGIVENESS

>1 John 1:9<

If we confess our sins, he is faithful and just and will forgive us our sins and purify us from all unrighteousness.

Taking, or accepting, forgiveness can often be one of the most difficult things we can do. With God, forgiveness is a pretty simple thing. "You're forgiven." That's it. When people get involved, it gets complicated.

It gets tricky when people are involved partly because we have a very tough time believing that we're really forgiven. We feel like we have to do something in order to earn it or even have to suffer or pay something in order to really receive forgiveness. We make it sooooo complicated. We bargain with God and tell Him that we'll do this or that so that we can be forgiven. And yet God still looks at us and gives forgiveness away freely, without penalty or strings attached. From cheating on a test to murder, God's forgiveness is exactly the same. "You're forgiven." That's it.

It seems just too simple, right? Surely there has to be more to it than that. The problem for us is that there's nothing else. So, start learning how to take forgivingness. Start learning how to accept this free gift. Maybe even more importantly, start learning how to forgive yourself. God has, so should you.

TAKING 3
TAKING NO

>*Ephesians 3:20-21*<

Now to him who is able to do immeasurably more than all we ask or imagine. according to his power that is at work within us. to him be glory in the church and in Christ Jesus throughout all generations. for ever and ever! Amen.

There's this old country song called "Unanswered Prayers." It's a song where the singer thanks God for unanswered prayers and how his life worked out better because God didn't answer his prayers. While I'm not a huge fan of that theology, there's something to that song. The problem is that I don't believe that there is such a thing as an unanswered prayer. I just think that God tells us no sometimes.

We're usually not good at taking no for an answer. It's hard right? You would not be asking for something unless you really wanted it. And or the most part we're people who get what we want. There are preachers and churches who tell the lie that if we just believe enough or have enough faith then God will give us our every desire. But this is just not the God that we see in the Bible. Our God isn't a God that buys into our consumeristic way of understanding the world. God has no problem saying "no" to us, and that's good.

When I study parenting, the children who grow up to be the best, most well rounded and responsible adults are the ones whose parents had no problem saying "no" to them. They had parents who didn't give them everything they wanted. These kids learned early that they couldn't have their every desire and they were better for it. Our God works the same way. Just like the verse in Ephesians says, it's not that God can't do these things, it's just that in many cases God chooses not to do these things. Just remember it's not that we should thank God for unanswered prayers. We should really thank God for answered prayers, even when the answer is "no."

TAKING REJECTION

> *Matthew 5:11-12* <

"Blessed are you when people insult you, persecute you and falsely say all kinds of evil against you because of me. Rejoice and be glad, because great is your reward in heaven, for in the same way they persecuted the prophets who were before you.

Lets face it: Rejection isn't easy. To be honest not only is it not easy, it hurts a lot. When someone rejects us we feel like it's a rejection of all that we are, our passions, dreams, plans, and so on. "Why am I not good enough"? "What don't I have what someone else has"? These are words that stick with us for years and questions that can drive us into low self worth and even depression. The hope that we can trust in is that Jesus experienced rejection too. Here's where my logic goes: If Jesus can be rejected then so can anyone. He was awesome, He loved people, cared for them, healed them, and made the world a better place. Yet people still rejected Him.

So much of rejection has less to do with the person being rejected and more to do with the person doing the rejecting. Should we listen to others opinions? Yes; they can help make us better people and improve in areas of our life that we have blind spots in. However, as helpful as some of these comments on our life can be, they don't define us as a whole person. Should I exercise more? Yes! That's helpful, but it doesn't define the entirety of who I am as an individual and especially who I am in the love of God.

Jesus was rejected. If we follow God closely we too will experience rejection. But that's OK. Jesus told us from the beginning that if we follow Him our path wouldn't always be easy. Take rejection, take comments, and take criticism. But know when all is said and done you're not defined by any of these things, and knowing that should make it much easier to hear and accept them.

TAKING DISCIPLINE

> *Proverbs 12:1* <

Whoever loves discipline loves knowledge. but he who hates correction is stupid.

There are two different definitions of discipline. The first is when we're disciplined. This is when we've done something wrong and we have to pay a penalty for breaking the rules. The other definition is what we do or submit to that will ultimately make us better.

Think about it like an athlete. Athletes discipline their bodies in order to make them the strongest and the most fit they can possibly be. They will work diligently and push themselves in order to achieve a peak of performance and strength. We too must discipline ourselves. Our faith isn't one that we can be spiritually lazy with and expect to do well at. We must discipline ourselves to get in better spiritual shape.

So many of us view faith as an add-on that, if convenient, will benefit us. Nothing could be further from the truth. While faith and grace is completely free, in order to grow in it, we have to work and commit ourselves to work and focus. The verse in Proverbs 12 is awesome. It gets right to the point. "If you love discipline then you love knowledge, if not you are stupid." Ha! This is kind of funny, but it's also true! Discipline makes us better, it makes us stronger, and it gives us a greater ability to live out our faith. Do not reject discipline but submit yourselves to it and watch how you will grow.

TAKING PEACE

> Psalm 34:14 <

Turn from evil and do good; seek peace and pursue it.

Have you ever been in an argument and got so into it that you didn't want it to end? Have you been so deep into a disagreement that you actually began to enjoy it and even feed off of it? We can easily become addicted to conflict and stress. I know this sounds crazy, but look at television for your proof. The best-rated news channels aren't the ones that tell the news in plain and straightforward ways. It's the stations that sensationalize it and have a group of people yelling at each other about every topic under the sun. Look at reality television: it's all about conflict and drama. Think about your friends and those around you at school.

Many people make it their mission to cause drama at some point each day and most of us stand around and consume it because secretly it's exciting for us too. We have to learn to take peace. We have to learn that all of this conflict and sensationalizing are only distractions to the real problems in our world and do little more than take our sights off things that actually matter.

So no matter how difficult it may be, make sure that you're someone who takes peace and is grateful for it. Don't live from one drama to the next but find ways to let those things roll off your back. Know that there are things out there that really matter for you to be concerned with.

TAKING INITIATIVE

> *James 2:18* <

But someone will say, "You have faith; I have deeds." Show me your faith without deeds, and I will show you my faith by what I do.

We talk a lot about having faith. Churches will often talk about how important believing is and how we must have faith in certain things. The problem is that for many of these churches, their faith is something that only exists in their heads. Their faith is separated from action. It's a faith that doesn't manifest itself in their changed lives. This isn't the kind of faith Jesus called us to follow. Jesus called us into a faith that's full of action and initiative. Faith in Christ is a changing faith. It compels us to act.

James sums it up perfectly here when he calls other Christ-followers out and basically tells them to not tell him about their faith but show him faith through their actions. For James, and I would argue with Jesus, there's no such thing as an inactive faith. Faith is best shown through what we do, not just holding to a set of ideas or rules.

The ancient Hebrew understanding of faith is that it isn't something that should ever have to be talked about. Someone's true belief will always be evident in how they act and what they do. We're a culture that's all about talking and less about doing. Have faith. Take initiative. Live it out. As St. Francis said "preach the gospel at all times and, if necessary, use words."

TAKING THE HIGH ROAD

> *Philippians 2:12-15* <

Therefore, my dear friends, as you have always obeyed—not only in my presence, but now much more in my absence—continue to work out your salvation with fear and trembling, for it is God who works in you to will and to act according to his good purpose. Do everything without complaining or arguing, so that you may become blameless and pure, children of God without fault in a crooked and depraved generation, in which you shine like stars in the universe.

You know when people do mean stuff to you or talk about you behind your back? It hurts. It makes you mad and it makes you want to get revenge. It makes you want to do something intentionally mean to them, talk even worse about them behind their backs, and hurt them even worse. So what do we do? We get down into the mud with the people who started the mud slinging and join in the dirty fight. Right?

While this might feel like a good idea at the time, it's not something that a person of faith should let himself or herself get dragged into. While the phrase "taking the high road" doesn't come from a Bible verse, it is very Christian in its meaning. We, as people of faith, are called to restrain from dropping into these bitter and angry fights. We're also called not to use the tactics of those who pick these fights either. Tactics like having secret conversations, rallying others against your enemy, talking about them behind their backs, and trying to defame them to others are not the ways of Jesus. We are to be people whose ways are above those, and whose minds are set to better things.

We have to treat all people, even our enemies and those who sling mud, with the respect and dignity that they were created to have. When we let ourselves get drawn into the pit and start acting like they do then we've failed at showing others that Jesus has a better way for each of us to live. So remember to take the high road in situations of conflict. Take the high road, not so you can look down on others, but so you can help pull them up into a better way of being.

TAKING HELP

> *Genesis 2:18* <

The LORD God said. "It is not good for the man to be alone. I will make a helper suitable for him."

There are times in all of our lives where we're going to need help. For some this isn't a problem; they gladly welcome help. But for others, like me, help is a hard thing to accept. There's this little thing called pride that can often step in the way of receiving help from our friends, neighbors, and families.

Many of us have bought into this notion that we're islands and that we can do whatever we need to do by ourselves. This is a lie that we've been told that not only isolates us from those who care for us but also isolates us from God. This way of thinking is fueled by pride, not by the gospel that Jesus preached.

From the very beginning of creation, God knew that we could not do this alone. So He gave the first human another human so that they could help one another. Each of us has a certain set of strengths and skills, which means each of us also are lacking in certain strengths and skills. This is the way humanity works. We need each other! It's like we are a puzzle, we are all different pieces, and we need each other to fill in the gaps. When we do this well we create something much bigger and more beautiful than we could ever accomplish on our own.

TAKING PRAISE

> *James 4:6* <

But he gives us more grace. That is why Scripture says: "God opposes the proud but gives grace to the humble."

There's nothing wrong with someone telling you that you did a good job. That's a compliment and it's a way that others can tell you that they appreciate the work that you've done. This is good. It becomes a problem when we want the praise of others and this motivates our actions. When we do good things it should be because that's something we feel called to do. If we do these things because we want something then we are using what God intended for good to bring attention to ourselves.

It can be so easy to become addicted to this type of attention. So here's the warning: when you receive praise or congratulations, then you should appreciate it, be grateful for it, but at the same time not let it go to your head. You must remember that while these things are kind and good they should not be the things that drive you to do good in your world. God, the originator of goodness, not only should be our driving force but should also be the goal of our work. When we do good, it's not because we thought it was a good idea, it's because we first learned from our God that these thing are good and were enabled by the gifts from our God to do them. So as we take praise for our actions we should also take an equal dose of humility, knowing that we can do what we do only because of a God who loves us.

LIFE *pg. 159-168*

In John 10:10 Jesus calls us to live life and live it more abundantly. In this set of devotions you'll be challenged with this same call. You'll spend ten days working through the Gospel of John to discover what it means to really be alive in Christ.

DEATH *pg. 169-178*

It's inevitable. You'll experience death. It might be a
relative, friend, or even a member of your immediate
family. But death is something that affects us all. If
you're reading this section there is a good chance
you've recently experienced this and may be looking
for some help. Over the next ten days you'll explore
not only what the Bible says about death
but also how Jesus calls us to face it.

REALLY LIVING

> *John 10:10* <

The thief comes only to steal and kill and destroy; I have come that they may have life, and have it to the full.

We know what it means to live. There are scientific standards that tell us if people are technically alive or if they're deceased. We don't have much choice in this matter; either we're breathing or we aren't. In this passage in John, Jesus begins talking about life. However, He calls us to think about something much larger that just breathing.

What does it mean to really live, not to just be alive? Most of us walk through life everyday just going through the motions. We know the things we have to do, our routines, schedules, and obligations and we do them with little thought or purpose. Many of us are alive but aren't fully living. John 10:10 tells us that every breath is an opportunity. Every moment that we're alive is a chance to really live. We have the opportunity to make choices that matter and that will do good in our world. We have the opportunity to really notice people, to talk to them, and see their faces. We have the chance to look at a world around us that's hurting and be people of healing. We have the chance to be alive and to bring that life to others.

I remember a movie from a number of years ago called Pleasantville. The entire movie was in black and white. Everyone went through life, going through the motions, and doing what they had always done. Then one day one of the characters "woke up" and for the first time saw something in color. The character began to embrace life instead of just going through the motions. It changed his world. Today, choose life, wake up, and watch the world around you become an amazing place!

MORE THAN A FEELING

> John 4:14 <

But whoever drinks the water I give him will never thirst. Indeed, the water I give him will become in him a spring of water welling up to eternal life.

Sometimes, as Christ-followers, we become caught up in wanting to always "feel" our faith. What I mean is that many modern Christ-followers judge their closeness or relationship to God by how they feel at a certain moment. If we feel emotionally connected to God, inspired, or excited about our faith we assume that we're in good relationship with God. If we don't feel those things many of us believe that we've drifted from God and have become distant from God's grace and love. I think this is an error on our part.

When we look at Scripture, it's rare that we ever see God promising a certain "feeling" when He is close. Yet, our religious culture places a large emphasis on what we feel and how close God is based on that feeling. I love the promise that we find in this passage in John 4. Jesus is talking to a woman who has had a very difficult life. She was rejected in a number of ways and was alone in this world. I'm certain she wasn't feeling too great about her life or her relationship with God. They had met by a well where the woman was drawing out water for the day, something she did everyday. Jesus used the water as a metaphor. He told the woman that the way she lived her life caused her to continually come back to refill her buckets. It's an endless pursuit. She would continually be thirsty, and would continually have to come back. He then told her that He had living water, that once she drank, she would never thirst again.

I think that our emotional pursuit of God is much like the water Jesus was telling the woman she was drinking. If we believe that the gauge for our relationship with God is how we feel emotionally, we'll be continually disappointed. We have to know that our relationship with God is not fleeting. It's not something that comes and goes like a thirst. Stop drinking from the well of an emotions-based faith. Trust that, beyond our emotional connections, God is there at work and in relationship with each of us.

LIFE 3
YOUR MOST IMPORTANT COMMITMENT

> John 6:48-51 <

I am the bread of life. Your forefathers ate the manna in the desert, yet they died. But here is the bread that comes down from heaven, which a man may eat and not die. I am the living bread that came down from heaven. If anyone eats of this bread, he will live forever. This bread is my flesh, which I will give for the life of the world."

We have a lot of opportunities to invest ourselves in our world. We can invest in our schools, sports, scholarship, jobs, friends, family, music, hobbies, and dozens of other things. There is no lack of good things we can occupy our lives with. There's an especially strong push in high school to be "well rounded," and to develop your college resume so you can get into the best school. In doing this you're encouraged to have lots of extracurricular activities. Again, a lot of these things are good, but they're not the most important things you can invest yourself in.

As Christ-followers we must have our faith and commitment to the way of life that Jesus called us to as our first commitment. Too often we act as though our faith is an add-on or yet another extra curricular activity that we can do if we have the time. This isn't the way Jesus intends for us to practice our devotion to Him. In John 6 we see Jesus calling himself the "bread of life." He then takes the metaphor to an extreme and tells us that if we're going to be a follower of His, that we must ingest him. This was shocking to Jesus' contemporaries. Not only was Jesus saying that He was sent from heaven, now we're supposed to eat him too? I think Jesus was sending a distinct message to us. "Hey, if you're going to follow me, really call yourself my followers, you can't put me on and take me off like a jacket. I have to be a living part of you and you have to be a living part of me."

He is serious. Jesus has to be a part of our DNA. Something that's inside of us and can't be extracted. Jesus said that He is the bread of life. Now let Him nourish and sustain you and know that everything else can be a wonderful add on.

LIFE 4
BRINGING LIGHT

> *John 1:3-5* <

Through him all things were made; without him nothing was made that has been made. In him was life, and that life was the light of men. The light shines in the darkness, but the darkness has not understood it.

The opening of the Gospel of John is a beautiful first century poem that many believe the early church would say together as a part of their early worship. These verses were a very important part of what the church was and what they wanted to be in the world in which they lived. These verses shaped them in their daily lives and how they understood their mission in the world. In this section Jesus is lifted up as life, which is the light of all people, and that is a light into a dark world.

These early Christians were affirming Jesus as life and light, but they were also reminding each other that they, too, are supposed to be these things in the world. So the question we have to ask ourselves is the same one the early church asked, "Do I bring life and light in the world in which I live"? We know the world that we live in can be a dark and scary place. We, as imitators of Christ, are called to bring light into those dark places. Places where there is fear, anxiety, and depression. Jesus came into our world and showed us a better way. We have the calling to do the same in our world today.

So where are the dark places in your world? Is it in your school? Is that a place where bullying is happening? Are people struggling with balancing school with life? Are there large cultures of partying and abuse? Are there a lot of lonely people? What about in your city? Is there hunger? Are there groups of people who are hated or segregated against in your town? Is there poverty? Go and look at your world. Find the places where there is darkness and live the light of Christ in that world.

A FAMILIAR TRUTH

> *John 3:16* <

For God so loved the world that he gave his one and only Son, that whoever believes in him shall not perish but have eternal life.

You know this verse. You have probably known it from the time you were little. It's the most recited verse in the world. Sometimes when we hear something over and over it can loose its impact and meaning. Many have read or heard it, but how many us have really listened to the words of this deeply important verse?

- God - This gives massive importance to this verse. God is acting. Listen up.

- So loved - The action that God is doing is loving, not hating or judging, but loving. Follow this example.

- The world - The object of God's love is the world, not a group, not a color, not a gender, not a political party, not a nation, not a language . . . the WHOLE world.

- He gave - Because God loved, God gives. God's giving is the outpouring of His love.

- His only son - What more cherished gift could God give than His only child?

- Whoever believes in Him - God's desired response to His love is that we believe in Him.

- Will not perish but have eternal life - Our belief in God gives us life. We can live because God has given it to us. Be thankful.

We have a chance to look at this verse and not see the familiar old verse that is pasted on billboards, shirts, and is carried by some rainbow-haired guy at a football game. We have the chance to read this verse, bit-by-bit, word-by-word and rest safe in the love of God for this world.

TO OBEY IS TO LIVE

> *John 3:36* <

Whoever believes in the Son has eternal life, but whoever rejects the Son will not see life, for God's wrath remains on him."

The word "obey" is a very scary word for most of us. It makes us think of being little children who have to obey our parents or a teacher or else we might get into trouble. Usually when we hear that word it's also something that we might not want to do. Rarely does someone use the word obey outside of telling someone something that they aren't already doing or want to do.

It also, for good reason I think, raises a red flag for us. Throughout history we have seen cases over and over where the person who is talking about obeying is a ruthless person, often holding an abusive power over a person or a group of people. I think all of the above play into why it's difficult for us as Christ-followers to feel comfortable with the word when it's used in Scripture to talk about our relationship with God.

What we must remember is that God isn't a ruthless dictator and that to obey doesn't mean that we're children who are having to be looked after. When we see the word used in the Bible we must understand that to "obey" is to gain life. God wants our lives to fulfill His mission in the world. God wants bigger and better things for and through us than what our selfish pursuits can provide. So God calls us to obey. God gives us a way of life. Not a trite set of rules that are there for the sake of having rules. God gives us an ethic, a practice, and a focus that will provide a life that makes a difference. That life is not only good for the sake of God, it's also the best possible life we could ever imagine living.

OUR NAME ON THE LINE

> *John 8:12-13* <

When Jesus spoke again to the people. he said. "I am the light of the world. Whoever follows me will never walk in darkness. but will have the light of life." The Pharisees challenged him. "Here you are. appearing as your own witness: your testimony is not valid.

Again, we see Jesus being referred to as the light of life, just as we saw in the opening paragraphs of the Gospel of John. Where the early church was testifying to Him as light, Jesus is now calling Himself the light of life. While verse 12 is significant, I want to focus on verse 13. The Pharisees were talking with Jesus as was their custom, and debating interpretations of the Jewish faith. Jesus then makes a pretty profound and gutsy statement: "I am the light of life." The Pharisees had to be shocked! Who in the world proclaims that they are the light of life?

I love what the Pharisees tell Jesus, they say, "You're testifying on your own behalf, therefore your testimony isn't valid." It's not that I agree with the Pharisees but I do think they make a very good point. It's not enough that Jesus tells us who He is. We're called to give testimony of who He is, what He has taught, and what He has called each of us to do. We're also called to talk about this in a personal way. It's not enough that we can spout off facts or teaching; Jesus' light has to be present in our lives.

When we do this, talk from our own experience, we also put our own reputation on the line. When we align ourselves with Jesus and speak to the things He has done, we're putting our name on the line for who He is. This is an important decision and one that we shouldn't take lightly. Think about if you were to testify in court on someone's behalf. You had better believe in what you're testifying to. So not only should we take on the call to speak on behalf of Jesus, we had also better make sure that we're invested in what we say.

LIFE 8
BACK FROM THE DEAD

> John 11:43-44 <

When he had said this, Jesus called in a loud voice, "Lazarus, come out!" The dead man came out, his hands and feet wrapped with strips of linen, and a cloth around his face. Jesus said to them, "Take off the grave clothes and let him go."

Read John 11:28-44. This is one of the most amazing stories in the Bible. A man, Lazarus, who was a close friend of Jesus, had died and had been dead for four days. Jesus hears of his death and is so deeply moved He cried over His friend. Then in an unprecedented move, Jesus goes, asks that the stone be removed, and calls Lazarus out of death and into life.

Jesus still resurrects the dead today. Now I'm not necessarily talking about people coming out of their graves and walking around; that sounds more like some blockbuster movie. I'm talking about parts of our lives that we believe are beyond repair. Jesus has the power to bring them back to life. Things like relationships, emotional wounds, personal pain, impossible situations, and guilt. Jesus has an incredible ability to take those things in our lives which seem to be beyond resuscitation and bring them back to life.

I have seen it throughout my life, both in my own life and in the lives of others. I can think of a couple of times where I believed a relationship or my own personal feelings of death and loss were absolutely too great to overcome. Then the impossible happened: those aspects in my life were brought back to life in new and fresh ways. I can remember being in very deep and dark depression believing that I would never find a way out. Through it all Jesus never gave up on me, and slowly called me out of my tomb and into life. He still rolls away stones today.

LIFE 9
TRUE LIFE

>*John 14:6-7*<

Jesus answered. "I am the way and the truth and the life. No one comes to the Father except through me. If you really knew me. you would know my Father as well. From now on. you do know him and have seen him."

This is a very well known, passage where Jesus is once again teaching on how we can know God though Him. Jesus speaks very clearly that if we believe in Him and follow what He teaches, we will know and be in relationship with God. He uses three words to talk about Himself: "the way," "the truth," and "the life."

The early church often referred to themselves as followers of "the Way." It was a group of people who followed Jesus' teachings and often lived in intimate community with each other. They called themselves the Way because they followed the way, or the path, that Jesus taught them. Jesus also calls Himself the truth. I love this because He seems to be saying that He's the standard for what is true, good, and right. It is Jesus' ways and His words that should set our standards. What we see revealed in his life is something that we can count on and live our lives by. Finally, He talks about the life. This one is a little trickier. If we look around the world we can see people who are completely disconnected from Jesus who have life, and if we're honest, have pretty good ones. I think Jesus isn't talking about life as living and breathing or even doing good. I think He's talking about living life to the ultimate or the best way possible. The life that Jesus calls us to is a life that's full of giving, sacrifice, and love. These are things that are often counterintuitive to us. Most of us want to get as much as we can, not give it away. Jesus gives us a new standard for what life is and shows it to us through His life, death, and resurrection. It's through that life, death, and resurrection that He's calling the world into relationship with God.

YOUR FAITH IN ACTION

> John 20:30-31 <

Jesus did many other miraculous signs in the presence of his disciples, which are not recorded in this book. But these are written that you may believe that Jesus is the Christ, the Son of God, and that by believing you may have life in his name.

The end of the Gospel of Luke tells that there are many more things that Jesus did and there's no way to record them all in this book. It then finishes by making one final plea to the reader that if we will just believe, then we will have life in His name. Unfortunately the word "believe" means something different to us than it would have meant to someone reading this book 2,000 years ago. When we think of believe we usually think of something that happens in our heads. In our understanding we can believe in something by primarily using our minds. In Jesus' day this meant something all together different.

To believe in the first century, especially to a first century Jew, had little to do with what happens in their minds and a whole lot to do with what happens through their actions, their hands, feet, mouths, and words. Belief for a first century Jew was an action. In order to know what someone believed you never had to ask them, you just observed what they did and that told you what they believed in.

When we look at our lives do our actions line up with what's in our hearts and our heads? Can people look at our lives and know what we believe without us even saying a word? Do our lives speak of love, grace, and life? Or do they speak of selfishness, hate, pride, and greed? What does your life say? Examine your life and see what your actions say. That will tell you what you really believe without ever having to say a word.

DEATH 1
A SPIRITUAL DEATH

> *Genesis 3:3-5* <

But God did say. 'You must not eat fruit from the tree that is in the middle of the garden. and you must not touch it. or you will die.'" "You will not surely die." the serpent said to the woman. "For God knows that when you eat of it your eyes will be opened. and you will be like God. knowing good and evil."

From the earliest chapters of the Bible, death has been a part of human life. It seems that death isn't always about the actual physical death that most of us think about where our breathing stops, our heart ceases to beat, and we become lifeless. There are many understandings of death that we find in the Bible.

It's interesting that when death is talked about in Genesis 3 it seems to be a little different than physical death. When the woman in the verse, Eve, is talking to the serpent it seems she believes that as soon as she touches or eats the fruit that she will die. This doesn't happen. Instead we see one of the other major biblical understandings of death: separation from God. When she and the man, Adam, ate the fruit, they were cast out of the presence of God and out of the garden. This transgression toward God caused a divide between humanity and God where the humans were separated from God in a way they hadn't experienced before. This was a death they brought on themselves.

Sometimes we bring this same death upon ourselves. We do things where we distance ourselves from God. Through our actions, speech, and choices we push away from God and the ways that God has called us to live. Now, don't get me wrong: God doesn't leave us or push us away. We're the ones who do the pushing. As we begin a 10-day look at death, I want us to think about how we oftentimes push away from God and bring about this sort of death in our lives. We'll also look at the more common understanding of death and see how the two actually both have a similar ending.

A BEGINNING AND AN END

>*Genesis 3:19*<

By the sweat of your brow you will eat your food until you return to the ground.
since from it you were taken; for dust you are and to dust you will return.

We all have a beginning and an end. It's definite. If you're reading this now you had a beginning and you'll some day--maybe sooner, maybe later--have an end. This verse is beautifully simple Hebrew poetry. It helps us connect both life and death. This is a very humbling verse. It makes us realize that we came from almost nothing and we will return to almost nothing.

Sometimes we look around at others and think how special, amazing, talented, and incredible they are. We often forget that we all came from the same place and we'll all return to the same place. For many this makes us nervous. It makes us think that we have to prove our-selves even more and do even greater things. For others it actually causes them to relax a little and causes them to re-prioritize their lives. For me, I get nervous. I want to do something. I want to be remembered. I want to accomplish. However, when I think about it, I realize that the things I really want to do aren't things like being famous, rich, or the best at what I do. I want to be remembered as a good dad, a devoted husband, a minister with integrity. I want to be remembered as someone who invested in relationships and the life that God has called me to live.

When I think about the dust to which I will return I want it to be said of my life that I love a lot, gave a lot, and learned a lot. We're all head-ing back to dust, there's no getting around it. So what are your pri-orities before that happens? What are the things that really matter? How does your life reflect these things?

A GOOD LIFE

> Deuteronomy 34:5 <

And Moses the servant of the LORD died there in Moab, as the LORD had said.

Moses is a really interesting character in the Old Testament. He was a lot like each of us. He was a normal guy, living his normal life as an infant in his mothers care, then the world around him changed dramatically and nothing was normal again. Moses' life became this crazy story of being left by his mother, adopted by the Pharaoh of Egypt, killing a man, running away, trying to live a normal life again, getting married . . . and then out of nowhere God calls him to stand up against the most powerful person in the land. Moses ends up leading his people on a great exodus from captivity and through years and years of a desert journey.

Read Deuteronomy 34:1-8. Through this journey Moses has had many encounters with God and many tense moments with the people Moses was leading. Then after years and years of this journey, he climbs to the top of Mount Nebo, looks across the place he had been traveling to for all of these years, and dies. It's an amazing story with an amazing lead character. Sometimes people like to call Moses and some of the other biblical figures "heroes" and act like they were all clean and spotless. They were anything but perfect. I bet at the end of Moses' life, as he looked over the promised land he would never step foot in, he thought about his journey. I bet he thought about the things he did well and the things he did poorly. I bet he looked at his life with joy and also with regret. Our lives will be similar. We'll have both regrets and wins.

There will be a point for all of us where we will sit and think back on our lives. My prayer is that at that time, you'll be able to look back with more joy than regret, more happiness than sorrow, and see a life that was well lived for others and for God.

WALKING WITH OTHERS

>2 Kings 2:11-13<

As they were walking along and talking together, suddenly a chariot of fire and horses of fire appeared and separated the two of them, and Elijah went up to heaven in a whirlwind. Elisha saw this and cried out, "My father! My father! The chariots and horsemen of Israel!" And Elisha saw him no more. Then he took hold of his own clothes and tore them apart. He picked up the cloak that had fallen from Elijah and went back and stood on the bank of the Jordan.

We don't walk through this life alone. In some parts of life we'll walk beside others. In some parts we'll lead others. And in other times we'll be lead by others. In this story from 2 Kings we see one of those times. Elijah is a prophet of God. Elijah goes around and helps individuals and communities follow God more closely and in the best ways possible. This isn't an easy job. He also has a protégé, named Elisha. Elisha would follow Elijah around, listening, learning, helping, and ultimately mirroring what he did. Then out of nowhere Elijah is taken from him. He's taken up in a chariot of fire to never be seen again.

All of the sudden Elisha is thrust from being the learner to being the leader. He can't rely on the wisdom, know-how, or experience of Elijah. He must now do it on his own. I love in the passage, where it says that that Elisha "took up the mantle of Elijah." Whose mantle are you taking up? Who are the people in your life that you're learning from, being led by, and mirroring? Who are those people who are teaching you the ways of God and are empowering you to teach others?

If you have those people who you can name, that's good. Stay close to them and make sure that you're learning from them. If you don't, it's time you find someone or several persons who can mentor you and lead you in the faith. This isn't a journey that we have to travel alone, nor should we. The death of Elijah marked the beginning of Elisha's new journey where he would wear the mantle and would lead others. I can think of several people in my life who have passed their mantle on to me, and I work to carry it proudly. Whose mantle will you carry?

DEATH 5
A VALUABLE LIFE

> Psalm 89:47-48 <

Remember how fleeting is my life. For what futility you have created all men! What man can live and not see death, or save himself from the power of the grave?

I can remember driving too fast down old country roads. I can also remember jumping off of really tall waterfalls with many butterflies in my stomach, a little concern on my brain. I can remember doing a lot of things that, at the time, seemed like a lot of fun, but now seems like an unnecessary chance with my life.

For some reason, when we're young, we don't realize how fragile and precious life really is. I'm in no way saying that we should live in a bubble or never do things that are exhilarating. But at the same time we must value life and hold ours and other's lives dear. We live in this tricky balance of enjoying life to its fullest and at the same time holding it closely, protecting it, and valuing as a precious gift. It's especially important to remember how important life is when we're down. It's not enough to make sure to value life when things are going well. We also must value it when we're at our lowest.

There are times in all of our lives where we feel the value of our life is less than it should be. In the worst of these instances we devalue our lives to the point of believing that we no longer want to live. No matter where you are in life, no matter how bad or how good things feel, your life is worth so much. So, in all you do, treasure, value, and take care of the life that you're given. If you feel great, or gloomy, fantastic or like a failure, remember that you're a loved, cherished and precious child of God.

DEATH 6
LIFE AFTER DEATH

> *John 11:25-26* <

Jesus said to her. "I am the resurrection and the life. He who believes in me will live. even though he dies: and whoever lives and believes in me will never die. Do you believe this?"

Here's the scene: Jesus is teaching and performing miracles. He gets word that His beloved friend Lazarus has died. He goes to be with the family. One of the sisters, Martha, met Jesus as He arrived and updated Him on the situation. Jesus began to engage her. He began to console her, speaking about how Lazarus would one day live again. She immediately responded that she knew of and believed in the resurrection that came through Jesus. Jesus affirmed her belief.

This life is the only life we have. We're called to live it to the fullest and treasure it. We're promised that there's something after this amazing life, and that something is beyond our wildest dreams. As we think about death, it's important to remember as Christ-followers that the physical ceasing of breath and brain function doesn't put a period on our life. It merely acts as a comma. Death is a transition from one part of our life to the next.

There's something more. If you're reading this you're very likely dealing with some sort of death or situation where someone is dying. When I read this passage I find comfort that just as I have lost friends and loved ones, so did Jesus. Jesus was in mourning in this passage. Just a few verses down we see Jesus weeping. He was hurting. And yet even in the midst of Jesus' hurting we see Him remembering and reminding us that what feels like the end is only a pause or a transition. Death is not the end.

HOPE IN LOSS

>1 Thessalonians 4:13-14<

Brothers. we do not want you to be ignorant about those who fall asleep, or to grieve like the rest of men, who have no hope. We believe that Jesus died and rose again and so we believe that God will bring with Jesus those who have fallen asleep in him.

Funerals are very difficult. They're especially difficult if the person who passed away did so suddenly or at a young age. No matter what, they're extremely tough times where we're drained emotionally, physically, and mentally. In this letter to the church at Thessalonica, the Apostle Paul is comforting a grieving church. They have lost people who are close to them and are both saddened and confused by their deaths. Paul is writing to comfort them and ease their confusion. He tells them first to not worry about their friends. Then he tried to change their perspective on how they approached death. This is a good perspective shift for us too.

Our first response to death, especially untimely death, is a response of shock and hopelessness. We deal with anger, denial, regret, blame, and fear. Paul doesn't tell us that we shouldn't have these emotions or that we shouldn't mourn. He actually encourages us to mourn but to mourn in a different way. He tells us to mourn as those with hope. Hope that this isn't the end, this isn't the last time we will see them. Death is not the final word. We get to mourn but we get to mourn differently, as those with something to look forward to after death.

If you're reading this and you're hurting, it's OK to feel pain and loss. But do so with hope that the loss and pain aren't permanent. If your loved one had a saving relationship with Christ, his or her existence isn't finished. Your loved one lives on with God. Mourn with hope, expectancy, and courage. Mourn with an empty tomb at the front of your mind.

DEATH 8
WHY?

>*Ecclesiastes 3:1-2*<

There is a time for everything, and a season for every activity under heaven: a time to be born and a time to die, a time to plant and a time to uproot.

Often when we deal with the question of death we find ourselves asking why. Why did this happen? Why now? We ask these questions because dying is a very confusing part of our lives. The thing to remember is that it *is* a part of our lives. It always has been and always will be as long as we're on this earth. And yet it's natural to ask why. It's natural to not understand the reasoning or the timing of death. But we should never question whether death will happen or not. It will happen to each of us, and that's OK. Ecclesiastes puts it very simply: "there's a time to be born and there's a time to die."

When some people realize this truth they become wrongfully preoccupied with death. They live lives that are fearful, worrisome, and paralyzed. This is unhealthy. Many would argue that if you live this sort of life, in many ways, you've already died. So ignoring the possibility isn't good and at the same time constantly focusing on its inevitability is also problematic. We have to live our lives in the middle of that tension, waking up every day ready to take full advantage of life while at the same knowing that each breath is a gift and that we're not promised the next. Never fearful but always grateful. A great way to think about it is living in the simple tension of Ecclesiastes 3:2; we all live and we all die. One of my mentors would always say that our first breath is due to us; every breath after that should be counted as a gift. Live a grateful life for all of your many gifts.

NO FEAR

>1 Corinthians 15:54-55<

When the perishable has been clothed with the imperishable, and the mortal with immortality, then the saying that is written will come true: "Death has been swallowed up in victory." "Where, O death, is your victory? Where, O death, is your sting?"

Death is a temporary thing, at least in an eternal sense. I don't pretend to know exactly what happens when we die. No one knows for sure. But we can have hope that it won't end with a forever death; what is to come is good and will last eternally.

For so many people their lives are this dreaded march towards death, and in the end death wins. Every time. Paul calls us to not think of it this way, because it's not a reality for Christ-followers. Paul, in his letter to the church at Corinth, even goes as far as to taunt death. He is almost making fun of it and calling it out saying "Hey Death! Where's your sting? Huh? Who's winning now, Death?" Now that's the Stephen translation. But it's pretty close!

We get to live our lives knowing that we're not on this inevitable path toward a dreaded destination. We get to wake up every day not fearing the sting of dying. We have the opportunity at the ends of our lives to welcome dying as a natural part of life that will lead us into our next phase of being with God. As we've seen time and time again, dying and death don't have the final word. There's hope beyond the grave. Beyond the grave is a God with open arms waiting to embrace His children.

WINNING IN THE END

>*Revelation 21:3-4*<

And I heard a loud voice from the throne saying. "Now the dwelling of God is with men. and he will live with them. They will be his people. and God himself will be with them and be their God. He will wipe every tear from their eyes. There will be no more death or mourning or crying or pain. for the old order of things has passed away."

I want to leave you with this final thought: with all of the talk of hope, promises of being with God, and death not having the final word, it still remains that when we loose someone, especially someone who is close to us, death really hurts. It's painful, miserable, you loose your appetite, feel like you're in a fog, and are full of sadness. It's hard. Never feel that you're wrong for feeling these things. They're healthy emotions and feelings. For some people the death of a love one takes years to recover from and that's OK.

I do want to leave you with this one last thought: In the final book of the Bible, Revelation, in one of the last chapters, John talks about how death is understood in the new Jerusalem and new earth. Death hurts but it does get better.

Read the verses at the top of this page. If you haven't already, let the words of John comfort you today.

FLOOD *pg. 181–190*

What happens when life is amazing? What do you do when God's goodness feels like a flood coming down on your life? You spend time with these ten devotions, that's what! There are so many positives during these times, but there are also some pitfalls that you should watch out for. So dig in with these devotions and enjoy the flood!

DESERT *pg. 191-200*

Sometimes life's a feast, other times it's a famine. These desert times can feel like there is nothing nourishing or helpful in life. You may feel dried up spiritually. These devotions are a spring in the spiritual desert that we all go through at some time or another.

BLESSED AND CALLED IN THE PRESENCE OF GOD

>*Isaiah 6:8*<

Then I heard the voice of the Lord saying. "Whom shall I send? And who will go for us?" And I said. "Here am I. Send me!"

Read Isaiah 6:1-8. This passage in Isaiah is one of the most powerful and descriptive passages describing the presence of God in the entire Bible. We see Isaiah, a prophet of God, called in a vision where God is an all-consuming presence in the Temple. God's presence fills up the entire structure. There are angels who are worshiping God and singing out His praises. Then Isaiah begins to interact with God, crying out because he sees and understands his own shortcomings in a new way, and confessing them to God.

Worship has the potential to bring us to this point. No matter whether worship is with a big band and hands in the air, or with robes, chants, and silence, God inhabits praise of all kinds. In these holy, sacred moments we are connected to God. There's a beautiful clarity that many of us have in these moments where we see God and ourselves in clearer, more real ways. These moments have a way of cutting through all of the masks we wear and getting to the deepest parts of who we are. It's in these moments where we cry out to God, confess, and ask for forgiveness.

I love how this interaction finished. It says that an angel takes a coal and touches the lips of Isaiah and his sin is made right and forgiven. Then God calls Isaiah to go out and do what Isaiah was made to do. Our worship can often bring about these moments of clarity and confession, but in the end God always calls us to go out do what He made us to do. Let these moments of blessing change you, not for a short time but for the rest of your life.

THE UNEXPECTED BLESSING

> *John 4:13-14* <

Jesus answered. "Everyone who drinks this water will be thirsty again. but whoever drinks the water I give him will never thirst. Indeed. the water I give him will become in him a spring of water welling up to eternal life."

Read John 4:1-26. This story happens on a normal day. Nothing new, nothing exciting. The woman, a Samaritan, was just going about her daily chores. Alone again, in the hottest part of the day. It was just another normal, uneventful, and somewhat depressing day. Things were not good at home. Friends were non-existent. She was alone. Not only this, but now someone, a Jew no less (the Jews and the Samaritans did NOT like each other at all), was asking her for water. Could this day really get any worse?

Then it happened. Out of nowhere she got into a conversation with this guy who was asking her for some water, and he begins to tell her everything about herself, stuff no one else knew. What was a terribly normal day all of the sudden turned into a day full of surprises and blessing.

While God certainly operates in worship settings to speak to us and bless us, God also works in the mundane places of everyday life. It's in these places where we find ourselves most commonly doing life. How often do we truly expect to see the work of God in these moments? There's a very unexpected feeling to Moses seeing a bush on fire in the desert, David tending sheep, and some guys mending their fishing nets. For some reason God loves to take ordinary situations and turn them on their heads. Everyday, mundane, simple, turned into miraculous, unexpected, and life changing. So what ordinary thing are you doing today that God can make extraordinary?

REMINDED OF BLESSING ALL AROUND

> *Psalm 36:5* <

Your love, O LORD, reaches to the heavens, your faithfulness
to the skies.

Have you ever found yourself in love? It's interesting, when you first fall in love, how everything is just a little better. You know what I mean. The sunsets are prettier, the air is a little fresher, the water tastes a little sweeter, and the world around you just seems to be a whole lot better.

In this psalm, David finds himself in a very similar place, although it's not a romantic love but his love of God. David looks around his world and everything he sees is seen through the lens of a creation that reflects God's goodness and blessing. God's love reaches to the heavens. It's like a high mountain. God's justice goes as deep as the deepest oceans. We can take refuge in the wings of God's love. It's almost like creation is singing a love song to its creator and David is there recording it.

It's funny to think about being in love with God. Loving God is one thing but being in love with Him can sometimes seem a little awkward. But it's with that passion and zeal that we are to love God. There's an intoxicating nature to our relationship with our creator where we're able to see the whole world in a way that sings out verses of love. This is just one way that we can see the presence of God all around us, and when we see creation sing out to God, we can't help but follow. Let this song of creation remind you of all of the blessings that are around you and the goodness that God surrounds each of us with.

BLESSING IN THE MIDST OF FEAR

> *Psalm 27:1* <

The LORD is my light and my salvation—whom shall I fear? The LORD is the stronghold of my life—of whom shall I be afraid?

Sometimes we forget. I know I do. I find myself in a scary situation. Not like Scooby-Doo cartoon scary, but real life "I don't know how I'm going to get through this and still have my world intact" scary. Sometimes it's because of something that I've done. Other times it's because someone is trying to discredit or hurt me. Either way, these are scary places.

When I'm in these places it's so easy to forget that we can trust God with both the situation and with our fears. It's so powerful how David so plainly states who God is and how strongly he trusts God. He makes the statement "God is my light and salvation." First David recognizes who God is to him personally. Then David makes a very simple statement, "So because of who God is, who in the world should I fear?" What if we approached our fears this way? What if, first, we remembered who God is and secondly we forgot about who we are not?

Too often we approach our scary times from the opposite way. First we remember who we're not; I'm not strong enough, smart enough, pretty enough, popular enough, and so on. Many times we never even make it to who God is because we're so preoccupied with who we're not. When we face fear, anxiety, and tough situations we can't begin with who we're not. We have to begin with who God is and know that who God is will always be bigger than what you aren't. When you do this you'll realize just how blessed, even in the midst of fear, you really are.

FLOOD 5
WHEN GOD BLESSES THE UNEXPECTED WHO IS EXPECTING

>Luke 1:46-47<

And Mary said: "My soul glorifies the Lord and my spirit rejoices in God my Savior.
for he has been mindful of the humble state of his servant."

There are a lot of seemingly scandalous stories in the Bible. Ones that would make for some pretty good movies, even some that your parents wouldn't let you see. But beyond all of the cheek blushing stories, there's one that tops them all. It's about a young, unmarried, pregnant, teenage girl who God blesses above all others. We all know her as a pretty young woman with a solemn smile on her face, usually in a blue robe, who appears once a year in plastic manger scenes in front yards. But there's so much more to Mary.

God takes what should have gotten Mary killed in that time (namely, being pregnant outside of marriage) and brings about the salvation of the world through her. It's hard to imagine a young, unwed, pregnant teenager could see anything about her life as a blessing. But as we see from the verses in Luke, she saw her entire world as a blessing.

Sometimes we fool ourselves into believing that we can only see or feel God's blessing when everything is going the way we want or expect it to go. The story of Mary changes all of that. She was just a young teenager with her whole life sitting before her. Out of nowhere all of that changed. It had to be super scary. Yet through it all she stays faithful, even singing a song of praise to God. It's true: God blesses when we least expect it.

BEING BLESSED BY BLESSING OTHERS

> *John 6:10-11* <

Jesus said. "Have the people sit down." There was plenty of grass in that place. and the men sat down. about five thousand of them. Jesus then took the loaves. gave thanks. and distributed to those who were seated as much as they wanted. He did the same with the fish.

You are never too young and the situation is never too normal for God to invite you into the work of blessing others with what you have. Today's devotion is a story about a young person who was going about his business doing something he probably would do every day. The difference is that he made himself available.

I was talking with someone a few years back (well we were arguing more than talking) about when you could actually "make a difference." He told me that youth were not supposed to do service until they were much older and more established. He said that the most efficient way for us to be able to serve God was to go to college, establish yourself in a career, make lots of money then, once you were comfortable and well established, you could serve God best. I argued and argued with him and eventually brought up this story. This is a story of a young boy who, as far as we know, was not well established or rich, but gave what he had when he could and God did amazing things with his gift.

You have all you need to do what God wants to do with you and through you right now. You don't have to "get enough" before God can do miraculous things through you. You just have to use what you have and trust that God can do the rest. Can you imagine the surprise on the boy's face when his tiny offering, 2 fish and 5 loaves of bread, was able to feed over 5,000 people? I'm sure he only believed that he was giving a small amount and probably hoped that it would help a little. He used what he was blessed with, not matter his small it was, to bless others. Look at your life. Don't ask what you can do with it, but imagine what God can do with it.

FLOOD 7
SUFFERING AS BLESSING

>*Romans 8:18*<

I consider that our present sufferings are not worth comparing with the glory that will be revealed in us.

We often look at floods of God's blessing as being times when everything is going our way. I can't tell you how many times I've asked someone the simple question "how are you doing?" and they answer with "blessed." The answer isn't the same when they're down. When they're in the dumps, they'll talk about being beaten up, hurt, sad, or afraid. Too often we only associate the word "blessed" with good times where we're happy, healthy, and finding fulfillment in what we're doing at that moment.

Paul continually challenges our understanding of this notion. Paul spent the better part of six years in and out of prison, not to mention his narrow escapes from death and the regular beatings he received. Yet, despite all of this he still sees his life as blessed. In his letter to the Romans, the place where he would ultimately be put to death, Paul states very clearly that nothing that he is suffering in the present is anything when compared to the blessing of what God was doing through him and the glory of what is to come.

I know if you're reading this, more than likely you're a teenager or a college student. One of the things I've experienced that causes people your age the most trouble is the lack of a long term view. In other words it's often very difficult to see beyond your present circumstance; it can often feel like what is going on now will last forever. I want to encourage you, like Paul does, to not look at the chains that bind you, but look to the future and what God is doing in those chains. See the blessing in the midst of the suffering and believe that through God there's a goodness that awaits you. Remember being blessed is not always what it seems.

FLOOD 8
THANKSGIVING IN BLESSING

> *Luke 17:17-19* <

Jesus asked. "Were not all ten cleansed? Where are the other nine? Was no one found to return and give praise to God except this foreigner?" Then he said to him. "Rise and go: your faith has made you well."

It's funny how our brains work. When things are bad we pray. I remember when September 11 happened; it was amazing how many people were in church that day and the days following that horrible tragedy. When we are sick or those who are close to us are dying, we often find ourselves in close communication with God. There's nothing wrong with this. God is there for us even when we're not communicating very frequently with Him. It's also very interesting that when things are going extremely well we rarely ever think of the need to communicate with God. When things are bad, we pray; when things are good we don't.

I love the story of the 10 lepers for this very reason. It shows our human tendency when it comes to prayer and thanksgiving in the midst of suffering and blessing. They are begging Jesus to heal them when they are in the middle of suffering. Then when they find themselves healed, they leave and don't return, that is except for one of them. There's that one lonely leper who finds his way back to Jesus, throws himself down at His feet, and thanks Him for what He's done.

Too often when things are going well in our lives, we find ourselves walking away. We walk away blessed but not thankful to the one who blessed us. Jesus makes a startling statement when the one returns, "Rise and go, your faith has made you well." Jesus lets us know that part of healing is being thankful to the one who healed us to begin with. Too often we can live life believing that we're the cause of all of our own fortune. This isn't the life of the Christ-follower. The life of a follower of Jesus is a life that continually goes back to God thankful for the goodness that's in our lives. Don't be like the nine that walked away.

GOD BLESSES ALL

> *Matthew 5:45* <

That you may be sons of your Father in heaven. He causes his sun to rise on the evil and the good, and sends rain on the righteous and the unrighteous.

You've seen it before. Something good happens to someone around you and you wonder, "How in the world do all of those good things happen to such a mean, unpleasant person?" I know that I've felt that way in my life. It's also hard when those people try to tell the world that all of their "blessing" is coming from God because they're in the center of "God's will." Those instances make me really question God, because many of these people seem to live lives far from the life God tells us to live.

In Jesus' Sermon on the Mount, He addresses some of these concerns. I mean think about it: It must have been a very real concern of His followers as to how Caesar had so much wealth and power while Jesus and His followers had so little. Jesus makes it pretty clear that the good prosper and so do the bad. The bad will suffer and so will the good. When I read this it seems to say that our standing with God can't and shouldn't be measured by material gain or loss.

When we're blessed it goes far beyond anything we can put our hands on or buy and sale. There will always be those who have more and there will always be more of those who have less. That's not what we're supposed to be focused on. Jesus tries to deter us from that focus in this passage. Remember, when we feel blessed it's not our prerogative to try to determine the how or the why, but to focus on being grateful and figuring out how we can best glorify our God with the blessings that we receive.

A DIFFERENT WAY OF UNDERSTANDING BLESSING

> *Matthew 5:6* <

Blessed are those who hunger and thirst for righteousness, for they will be filled.

Jesus completely uprooted our understanding of what being blessed looks like. He does so in a beautiful and poetic section of 12 verses in the beginning of the Sermon on the Mount. I want you to read Matthew 5:1-12 and see if any of the following words equate to our world's way of understanding the idea of being blessed: Poor in Spirit, Mourners, Meek, Hungry and Thirsty, Merciful, Pure in Heart, Peacemakers, Persecuted, Insulted, and Slandered. Those don't sound like titles that any of us were taught we should aspire to hold.

In most cases these are words that we try to avoid. Let's be honest: who really wants to be persecuted, slandered, and insulted? It's interesting because Jesus tells us just the opposite: "Do you want to know when you are being really blessed? See if any of these fit you right now." Remember Jesus seems to be pointing away from those things that are tangible and fall under the way the rest of the world sees blessing. These aren't things that are desirable, profitable, or valuable. These are things the majority of the rest of the world avoids at all cost and yet Jesus tells us that they are the markers for a blessed life.

You probably decided to read this section because you felt as though things were going well in your life. That's wonderful. Count that as a blessing. While you count those things as blessings, it's so important to also look at your life through the lens of the beatitudes and see how your life looks when compared to Jesus' standard of blessing. Remember that all of these "blessings" come about not because of what we do, but because who Jesus is. How closely are we seeing out God's ways in the world around us?

ANSWERING IN THE DESERT

>*Exodus 3:4*<

When the LORD saw that he had gone over to look. God called to him from within
the bush. "Moses! Moses!" And Moses said. "Here I am."

It was a desperate time for the Jewish people. They had been slaves in
Egypt for as long as they could remember. It was all they had known
and all that they could see for their future. They were not hearing
from their God and they were in a lonely dry, desert place. There are
times where we feel alone, abandoned, and forgotten about. These
desert experiences where God's presences seems very far away can
be discouraging, and can often lead us to forget who we are as people of God. This section of devotions is for when you're in those desert places.

Moses was in a desert place. He was abandoned by his mother, then
was banished from his adopted home. He found his way to a new
family, his wife's, while in the desert. While he was tending to his father in law's sheep he heard a voice. It was God. This is the first time
we see Moses hear the voice of God. Can you imagine going through
all Moses had without any sense of the presence of God? What Moses
did next was incredibly important. Not only did he hear God calling,
he answered that calling.

When we're in desert places we can feel as though God has abandoned us and that we'll never feel close to God again. God hasn't
abandoned you. God hasn't left you alone. God is calling you. Moses
answered God's call, no matter how unlikely it seemed, even though
it was coming from a bush. The first thing to remember is that even
in those lonely desert places, you're never really alone. As distant as
God may feel, God is always right there just waiting to listen, talk, and
call you to something more.

OBEYING IN THE DESERT

>*Exodus 3:5*<

"Do not come any closer." God said. "Take off your sandals, for the place where you are standing is holy ground."

Some of the most foolish mistakes I've made in my life are when I'm in desert places. When I would feel alone and disconnected from God, my mind would wonder and become focused on things that weren't what God was calling me to do. I would find myself focused on things like popularity, acceptance, and money. It's not that any of these things are inherently bad, but they were distracting me from the calling that I had from God.

When we're in the desert places in our lives we have to remember that we are still called to do what God says and to not stray from that path. I think the reason many of us will begin to mess up when we're in the desert places is because we begin to feel sorry for ourselves. We often feel that God has abandoned us, and since God has abandoned us, that we can also turn our backs on God. When we're in the desert we're called to stay close to God even when we don't feel that God is there. We have to listen, but we also have to obey.

Don't let your fear, anxiety, and hurt in these times come between you and God. Even more so, don't let yourself make foolish mistakes that you'll have to spend valuable time and energy fixing and recovering from. Whether you feel like God is speaking to you or God feels silent, follow what God has called you to do. John Wesley said, "Preach faith until you have it, and then because you have it, you will preach faith." So, live your faith even when you don't "feel" it. Obey God even in the desert.

WORSHIPPING IN THE DESERT

>Exodus 3:6<

Then he said. "I am the God of your father. the God of Abraham. the God of Isaac and the God of Jacob." At this. Moses hid his face. because he was afraid to look at God.

In the same way we're called to obey in the desert, we're also called to worship in those lonely places. Unfortunately in recent years, the word worship has been very narrowly defined. Lately the idea of worship has been focused around a service of some sort with a lot of music, prayers, and preaching. All of these are good things. But they don't fully define what worship is.

Worship, at its core, is a recognition that we're not God and that God is more than we ever could be. After Moses sees the burning bush and God calls him to recognize that the ground he's on is holy, Moses understands two things: 1) He's not God and 2) God is more than Moses could ever be. In recognition of this, Moses worshiped God by hiding his face. The verse said that he did this out of fear, which can be confusing at times. His fear came from his worship. I know that sounds crazy, but when we realize that we are not the center of the universe, when we realize that we are not God and could never be God, we might become a little scared of what all we've done in our lives. Those things that we're not proud of and wish we could hide will often come back to us and we'll be ashamed.

When we encounter God after a time in the desert there's a time of recognizing who we are and who we aren't. Have you forgotten who you are? Even more importantly, have you forgotten who God is? Spend today remembering who God is and let that be your act of worship.

LISTENING IN THE DESERT

>*Exodus 3:11-12*<

But Moses said to God. "Who am I. that I should go to Pharaoh and bring the Israelites out of Egypt?" And God said. "I will be with you. And this will be the sign to you that it is I who have sent you: When you have brought the people out of Egypt. you will worship God on this mountain."

God doesn't leave us in the desert. We have to remember this fact. God wants more for you than to be wondering around feeling alone and lost. When God calls us we must listen. In Exodus 3:7-11 God does all of the talking. Then in verse 12 Moses asks a question and God answers. We have to be prepared that when God begins to call us to go, we have to listen and be ready to be challenged.

You have to remember that Moses was just going about his business, taking care of the sheep his father-in-law had trusted him with. He wasn't wandering around looking for some great mission, and then without warning was being called to be the greatest leader his people had ever known. It reminds me a lot of another leader who has often been compared to Moses. Martin Luther King Jr. was just going about his business. He was following in his father's footsteps as a preacher to the African American church in the Deep South. He, like Moses was just tending to his sheep, taking care of them, and going about his business in a region that, for African Americans in the 1950s and 1960s, was very much a desert place. King, like Moses, began to hear God's voice in the desert. And like Moses, God was calling him to go and do something very significant. God was calling him to go and free his people, so to speak.

When you begin to listen to God you have to know that there's no limit on what He will call you to do. It may seem small or it may seem massive. But no matter what, God won't call you to do something that He's not willing to do with you.

MAKING EXCUSES IN THE DESERT

>Exodus 4:1<

Moses answered. "What if they do not believe me or listen to me and say, 'The LORD did not appear to you'?"

It's only human. When we see ourselves against something that seems massive and so intimidating our first inclination is to begin making excuses. We make excuses about why we are not qualified, how we do not have the gifts, why others would be better at it than we would. Moses was just the same.

Read Exodus 3:13-4:17. Moses spends almost two chapters explaining to God why God has gotten the wrong guy. "Well, what if they don't believe me?" "What if I stutter?" "Why not someone else?" It is not uncommon, when God is calling us to do something, that we make excuses and will shy away from our calling. There have been great men and women in history who were tasked with great responsibility who made excuses at first. What we have to remember is that God isn't calling us to do something because we can do it on our own, but because we can do it with God.

What we have to remember, what Moses had to learn, is that our excuses don't matter to God. We're not going to be able to reason our way out of what God is calling us to do when talking to God. Try as we might, there will never be a time where we make a point and God says, "You know, I haven't thought of that before. You're right, I'll let you off the hook on this one." It's just not going to happen. Live into what God is calling you to do, stop making excuses, and start making a difference.

BRAVERY IN THE DESERT

>Exodus 4:19-20<

Now the LORD had said to Moses in Midian, "Go back to Egypt, for all the men who wanted to kill you are dead." So Moses took his wife and sons, put them on a donkey and started back to Egypt. And he took the staff of God in his hand.

Sometimes when we're in the desert we're there because something has happened and we've run into the desert to hide. Oftentimes we find ourselves in places of loneliness and fear because we've run from a situation that's causing us stress. This was Moses' story.

Read Exodus 4:19-23. Moses had become angry and killed a man. As a result, he ran. A lot of times his story is our story. Something that we've done or that's been done to us places us on a journey into loneliness. There are those times when we're in the desert where we know we can hide no longer and we know that God is calling us to come out of hiding and face our fears. This calls for bravery, courage, and a trust that God will not abandon us when we leave the perceived safety of our hidden places. It not only takes courage to leave these places, it also takes courage to face what's on the other side. For Moses it was Pharaoh, the slavery of his people, and a shameful past. No matter what it is that we have to face it's often very painful and full of uncertainties. I can remember many times in my life where I knew, deep down in my gut, that I had to face what had sent me into exile.

What is it that made you read this section of the devotion on being in a desert place? What is it that drove you here? Was it something you did, or something that was done to you? No matter what it is, we can take comfort that God will provide us what we need when we come out of hiding. I love how God tells Moses that He will provide what Moses needs when he needs it. We have to trust that the God who is calling us out of the desert will not send us back in shame and humiliation.

COMMUNITY IN THE DESERT

>*Exodus* 4:29-31<

Moses and Aaron brought together all the elders of the Israelites. and Aaron told them everything the LORD had said to Moses. He also performed the signs before the people. and they believed. And when they heard that the LORD was concerned about them and had seen their misery. they bowed down and worshiped.

Oftentimes when we're in a desert place we think that we're the only ones there. We fool ourselves into believing that we're the only ones lonely, afraid, willing to make a stand, or that want to see change in the world. It's only when we summon the courage to leave the desert that we find there are whole throngs of others who either believe the same, feel the same, or want the same things.

Often we think we're in the desert places, where we feel like God isn't talking to us, and when we come out we realize that God was speaking the entire time. The things we were thinking and feeling that we believed separated us from others and from God can often be the things that God was speaking into the entire time. Sometimes it's only when we leave those desert places and come into community that we realize we were not the only ones that God was softly speaking to. It's incredible how when we feel something down deep, something that feels alienating, it can actually be a common feeling among so many people.

When Moses went to the Israelite encampment, He found people wanting to hear the message that God was calling him to bring. What is it that you're learning in the desert places that you'll be taking with you when you leave? How is God calling you into community that will help those stories come forth and bring light and goodness into the world?

RESOLVE IN THE DESERT

>*Exodus 5:1-3*<

Afterward Moses and Aaron went to Pharaoh and said. "This is what the LORD. the God of Israel. says: 'Let my people go. so that they may hold a festival to me in the desert.'" Pharaoh said. "Who is the LORD. that I should obey him and let Israel go? I do not know the LORD and I will not let Israel go.' Then they said. "The God of the Hebrews has met with us. Now let us take a three-day journey into the desert to offer sacrifices to the LORD our God. or he may strike us with plagues or with the sword."

So here's the deal: It's not always going to be peachy and full of community when you come from the desert places. You won't always find everyone so receptive to you coming out of that place. You may meet resistance. It's part of life, especially the life of a person of faith who is challenging norms with who you are and with what God is calling you to say and do.

When you're in these situations you must have resolve. You must have resolve that when God calls us out of those places, that He's doing so for a reason. We have a very real mission that we're called to fulfill and a very real word that God is calling is to take to the world. Too often, though, we are people who get very scared when we meet resistance. Too often we cower at the smallest sign of rejection or fear of persecution. Your resolve in these situations is the thing that will determine whether you move forward with God's goodness into the world, or you return back to a desert place where you feel isolated from God and from the world.

God speaks to us in these lonely places, we know that. Sometimes, God even speaks to us more clearly in these places because we are more apt to hear. The clear and resolute voice of God that you experienced in the desert isn't going to change or waver. It speaks the same message as it spoke in what will hopefully one day seem like a far and distance place. Don't let fear and conflict dilute that moment and the call that you know is so very real.

DIFFICULTY IN THE DESERT

>*Exodus 5:20-21*<

When they left Pharaoh, they found Moses and Aaron waiting to meet them, and they said, "May the LORD look upon you and judge you! You have made us a stench to Pharaoh and his officials and have put a sword in their hand to kill us."

Sometimes things are going to get worse before they get better. Not all roads out of the desert are straight and smooth. Many are full of setbacks and times where you're going to want to turn back and quit. I have friends who deal with addiction and their journey out of the desert often has relapses and deep temptation. Most of these journeys are full of unexpected circumstances and difficult situations that will cause us to doubt and question everything. We see this with the story of Moses.

Read Exodus 5:4-21. God was calling Moses to do something. Finally after some arguing Moses did it. Moses believed that God could do what God wanted to do. Moses had resolve. Then we get to these verses, Moses spoke to Pharaoh what God had told him to, and everything should have gone well, right? Nope it didn't. The Israelites were punished, and punished hard. They not only had to work harder but had to do so with less materials and the scorn of their masters.

It would have been very easy for people to look at the situation and said that it didn't matter that what they were doing was right because it was causing so much suffering. I have seen many situations where this doubt has happened because people didn't understand that, often, it will get worse before it gets better. If it's good, if it's right, then keep on, move forward, and do what God is calling you to do.

DELIVERANCE FROM THE DESERT

>*Exodus 6:7-8*<

I will take you as my own people, and I will be your God. Then you will know that I am the LORD your God, who brought you out from under the yoke of the Egyptians. And I will bring you to the land I swore with uplifted hand to give to Abraham, to Isaac and to Jacob. I will give it to you as a possession. I am the LORD.

You're not meant to live in desert places. You're not meant to live in suffering, fear, anxiety, and loneliness for the rest of your life. Beyond the doubt things seem to only get worse. Don't fear. You're being called out of the desert. You're being called to something more and to a place where God has promised.

Read Exodus 6:1-8. It's important when we leave these places to make sure that we not forget where we've been, the God we met there, and the way that He delivered us from those places. We must also remember the lessons we learned and the new ways God revealed Himself to us.

On this, the 10th day of this devotion, I want you to spend some time reflecting on these things. Write down your journey and those things learned, mistakes made, and the ways you saw God delivering you. Take the time to do this and mark it as a time of God's deliverance from your desert place.

CONFIDENT *pg. 203-212*

Feeling like you have it all figured out? Does it seem like you can do no wrong? That's great! What an awesome feeling. While we understand enough about life to know that we don't really have it all figured out and we certainly can still do wrong, it's fun to feel this way when things are going well. If this describes you, then take a couple of weeks to focus on ten spiritual disciplines that have been practiced through out the 2000 years of our faith. Not only will they inspire you, but they'll also help you keep your head level and your eyes focused on your God.

CONFUSED *pg. 213-222*

Life can sometimes be confusing. And when we're most confused is when we need to focus on listening to our God most diligently. One of the ways that Christians throughout the centuries have done this is through spiritual disciplines. Over the next ten days, you'll learn about (and be challenged by) a different spiritual discipline that will help you hone in and focus on what God is calling you to do. Confusion is a normal part of life. Good thing God is here to help clarify things for you.

CONFIDENT 1
PRAYER

>Matthew 6:5, 9-13<

And when you pray, do not be like the hypocrites, for they love to pray standing in the synagogues and on the street corners to be seen by men. I tell you the truth, they have received their reward in full . . . This, then, is how you should pray: 'Our Father in heaven, hallowed be your name, your kingdom come, your will be done on earth as it is in heaven. Give us today our daily bread. Forgive us our debts, as we also have forgiven our debtors. And lead us not into temptation, but deliver us from the evil one.'

Confidence is one of the greatest deterrents of prayer. When things are going well, we know our course and certainty abounds. Prayer has little room. Most people come to prayer in times of uncertainty and confusion. There's a natural proclivity towards prayer during these times. It's in these times where we're grasping for any help. When we're confident we grasp for nothing. That's why prayer can be even more important during times of confidence than when we're struggling.

It's very easy to forget that while we're successful and strong we still need God. During these times prayer can act as an agent of humility. When we pray we admit first and foremost that there's something that's greater than we are. Prayer also admits that we don't have it all figured out. Prayer is wildly important when we're at our best, not so we can stay our best, but so we can remember where we are in the grand scheme of things. In the grand scheme of things we're still mortal, and still able to make mistakes. So, when things are going great, don't forget to pray. When it seems that you can't lose, don't forget to pray. When it seems you can't make a wrong move, don't forget to pray. Because at the end of the day, it won't always be this way.

Don't pray as though it were some magic that keeps you on top. That's superstition. Pray because in truth you're never on top; God is and that's important to remember.

FASTING

> *Matthew 6:16* <

When you fast, do not look somber as the hypocrites do, for they disfigure their faces to show men they are fasting. I tell you the truth, they have received their reward in full.

When things are going our way it can be easy to tell ourselves that we're the kings and queens of the world. As the kings and queens of the world there's often the temptation to believe that we deserve the things we want and desire. This is called false entitlement. False entitlement is when we think that there are all of these things we're entitled to simply because, well, just because. Rarely during these times do we withhold things from ourselves. Oftentimes when we're confident and on top of the world we'll lavish ourselves with pleasures because we feel like we've earned it or deserve it. Fasting is one way to deny ourselves and remember that everything is a gift from God; nothing is a given. It's a way of not submitting ourselves to our every desire and choosing to live in such a way where our every want is not our first priority.

Fasting doesn't have to be food-based either. We can fast from anything. The intention of it is to take something away that we usually depend on or want in order to admit our dependence on God. It's also a way of remembering that we too are mortal. When you fast it's an act of humility. It reminds us that we're not owed anything and that all we have is a gift. So, when you're in confident moments like you might be now, think to yourself, "What can I take away to make sure that I'm not becoming falsely entitled? What can I do to remember my own mortality?"

CONFIDENT 3
GUIDANCE

> *Proverbs 11:14* <

For lack of guidance a nation falls, but many advisers make victory sure.

There will come a time when the student becomes the teacher. That time might be happening for you right now. You've been successful. You're now longer the newbie. You've achieved a level of maturity and others have noticed. Now you're being looked to for wisdom, guidance, and inspiration. It would be easy with others looking to you now, to believe that you have all of the answers. It would be very easy for you to put yourself at the top of the food chain. But don't do this.

The greatest leaders and teachers still need guidance. The most knowledgeable men and women in our world still seek council from trusted friends and teachers. Even our most talented and brightest leaders have people who help them choose the right course of action, to check their motives, and to give them different perspectives on situations. The greatest leaders don't lead alone; they lead with the council of those who are collectively wiser than themselves.

When we choose to lead without influence, then we've proven that we're not wise enough to lead at all. Contrary to what some might tell you, leadership with council and guidance is not showing weakness; it shows wisdom, humility, and strength. You'll ALWAYS need the council of others. Whether you're the captain of the basketball team or the President of the United States, you'll need those around you to help you see the task in front of you and to council you well on that task.

The thing that keeps us from guidance is not an abundance of knowledge. It's a lack of understanding and self awareness. Always seek out guidance in all you do.

CONFIDENT 4
SILENCE

> *Psalm 62:5* <

Find rest, O my soul, in God alone; my hope comes from him.

When I'm doing well and confident in what I'm doing, I often find myself talking a lot more. It's natural if you think about it. The more confident you are, the more people are going to want to know what you have to say, and what's supporting your confidence. You'll also be more apt to lead from up front, which necessitates another level of speaking and instructing. It can often be the case that the more successful and confident we become, the less silent we find ourselves. This isn't a great thing.

When we're silent a few things happen. The first is that we're able to listen. We live in a time and place where people are much happier to sit and talk about their opinions and thoughts than listen to the thoughts and ideas of others. The second is that when we're silent we have a much better chance of hearing that still, small voice of God. When we talk, and talk incessantly, the only voice we're able to hear is our own. God wants us to hear His voice and hear it clearly. It's very difficult to do this when we do all of the talking. Silence also allows us to rest and find peace in ways that talking does not.

Remember silence, as a spiritual practice is not only about not talking, but also about being in quiet places where we're not inundated with all of the many things that tug and pull at our attention. So whether it's audible silence or physical silence, make sure that even in the best of times that you find time and places to simply be . . . silent.

CONFIDENT 5
READING

> *Acts 8:26-31* <

Now an angel of the Lord said to Philip. "Go south to the road—the desert road—that goes down from Jerusalem to Gaza." So he started out. and on his way he met an Ethiopian eunuch. an important official in charge of all the treasury of Candace. queen of the Ethiopians. This man had gone to Jerusalem to worship. and on his way home was sitting in his chariot reading the book of Isaiah the prophet. The Spirit told Philip. "Go to that chariot and stay near it." Then Philip ran up to the chariot and heard the man reading Isaiah the prophet. "Do you understand what you are reading?" Philip asked. "How can I." he said. "unless someone explains it to me?" So he invited Philip to come up and sit with him.

Much like prayer, reading is something that we find ourselves doing a lot more when we're struggling with a situation or our faith. Reading (especially the Bible) is one of those spiritual practices that occurs more when we're frightened, confused, or are seeking answers. While many read the Bible or devotionals or other spiritual readings daily, most find themselves deepest in this spiritual practice when times are most difficult.

Success is often a double-edged sword. The more successful we are, the more confident we become in our way of doing things. This is good in many ways. Confidence is an important factor in our lives. However, when we become too confident in just "our" way we often forget that we follow "The Way." Reading the Bible and other books that help us understand our faith is imperative in making sure that our way doesn't become the only way.

The way Jesus taught us was a way that often went against social norms, was a little counter intuitive, and not very popular. The more successful we become, the more difficult it becomes to keep to these unpopular ways. Oftentimes our ways seem to make much more sense and are much more "realistic." The teachings, especially the more difficult teachings, of Jesus can often be disregarded is lofty ideals and not practical for our modern minds and rhythms. Our ways, which are usually much more convenient and easy (because lets face it they are what we do anyways) take precedent and soon can become our standards instead of those set forth by Jesus. In reading the text, we're grounded in the text and then our standards and practices are the ones that are judged by the reading not the other way around.

CONFIDENT 6
SOLITUDE

> *Luke 6:12-13* <

One of those days Jesus went out to a mountainside to pray, and spent the night praying to God. When morning came, he called his disciples to him and chose twelve of them, whom he also designated apostles.

Being alone is tough, especially when we're doing well. When we're confident and successful we usually hear praise and accolades. This praise feels good. And it should. As good as it is, it can often become very addictive. When we're with those who praise us and cheer us on it's difficult to not feel good about ourselves. They cheer us on at those things that we're good at and are excelling with. They don't cheer us on but then also say, "Hey, you're doing fantastic at dance but your chemistry grade is below where you need it to be." No, they just praise what we're doing well at. When we're alone that's not the case.

When we find ourselves alone and not around those who encourage us, we will often hear our own voices, fears, and doubts. We also think about the things that aren't going as well and that worry us. When we're alone we have to deal with our worst critic: ourselves. But that doesn't have to be what solitude is about. Much of the purpose of solitude is so that we neither have the negative or the positive voices, only God's voice.

We need praise and we need critique. But solitude is for neither. It's for time to breathe and to be alone with God. Don't be afraid of solitude, you need it. We all need it. It's so easy to become addicted to having so many people surrounding us that being alone can feel like punishment. In true solitude, the only opinion that we should hear is that of God's. Find a place to be alone and listen closely.

CONFIDENT 7

SERVICE

>1 Peter 4:10<

Each one should use whatever gift he has received to serve others, faithfully administering God's grace in its various forms.

Very often people who find themselves confident at something, especially a sport or hobby, also find themselves with less time to serve in our world. It makes sense. The more successful you are at something, the more you'll do it, and the more it will compete with other things you spend your time doing. One of those things is service to others.

The spiritual practice of service is a deeply important part of a person of faith's life. One of the things I've seen happen to people, even ones with the best of intentions, is that they begin to think that service is something that's an option, add on, or in worst case scenarios, something that's not really valuable. It happens that when people become engaged in specific pursuits at which they are successful, they can look at their time and ask, "Is serving others worth my time?" While this is a good practice that helps us really think about where we invest our time, if done wrong, it can lead to a "our time is worth more than they are" attitude.

At the end of the day we're all called to serve, period. We're all called to spend our time and energy giving to others, period. No matter who we are and what we do, the call and expectation is just the same. We are to care for those who can't care for themselves. We are to love the unlovable and to align ourselves with the forgotten and the abused. In God's Kingdom there are not the successful and the unsuccessful. There are only God's children, and His love for all humankind.

CONFIDENT 8
PILGRIMAGE

>*Luke 2:41-42*<

Every year his parents went to Jerusalem for the Feast of the Passover. When he
was twelve years old, they went up to the Feast, according to the custom.

Confidence can be such a great thing. It can help us do more than
we ever thought we could and causes us to strive harder to achieve.
One of the drawbacks can also be that we can begin to think that we
made it to where we are by ourselves. Sometimes confidence can
lead us to believe that we are the sole reason for our own success.
It can cause us to become very self-centered. We have to remember
that none of us is an island, and all of our success is in at least some
way because of the work of someone else.

Pilgrimages are one way to remember that we're a part of something
much bigger than just our ambitions and us. We're locked into a specific time and place, and we should live our lives trying to make the
most impact possible. But at the end of the day we have to remember that we're a blip on the screen of history. This isn't to make us feel
insignificant but to help us understand that our lives are partly spent
advancing the mission of those who have gone before us.

When I walk the paths that have been walk for thousands of years
and worship in ways our the saints who went before us worshipped,
it helps me realize that each of us are a piece, a single but important
piece of a much bigger puzzle.

SABBATH

>*Exodus 20:8-11*<

"Remember the Sabbath day by keeping it holy. Six days you shall labor and do all your work, but the seventh day is a Sabbath to the LORD your God. On it you shall not do any work, neither you, nor your son or daughter, nor your manservant or maidservant, nor your animals, nor the alien within your gates. For in six days the LORD made the heavens and the earth, the sea, and all that is in them, but he rested on the seventh day. Therefore the LORD blessed the Sabbath day and made it holy.

There's probably no more difficult spiritual practice, for a confident successful person, than sabbath. Sabbath is the concept of rest. God-centered, reflective rest. And when things are going your way you don't want to hurt that momentum or really stop what you're doing because you're doing it well! There's a sense that, in order to maintain the good things that are going on, we must push relentlessly. Plus we usually don't mind because we enjoy the success. But no matter if things are going well or poorly we need sabbath.

God rested and so should we. We must learn to balance our lives and our time in such a way that allows for rest, reflection, and time away from those things we do, even when we really enjoy doing them. I love doing youth ministry, consulting, and writing. But unless I take breaks from those things I love, I'll become burned out on them and ultimately will resent them.

Sabbath is something that requires a lot of discipline. When we have things to do it takes a lot of self-restraint to put that on hold. No one wants to miss a good opportunity or to get behind. But unless we take time for ourselves, time to rest and to not do whatever it is we do, then we run the risk of burnout. Sabbath, when kept properly, sets a different order of priorities. It says that God requires a time each week for us and with us. It tells everything else that it can wait because there's something much more important, much more necessary. Rest and know that nothing else is as important than rest with God.

CONFIDENT 10
WONDER

> *Psalm 40:5* <

Many. O LORD my God. are the wonders you have done. The things you planned for us no one can recount to you: were I to speak and tell of them. they would be too many to declare.

When it's all said and done, we have to sit back and sit in wonder of what God continues to do. It can be very easy, when we're confident, to focus on what we've done. But when we focus on our accomplishments alone we miss an entire world of amazing things that God has done. No matter what we do, it will always pale in comparison to what God has done and continues to do.

I'm not only talking about what happened on the cross. I'm also talking about what God does every day. The songs the birds sing, the way a tree reaches towards the sun, and the love of a parent toward a child. These are just some of the things that I can't help but stand in awe of. Sometimes we can be so preoccupied with all of the awesome things we're doing that we forget to look up from our tasks and see all that is going on around us.

So, when you are confident, doing well, and feeling great, just make sure to take some time and remember the amazing world that exists around you. Take some time and find yourself in amazement of the simple things and the profound things, the noticed and the unnoticed. Don't let a day go by where you don't sit back and open your eyes wide, breathe in deeply, and know that in comparison, our lives are wonderfully small. In this smallness we can find some of our greatest inspiration and wonder.

PRAYER

> *Matthew 6:5, 9–13* <

And when you pray, do not be like the hypocrites, for they love to pray standing in the synagogues and on the street corners to be seen by men. I tell you the truth, they have received their reward in full . . . This, then, is how you should pray: 'Our Father in heaven, hallowed be your name, your kingdom come, your will be done on earth as it is in heaven. Give us today our daily bread. Forgive us our debts, as we also have forgiven our debtors. And lead us not into temptation, but deliver us from the evil one.'

Praying is natural when we're confused. When we find ourselves in places of indecision or out of options, prayer comes naturally. Prayer is, at its core, a conversation. It's a time where we can speak to God without pretense. It's a time for honesty, fear, anxiety, questions, petitions, and vulnerability. I love how in verse 5 Jesus doesn't say "if" you pray, but "when" you pray. Jesus assumes that as a follower of His, prayer is a natural part of who we are and what we do. He's not asking if we pray but more telling us how to pray when we do. Then Jesus gives a template, or a guide, for how we can and should order our prayers.

When you are in times where you don't know what to do, it's very easy for our prayers to only be focused on our needs. Sometimes this can be detrimental to our faith and to how we actually cope with our confusion. Even when we're in times of fear or indecision we must remember that our lives shouldn't be centered on us. There is a God we worship, a world that we're called to serve, and a Kingdom we're called to help usher in.

Too often our temptation is to put ourselves at the center of our prayers. Push against this temptation especially when you're in a trying situation.

FASTING

> *Matthew* 6:16 <

When you fast. do not look somber as the hypocrites do. for they disfigure their faces to show men they are fasting. I tell you the truth. they have received their reward in full.

Even when we find ourselves in confusion and uncertainty, too often we begin to develop bad habits. It's natural. In order to cope with the stress that we're encountering from the world we medicate ourselves with things we know aren't good for us. Or if nothing else, we slack on our self-discipline and stop the practices we know keep us healthy, focused, and strong. Stress and anxiety will cause people to sleep less, sleep too much, over eat, not eat enough, drink, make bad choices, stop exercising, and even loose our focus on our faith. It seems that in one of Jesus' most stressful times, just before He begins His ministry, He obediently undertakes a 40-day fast. He also assumes, like prayer, that His followers will fast as well. He says "when" you fast, and then gives instructions.

Fasting is something that's so difficult for us to understand. Why would we intentionally give something up, especially something that's not bad for us, like food? To be honest, I'm not entirely sure. Some will say it's so we will remember God when we feel hunger pains or want whatever we're fasting from. Others say that's a way of self-denial that brings us closer to God. No matter what the reason it seems to be something important to Jesus and something He expects from us. It also seems that in the culture fasting took place when there were decisions, stress, uncertainty, and mourning.

As you're dealing with confusion, take on this intentional practice. Find something you're going to give up as an intentional practice. You may not know the reason why, but you can trust that God understands and knows your heart.

GUIDANCE

> *Proverbs 11:14* <

For lack of guidance a nation falls, but many advisers make victory sure.

You're not a ship alone adrift in a sea. You're not an island with no others in sight. You don't have to do this alone, and in truth you shouldn't even try. Over and over again in the Bible the people who were shown as the most faithful followers of Christ were the ones who followed God alongside other Christ-followers. They had people who were close to them who could speak truth, sometimes hard truth, into their lives. Moses had Aaron. Ruth had Naomi. Elijah had Elisha. David had Jonathan. Peter had Paul. Paul had Timothy. Throughout Scripture we see people not going about this journey alone.

In every one of the relationships above, one of those people helped the other through terribly confusing times and trials. This verse in Proverbs speaks deep truth into our lives. You're crazy if you try to do this life alone, especially when you're confused. During this time, seek out guidance of those who you trust and believe are going to help you discern (a fancy world for thoughtfully decide) what path you should choose. God does amazing work through these relationships.

One of the reasons these are so important is that they can help us see new possibilities that we would've never considered before. We're too "in the weeds" to really see what's going on. These relationships bring about different perspectives that open up new possibilities and create close community. It's often through this community and these relationships that God not only does great things in your life but also in the world.

SILENCE

> *Psalm 62:5* <

Find rest, O my soul, in God alone; my hope comes from him.

Silence is hard for us. We live in a world that's anything but silent. Not only are we constantly surrounded by noise (radio, cell phones, music, chatter, conversations, airplanes, cars, the hum of electronics, television and every other imaginable device) we're also bombarded with visual noise. We can't walk five feet without seeing billboards, signs, advertisements and screens of every shape and size. That's a lot of noise.

There's something about being quiet that our culture just doesn't understand. In truth it often seems that the more anxious we are the more many of us talk. I can't tell you how many conversations I've been in where I knew someone was lying or covering up something by the sheer volume of words that were coming out of their mouths. When we never find ourselves in a quiet place we begin to believe all the voices that are around us and forget to listen to the voice of God that often comes in the most silent of situations. When we intentionally place ourselves in silence we also find that we're more relaxed and calmer.

Confusion doesn't always come from a situation or a decision. It often comes in the form of not enough time to simply think with a clear and focused head. Many of us run around with our heads spinning like tops, going from one thing to the next and never actually sitting to be in silence. In truth, many of us deeply fear silence. We fear what we might discover about ourselves or even what we might hear in those quiet moments. The verse in Lamentations encourages us that sometimes we just need to sit in silence and with God. When is the last time you actually did this? Try it now. Set an alarm on your phone for 10 minutes, find a quiet place, and turn the alarm on. Let your mind focus on nothing. Breathe and listen for the quiet voice of God.

CONFUSED 5
READING

> # >𝐴𝑐𝑡𝑠 8:26-31<

Now an angel of the Lord said to Philip. "Go south to the road—the desert road—that goes down from Jerusalem to Gaza." So he started out. and on his way he met an Ethiopian eunuch. an important official in charge of all the treasury of Candace. queen of the Ethiopians. This man had gone to Jerusalem to worship. and on his way home was sitting in his chariot reading the book of Isaiah the prophet. The Spirit told Philip. "Go to that chariot and stay near it." Then Philip ran up to the chariot and heard the man reading Isaiah the prophet. "Do you understand what you are reading?" Philip asked. "How can I." he said. "unless someone explains it to me?" So he invited Philip to come up and sit with him.

We can't forget to read the Bible. Hopefully through this devotional you've discovered a lot of new parts of the Bible as well as rediscovering parts that you've known but have a new and fresh take on. But, reading the Bible isn't enough. We have to let it read us. One of my favorite quotes is by the now deceased Rev. Peter Gomes. He said "Apply yourself closely to the text, and apply the text closely to yourself." I love this quote.

The Ethiopian in the passage in Acts was reading the Bible, but he wasn't letting the Bible read him. He was only reading the words on the page but didn't understand what they meant. Too often we find ourselves reading verses, doing a devotion, and going about our business. It's so important to let these verses settle over us, marinate in them, and allow them to shape us so that we're different because of them. It's so easy to look at them dissect them and analyze them. This isn't bad at all. But if this is all we do we've missed so much of the point of the Bible. It's a story book of the stories of our faith. It's a book of stories about this God who desperately loves His children and wants nothing more than to be with them in relationship. It's a story book that we must sit with by letting it speak to us. When we do, our confusion will turn to hope and our doubt will turn to courage. Let it read you.

SOLITUDE

>*Luke 6:12-13*<

One of those days Jesus went out to a mountainside to pray, and spent the night praying to God. When morning came, he called his disciples to him and chose twelve of them, whom he also designated apostles.

Throughout the Gospels we see Jesus getting away from everyone and spending time in solitude, completely alone. Solitude is very similar to silence in that it's just not something we as a culture hold very high on our priority list. It's something that we rarely experience or have time for. Just like silence or fasting, there's nothing magical about the actual act. But amazing things can happen through it.

In these verses, we see Jesus retreating to the mountain alone, to the wilderness by Himself and going away to pray and telling His disciples (His closest friends) to go on without Him so that He could be alone. If Jesus needed to be alone, don't you think we need it too? And, in truth, probably need it even more so? Solitude isn't just finding yourself alone. If it were we all could say that we practice solitude and silence when we go to bed each night. No, when I mention solitude, I'm talking about an intentional choice to be by yourself with the expectation and hope that our faith will grow and our relationship with God will benefit.

Solitude is tough because so many times we feel we have to have something "to do." When you choose solitude, that's what you're choosing to do, to be alone. When we're confused and trying to figure out our lives, solitude can often seem pointless because we might feel like we're not getting any closer to clarity on our problem. Don't fall into this trap, where we believe our confusion becomes less with the more we do. Oftentimes it's the opposite. Many times it's when we take time, stop, and are alone that we see things for how they actually are. While a part of our practices are focused on receiving guidance from close and trusted friends, we can never forget to make sure there's also time for us to be alone with God.

CONFUSED 7
SERVICE

>1 Peter 4:10<

Each one should use whatever gift he has received to serve others, faithfully administering God's grace in its various forms.

You might remember that earlier in this set of devotions on being confused I wrote about how prayer should not only focus on us but on others, as well. Here's the deal: so should our actions. Again, when we're confused it's often easy to just be the victim. No matter whether we're up or down, confident or confused, joyful or sad, we're called to use the gifts that God has given us to do His ministry in this world. It's amazing how many times I have worked with youth and adults who are terribly confused or depressed. Part of the reason they're so confused is because they have only focused on themselves and can only see their situation. They have lost perspective. They have lost a sense of purpose beyond their own selves and their own problems.

When you get to this place it can be very dangerous because it makes you more confused or sad. The more sad and confused you become, oftentimes the more you will focus on the things that make you sad and confused. It's a scary cycle. I've seen so much healing come about in people's lives when they stop focusing solely on their problems and confusing situations and beginning to focus on the problems and situations of those who God has put in their paths.

So often our healing comes through the service to and healing of others. I believe this is in our DNA. When we help others and do good in our world, there's often a trigger in us that begins to heal us, as well. Even when you're confused, you can know for certain that you're still called to serve this world.

CONFUSED 8
PILGRIMAGE

>*Luke 2:41-42*<

Every year his parents went to Jerusalem for the Feast of the Passover. When he was twelve years old, they went up to the Feast, according to the custom.

I know. This one seems a little crazy right? How in the world can you, a teenager, take a pilgrimage (a intentional journey to a holy place to be with and experience God) by yourself? Oftentimes when we think about pilgrimages, we think of holy places like those in Jerusalem, the Judean desert, and along the Jordan River valley. We might also think of places where Paul traveled like Ephesus, Corinth, and Rome. While these are certainly holy places (and if you have the chance you should go), they're not the only places where you can experience pilgrimage.

While our faith specifies holy places, we as individuals also have places that are holy to us in our lives. There are places where we have experienced God in significant ways that we know are different and that stick out in our minds more than others. For some of us it might be a retreat that we go on every year, or a camp where we experienced God in a special way. You might have a church where you first understood or felt God. There might be a path in the woods where you walked and something inside you changed. As we journey through our faith we experience these holy places.

When we're confused it's important sometimes to go back to these places. Sometimes these places are where our faith was birthed. We can return to them to be reminded of what was so we can know what can be. Taking an intentional trip back to a place where God moved in a special way is a way to refresh our faith and see the world in a new way. It can often provide clarity in confusion and re-inspire us in ways that gives us a new sense of what we're supposed to do. Identify these places, why they are special, and how you can make your pilgrimage to reconnect with God in unique ways.

SABBATH

>*Exodus 20:8-11*<

"Remember the Sabbath day by keeping it holy. Six days you shall labor and do all your work, but the seventh day is a Sabbath to the LORD your God. On it you shall not do any work, neither you, nor your son or daughter, nor your manservant or maidservant, nor your animals, nor the alien within your gates. For in six days the LORD made the heavens and the earth, the sea, and all that is in them, but he rested on the seventh day. Therefore the LORD blessed the Sabbath day and made it holy.

Rest. I mean it. Just relax. You live in a time and place where, if you let it, the world will take every second of your time and fill it up with stuff. Some good, some not so good. If we don't watch it we'll go weeks and weeks going to sports practices, school, meetings, and so on and never have had a whole day where we just rested. Trust me when I write this, I'm preaching to myself!

There will always be more to do, trust me. There will always be another opportunity, deadline or thing demanding our attention. You'll probably never have a day in your life where there isn't something you can or should do. Don't buy into the lie that if you just do one more thing things will calm down. Through this chaos and stress we have to retake control of our lives and stop letting our activities and schedules determine our priority. We have to take the Bible seriously when it tells us that there must be one day a week where we stop and do nothing. It's not only good for our bodies it is also good for our souls.

Sabbath helps order our lives for us. When we take it seriously we begin to regain control over our lives and our time. When you go and go and don't stop, it's so hard to ever have a clear sense and understanding of where you should go and what you should do. God wants you to rest. It might take a while to clear your schedule and to regain control, but don't forget that this is so important that God actually included it as one of the 10 Commandments. That's pretty important.

WONDER

> *Psalm 40:5* <

Many. O LORD my God. are the wonders you have done. The things you planned for us no one can recount to you: were I to speak and tell of them. they would be too many to declare.

At the end of it all, sometimes we just have to sit back in wonder of what God does in our world. One of the most important parts of our relationship with God is that at the end of the day we're never going to get it all the way. We're never going to know the whole plan and we're never going to stop being surprised. I know it's frustrating when you're confused and don't know what direction you're supposed to go in. I am the type of person who always wants to know my options, have all of the information, and always be in control. I hate surprises. The hard part of faith for me is that I can't totally be in control and there are just sometimes where I have to sit back and wonder at God's wonder.

There are parts of our lives that we may never have an answer to and we will always have a question about. That's OK. We're not meant to understand everything in our lives. We aren't meant, nor could we handle, all of the ramifications of each of the events that happen to and around us. I know when you're confused you want answers and want to be less confused. You won't always feel this way, but at the same time there are situations where you'll never get the whole picture. You have to trust that God who bigger than your situation and bigger than your confusion. When all else fails, try just sitting in wonder.

GAIN *pg. 225-234*

What do we gain as Christ-followers? What are the fringe benefits of believing in God? In this section you will learn about all of the things that you gain by calling yourself a Christian. Some are pretty exciting, while others might feel like you have gotten more than you bargained for.

LOSS *pg. 235-244*

There are just times in our lives where we find ourselves losing. We might lose friends, lose the big game, lose courage, or lose our direction. Through these ten devotions you will begin to think about the things we lose and not only how we cope with them but also how God calls us to lose well.

WHEN YOU HAVE, YOU MUST GIVE

> *Luke 3:11* <

John answered. "The man with two tunics should share with him who has none. and the one who has food should do the same."

So you have this guy named John and people believe that he's pretty crazy. He's out in the desert, wearing crazy clothes, eating honey and grasshoppers, and preaching. A lot. They also think he's crazy because of the things he preaches. He's telling people that someone is coming who will forgive their sins. He's also telling them things like, "don't make extra money by taking advantage of people," and "if you have two shirts then give one to someone who needs it." People thought he was crazy. Until the "someone" John was talking about came along who may have been even bolder than John.

There's a consistent teaching throughout the Bible that calls people of God to use what they have not to benefit themselves, but to take care of others. In this passage we see John the Baptist preaching one of his first recorded sermons. In it he spends a considerable amount of time on taking care of those who can't take care of themselves. Jesus came along right after and started preaching the same message.

When we have, we must give. Most of us have way more than we need and yet we hoard it. We get more and more. Trust me I know this because I'm guilty of it too! But throughout Scripture we are told to give, not hoard. So what's the "second shirt" in your life? What are those things that people need, you don't need (because you have enough), and you can give? Think about that, but make sure to not just think about it, but do something about it.

THE REAL GAIN

> *Luke 9:23-25* <

Then he said to them all: "If anyone would come after me. he must deny himself and take up his cross daily and follow me. For whoever wants to save his life will lose it. but whoever loses his life for me will save it. What good is it for a man to gain the whole world. and yet lose or forfeit his very self?

I often hear preachers and authors talk about all of the things you gain when you become a follower of Jesus. I agree, you gain so much! The problem is, a lot of the time, I don't agree with them about what you gain. A lot of people will talk about the rewards of following Christ as being happiness, self fulfillment, money, prosperity, and confidence. These aren't the things I see Jesus talking about us gaining. One of the most prominent things I see Jesus tell us that we will gain is a cross.

Now, please hear me. I'm not talking about a pretty cross that hangs around your neck, or one that you wear on your shirt. I mean a cross, like the one people were killed on under the Roman government. The one that Jesus carried and ultimately died on. Not such a desirable gain as a new Lexus is it? I don't think that Jesus was trying to "sell us" on Christianity. I don't think that He was trying to convince us, with gimmicks and catchy phrases, that we should follow Him. I think Jesus wanted us to realize the difficult life that He was calling us to and I think that difficult life is personified in Luke 9:23-25.

Jesus tells His disciples, who knew all too well what the cross meant, that they had to pick it up and carry it, daily. He told them that in order to follow Him, they had to lose their life. Jesus wasn't painting a pretty picture. But that's what we gain: a cross. We give up the "normal" life that everyone else is living, and we take on a life that calls us to sacrifice, give, and love. It's not glamorous, attractive, or very marketable. But it's good and it gives us the ability to live a life that makes a real difference wherever we go.

WE GAIN BECAUSE HE GAVE

>*Matthew 27:50*<

And when Jesus had cried out again in a loud voice, he gave up his spirit.

Jesus calls us in Luke 9:23-25 to take up our cross. In Matthew 27 He not only calls us to do it, He does it Himself. We gained because He gave. That is how gain works. Someone has to give in order for someone to gain. Well that's the way it's supposed to work. Many people take and that's the way they gain. But the way that Jesus taught us is to give so that others can gain. When we do this it's called sacrifice.

Sacrifice isn't a bad word. Unfortunately most people think about it as some ancient tribal group sacrificing animals on an altar. This is different. When we give of ourselves we're sacrificing. But remember, when we sacrifice for others we don't do so in vain. We do so in order that they can have hope, food, clothes, a better tomorrow, and so that the Kingdom of God can be seen and felt closer today than it was yesterday.

Jesus gave so that we could gain. So that we could gain life, hope, and know that even in the face of certain death and evil, that God is still with us and that we can trust God's way. That's not how our world thinks though. Our world constantly talks about gaining and not giving. What they don't understand is that as people of faith, when we give, we're actually gaining. We become more like our Lord, following His actions and living His commands. We come closer to His way and embody His teaching. We gain everything when we give.

GAIN IN ANY SITUATION

> Philippians 1:20-21 <

I eagerly expect and hope that I will in no way be ashamed, but will have suffi-cient courage so that now as always Christ will be exalted in my body, whether by life or by death. For to me, to live is Christ and to die is gain.

We live in this interesting conundrum. We're here on earth, this place that God gave us to take care of and to show His love in. Yet, there's something beyond this place. There's a place that exists where we will be with God, where there will be no sickness, violence, and pain. We love the world that we live in and are called to serve and do good in it, but we also know that we won't always be here. This makes us long for what's to come. So what do we do? Do we focus on making the world the best that it can be constantly ushering in God's goodness, or do we focus on what is to come and constantly looking toward that place?

Paul, the author of the letter to the church in Philippi, says that we have to be faithful wherever we are. Paul says that he hopes that in whatever happens to him, life or death, that he wants God to be shown. He also has this small sentence that says "to live is Christ, to die is gain." We usually don't hear in our world that dying is gain. Paul looks at life a little differently. For the government, who was perse-cuting Christians at that time, death was something that they held over the heads of anyone who came against them. Paul took a differ-ent approach and told the church that if he's alive, he's serving Jesus. The worst thing that could happen is that the government could kill him, and at that point it's to Paul's advantage.

The way Paul looked at everything was that it could be considered gain, because he believed that God could work in any and all situa-tions. Not that God caused bad things to happen, but for those who trust in God, good or gain can come from any situation because of the goodness of God.

GAIN THE RIGHT WAY

>*Matthew 16:26*<

What good will it be for a man if he gains the whole world, yet forfeits his soul? Or what can a man give in exchange for his soul?

There is a train of thought in our world that says the end justifies the means. You may have heard this phrase before. Another way of saying this is that we should go after whatever we want, no matter what the cost, and as long as we succeed, whatever we did to actually achieve our goal was fair game. This type of thought has been applied to sports, business, jobs, and even religion. This thought process justifies athletes taking steroids, businesses abusing employees and child labor, employees stealing from companies, and even ministers taking advantage of people's fears and hopes.

The ends don't justify the means. How we go hitting our goal is every bit as important as our success. When we call ourselves people of faith, or followers of Jesus, we're committing to living a life by a certain sort of ethical code or standard. The standard of Jesus tells us that when we make decisions we have to make them based on His life and His teachings. When we're His followers we have to live our lives in such a way where people know who we follow, not just by what we say or look like but by every action that we take.

Jesus doesn't want someone to make millions of dollars in dishonest ways and then be a big giver to the church. It's not OK to take performance-enhancing drugs and then point to the sky every time you score a touchdown (or thank Jesus in your post game interview). Each time we deceive, lie, cheat or steal, we lose a little of who we are as people of faith. Jesus points it out plainly, "What good is it to gain the world and loose your soul?" So when you're driven to do well, it's just as important to do what you do in honest and truthful ways than it is to win or be the best.

MEASURING YOUR GAINS

> *Phillipians 3:7-8* <

But whatever was to my profit I now consider loss for the sake of Christ. What is more. I consider everything a loss compared to the surpassing greatness of knowing Christ Jesus my Lord. for whose sake I have lost all things. I consider them rubbish. that I may gain Christ.

Where do you find your greatest gains? What are you most proud of? Is it something that you've done in sports or art? Is it a play you were in or an instrument you perform with? Is it something people cheer you for? Or is it something you create and others admire? These things are wonderful and it's so important that you enjoy them and do the best you can at what you try.

Paul, the writer of two-thirds of the New Testament, had a lot of accomplishments as well. He was known as someone who was very religious, knowledgeable, and pious. In his letter to the church at Philippi he says that all of the things he's done and all of the things he's known for, he considers loss. That sounds weird. Why would you call all of the things you had worked for and spent your whole life doing garbage? He continues, "I consider them loss when I compare them to the surpassing worth of knowing Jesus." Ah . . . that's different isn't it?

It's not that Paul didn't care about the things he used to do, or had accomplished. It's just that his priorities had changed. Those things no longer meant the most to him. They weren't the things that defined him. His relationship with Jesus had become what defined him. Everything else is a distant second place. As Christians, we're called to see life as Paul sees life here. We're called to focus on Jesus. It's not that sports, arts, grades, and everything else is bad, not at all. It's just that now those things don't define us and set our priorities. What are the things in your life that most define you? How can you begin to let those things move into a supporting role, as your faith becomes the primary thing that defines you?

GAINING TO GIVE

>*Genesis 12:2-3*<

I will make you into a great nation and I will bless you; I will make your name great, and you will be a blessing. I will bless those who bless you, and whoever curses you I will curse; and all peoples on earth will be blessed through you.

From the first book of the Bible there's a precedent set; when you're blessed, you're supposed to be a blessing. When you have, you give. When you gain, you share. Now the crazy thing is that this is something that most of us learn from the time we're little. We don't learn the Biblical principle but we learn the importance of sharing. Anyone remember, "sharing is caring"?

God is constantly calling us, throughout Scripture, to share what we have with the rest of the world. From early gleaning laws (Leviticus 19:9-10) to the vision of Micah with everyone having enough (Micah 4:4); from Jesus and the feeding of the 5,000 with a young boy sharing his two fish and five loaves (Matthew 14:13-21), to the first church sharing everything they had with each other and taking care of the widows, the orphans, and the poor (Acts 2:44-45). Sharing really is caring. God calls us to not store up all we have and keep it all for ourselves.

Genesis 12 gives us a good understanding and a foundation for what we're to do with our gains. Ultimately there are always going to be poor people in the world, people who need help. The reverse is also true: there will always be people in the world with more than they need. As people of faith, as you grow up and have bank accounts and possessions, it's so important for you to remember this and live this calling of God out in your lives. Sharing is caring. Share a little more.

TO GAIN YOU HAVE TO LOSE

> *Mark 8:35* <

For whoever wants to save his life will lose it. but whoever loses his life for me and for the gospel will save it.

Have you ever heard the saying, "If you want to keep your love, you have to let it go"? I've never understood this saying. It's pretty confusing and a little frightening. It's interesting though that it's very similar to a verse found in Mark. Here Jesus is speaking in these complex ways about how we are to be His followers. In one of His almost riddle-like sentences Jesus tells us that if we want to gain our life then we have to lose it. At first glance, that just doesn't make sense! Why would I lose my life and expect to gain it? It doesn't make sense unless we've read the whole story of Jesus and His disciples.

Each disciple had a real life. They had jobs, families, and interests. Then Jesus came along. The life they knew is the life that they lost. When Jesus told them things like, "drop your nets and follow me" they did. They dropped everything they knew and they followed Him. We all have lives. They are made up of things we choose and things we don't choose. So what does it mean to lose your life? Does it mean that you drop out of school, sell all of your possessions, and leave your family to follow Jesus in the world? It might. It might mean a ton of different things.

It's important to notice that Jesus didn't tell each disciple to "drop their nets." He called each one differently. How is Jesus calling you? What is He calling you to leave behind in order to follow Him? How is Jesus calling you to lose your life? I've seen teenagers quit sports, after school clubs, and even change their whole career path because they felt that Jesus was calling them somewhere new. What is God calling you to? How is Jesus calling you to lose your life in order to gain His?

WHAT REALLY MATTERS?

> *Matthew 6:19-21* <

Do not store up for yourselves treasures on earth, where moth and rust destroy, and where thieves break in and steal. But store up for yourselves treasures in heaven, where moth and rust do not destroy, and where thieves do not break in and steal. For where your treasure is, there your heart will be also.

What is it? What are the most important things to you? What would you absolutely freak out about if you were to lose? Is it your phone, car, video game, or clothes? Is it something that can be bought or sold? If it is, I want you to rethink what's most important to you. I remember being a teenager and my clothes accidentally got bleach spilled all into the washer. All of my clothes were ruined. I was furious. I had an absolute meltdown. Most of us have seen the clip on You-Tube of the guy whose mom deleted his gaming account. He freaks out. What are your treasures?

In the past 10 or so years my treasures have changed significantly. The things I treasure most don't rust, can't be deleted, and aren't going to be ruined with bleach. My greatest treasures are relationships. They are my relationship with God, my wife and kids, my family and friends, and the students and parents I work with. These relationships are places where I find God and I find life. These are things that can't be destroyed by rust and moths, and they aren't something that can be easily taken away.

God is calling us to invest and treasure things that are valuable to Him. We know through the Bible that relationships are one of the important parts of our lives that God values. God walked with Adam and Eve in the garden and ultimately God sent Jesus to be in relationship with us so we could know God in a real, human way. God continues to be with us even now in that relationship. I want you to think about the things that are most important to you. How many of those things can rust, be burned up in a fire, or be stolen? Invest yourself in relationships and taking care of the world around you. You'll find that your treasures are more valuable than you could have ever imagined.

PUT YOUR GAINS IN PERSPECTIVE

> *Matthew 19:23-24* <

Then Jesus said to his disciples, "I tell you the truth, it is hard for a rich man to enter the kingdom of heaven. Again I tell you, it is easier for a camel to go through the eye of a needle than for a rich man to enter the kingdom of God."

Finally, a warning. Not just a warning, but a warning from Jesus. First let me say this: If you're reading this book and you're sitting somewhere in the United States of America, this verse applies to you. If you live in our country then, by default, you have more money and possessions than, at worst 80% of the world and in most cases 90% of the world. So, no, this verse isn't just talking about the family who lives in "that neighborhood" or the people you see on television who fly in private jets and live on the top floor of sky scrapers.

It's easy to look at these people and believe that Jesus is only talking about them, but He's not. He's talking about me and probably about you. When we gain, when we have a lot, it's very easy to become sidetracked with what we have. It's very easy to prioritize what we have and more often what we want instead of focusing on our God. When we have so much it's so easy to believe that we don't need anything from God. We fool ourselves that we have it together and that we're not in need of a God to show us what really matters.

It's so easy for us to buy into the lie that because we have so much and so many opportunities that we can do life by ourselves. The warning is this: No matter how much you gain, you'll always be in need. No matter how much you have, you'll still lack. No matter how good life is, it can always be better. We are all in need of our God. Never forget this need.

LOSS 1
LOSING FRIENDS

> John 15:18-19 <

If the world hates you, keep in mind that it hated me first. If you belonged to
the world, it would love you as its own. As it is, you do not belong to the world,
but I have chosen you out of the world. That is why the world hates you.

We have this interesting relationship with the world in which we live.
We're called to be in the world but not born of the world. This means
that yes, we are deeply connected and depend heavily on the world
that's around us. At the same time we're called to live by a different
set of standards and priorities than those around us. We're called to
follow the way in which Christ leads, and that's where it gets tricky.

Read John 15:18-23. Jesus says in the verses in John that there will be
times where people hate you because you follow Jesus. He tells us
that people hated Him. So if they hate Him, and we're trying to imitate
the way He lived, then they'll hate us too. It doesn't sound like a good
sales pitch for someone who's starting a religious movement does it?
"Hey guys, come follow me and you'll lose all your friends!" There are
going to be times where we lose people because of what we believe
and because of how we live. If we're not separated from people and
sometimes lose friends because of our faith, then we might want to
look at how closely we're following the way Jesus taught us.

It's nearly impossible not to get into trouble with people if we're following the way Jesus showed us in the gospels. When we love the
unlovable, stand up for the persecuted, and choose peace and love
over vengeance and hate, those things will get you into trouble in our
world. So, count it gain when you lose friends because of your faith
and your life. The way of Jesus never promised us friends, but it does
promise us so much more.

LOSING HOPE

>*Isaiah 40:29-31*<

He gives strength to the weary and increases the power of the weak. Even youths grow tired and weary, and young men stumble and fall; but those who hope in the LORD will renew their strength. They will soar on wings like eagles; they will run and not grow weary, they will walk and not be faint.

We all lose hope. Sometimes it's in that math class that we just can't seem to figure out. Other times it's losing hope that our parents will ever stop fighting. Some of us even get to a place where we're so hopeless we believe there's no point in continuing to try.

I went to Haiti just after the earthquake that devastated that country in 2011. It was a nightmare. Everywhere you looked it was pure destruction and death. I was constantly in tears from the devastation and heartache of that country. I would call my wife at night and tell her what I saw and confess to her that I saw no hope there, that I could not find a way to believe that it would ever get better. When we're Christians, that's a very scary place to be. The foundation of our faith is based on hope, and I had none.

Isaiah tells us that we all grow weary and stumble. He also tells us to not loose hope because God renews our strength, gives us energy, and the ability to go another day. Not only that but he compares the hope that God gives us to being like having wings like eagles and soaring. You'll lose hope at some point, never doubt that. It'll all come crashing down and the pain and despair will be very real, I promise. But take comfort that when you lose hope, hope isn't lost on you. We're a people whose faith it built on a hope that can't even be held by death or a tomb. So, trust that you can push on and not grow tired, that you can go another day and not fall. Don't ever believe that you are too far gone. You're always within the reach of the loving arms of our God.

LOSS 3
LOSING COURAGE

> *Joshua 1:9* <

Have I not commanded you? Be strong and courageous. Do not be terrified; do not be discouraged. for the LORD your God will be with you wherever you go.

Life can be pretty intimidating sometimes. If, we as Christ-followers were called to duck our heads, try not to be noticed, and tip toe through life, that would be one thing. That doesn't take a lot of courage. However, Jesus didn't call us to that kind of life. He called us to a life, and a life lived more abundantly. He called us to go into a world that isn't always too friendly and show them the love of God He called us to go to the ends of the earth spreading good news about God and the life that God is calling us to live. He told us that we would be persecuted, that our parents and families might disown us, and ultimately we would have to carry our own cross to be his disciples. Wow.

That kind of life takes courage. Sometimes when we find ourselves diving into that life we begin to lose faith and we especially begin to lose courage. The Book of Joshua starts and almost at the very beginning in chapter 1 verse 9 we're told to be strong and to know that the Lord our God is with us. The bottom line is that Jesus is calling us to a life where, if we're really doing what He says, we have to be courageous. You have to be courageous. It takes courage to stand up and live a life that isn't always popular, a life of sacrifice and love. So, will you flinch? Will you cower or retreat when adversity comes your way because of the faith you live, or will you take Joshua's advice and be brave, courageous and trust that our God is with us wherever we go? Be strong my friends.

LOSING THE GAME

>Ecclesiastes 4:4<

And I saw that all labor and all achievement spring from man's envy of his neighbor. This too is meaningless, a chasing after the wind.

You're not always going to win, and that's OK. Not only is it OK, it's good! We learn the best not when we win, but when we lose and it causes us to examine ourselves and work harder. But, even beyond that, beyond the idea that winning feels great, what good is winning? Or better yet, what is so bad about losing? Don't get me wrong, I can't stand to lose. It stinks to work hard and invest yourself in a project, game, or sport and come up short of your goal. Beyond those feelings, there isn't a lot that's terrible about losing at something.

If you worked your hardest, competed well, and did so with a good spirit, you've done something great! And, at the end of the day, the games we play, the projects we work on, and the competitions we enter, usually don't mean a lot in the grand scheme of things, especially our spirituality. Ecclesiastes 4:4 is a profound statement about what things we focus on and spend all of our time thinking about. The writer, most likely Solomon, talks about how so many of the things we spend all of our time doing, focusing on, and chasing after are really pretty meaningless in our lives. So meaningless that it's like chasing after the wind. Have you ever chased the wind? Probably not, but take a moment and imagine what that would look like. You, in a field, running with your arms wide yelling at the invisible wind to "stop," or "come back"! It's pretty silly. When we are constantly chasing after things that really don't mean a lot, it can be just as silly. When you lose, it's OK, no big deal. There are bigger, God-sized things, for you to chase.

LOSING A BOYFRIEND/GIRLFRIEND

>Song of Songs 8:7<

Many waters cannot quench love; rivers cannot wash it away. If one were to give all the wealth of his house for love, it would be utterly scorned.

Breakups are the worst. They're never fun for either party and can be pretty painful for some time. The writer of Song of Songs gets it. The writer gets the depth of that love and how it runs through every part of you and your mind and body. The writer talks about the unquenchable nature of love and how it rages within us. I want to tell you something, you might not believe it, but I promise it's true: You will probably love many times and be loved many times in your life.

I know it hurts right now. It hurts badly. Your stomach is in knots, your mind keeps going to back to him or her, and you constantly see things that remind you of him or her. You miss this person. You can't concentrate on school. It's tough in the aftermath of a relationship that has gone sour. Again, I want to tell you, this is most likely not the last person you will love, and it's not the last person that will love you.

This type of loss is hard! But it's OK. You have many years ahead of you. So, take your time and don't feel like you have to rush getting over this person. Let yourself mourn the loss and do so in your own time. But keep remembering, it will be OK, because you will love and be loved again.

LOSING TRUST

> *Matthew 5:37* <

Simply let your 'Yes' be 'Yes,' and your 'No,' 'No'; anything beyond this comes from the evil one.

Imagine this: You've done something stupid. You lied, snuck out, hid something, did something, got caught, and now you feel dumb. Beyond feeling dumb (and probably being grounded) you know that there's something more important, more hurtful happening; you've lost the trust of your parents.

I remember being your age (fortunately it was not too long ago) and losing my parents' trust. It was tough. You feel really bad. You might also feel like you might never get it back. Let me assure you of a couple of things. First, the distrust isn't permanent; your relationship will heal. Second, it might take a while, especially depending on what happened. Third, when it does come back, you have the responsibility to make sure it stays. It's one thing to lose their trust once, it's another thing to keep doing things that damages trust and undermines your relationship with them. Jesus is speaking very directly with His disciples in Matthew 5:37. He tells them to let their "yes" be "yes" and their "no" be "no." He's telling us that what we say must be truthful and reliable.

It's so important, as you get older, that people can count on what you say and trust you. Trust is one of the greatest gifts we can give someone. It's such a joy and relief when people know that they can depend on you and trust you for what you say. Do what you say you'll do, and be someone whose words are never second-guessed. It doesn't take a lot of work. It's as simple as telling the truth.

LOSS 7
LOSING HUMILITY

> *James 4:6* <

But he gives us more grace. That is why Scripture says: "God opposes the proud but gives grace to the humble."

Have you noticed that many times the people who are celebrated in our culture are often not the ones who give credit to their team, or talk about those who helped them achieve their goal? I bet you don't have to look at celebrities, musicians, or athletes to find examples. I bet you see it every day in your school. It seems like lately our culture doesn't place a high value on helping each other, celebrating each other, and picking others up when they're down. It seems like a very cutthroat, competitive, and "I'll take all of the glory" kind of culture . . . especially in your school.

I had several students tell me just the other day, that everyone around them in their school is just waiting on them to fail or stumble. They even went as far as to say that no one cares about them in their school; others are too concerned with being better than everybody else. That's really sad to me. So much of the time when we experience people who are like this (or if we are like this ourselves) it's because they're full of pride. Pride tells us that we're the best and we have to always be the best. Pride tells us that the only reason why we did well is because of our own hard work. Pride fails to recognize help, community, and grace. Pride is a dangerous, dangerous sin.

In the Book of James he restates what has already been made clear in Proverbs and Matthew: God doesn't like pride. Pride fails to take into consideration that we can't do it by ourselves and that there are always others to be grateful for. Pride disregards thankfulness as foolish and humility as weakness. We're probably all guilty of pride at some point or another. So, when you do well, celebrate it, be proud (not prideful) of it, and give credit where credit is due. Be grateful for what you have and be grateful for those helped you get where you are.

LOSS 8
LOSING INNOCENCE

> *Romans 3:23* <

For all have sinned and fall short of the glory of God.

There will come a time where you will mess up. Now I'm not talking about leaving the milk out or stuffing all your dirty clothes under your bed. I mean really messing up, where you know that you'll be in real trouble, the kind of trouble that will make you feel really bad. More than likely, there's a chance you find yourself in this spot at some point in the future.

You won't be alone. There's a time in all of our lives where we do something that we know we shouldn't do, something we may not ever really want to do. These times are really difficult. They're tough because we change a little. We enter into a new phase of life, one that has more consequences, guilt, responsibility, and sometimes fear. When we enter into this new phase of our lives, we can often feel like we're terrible people. Guilt becomes a major issue. And for some of us, there may even be the chance that some of our innocence is lost.

Take heart. Most everyone (including your parents and probably even your youth minister) has done something they wished they hadn't done. We all sin. That doesn't make it right, or even justified. You still have to deal with the consequences. But I want you to know that you're not unique. You don't have to feel like you're the only one who has ever messed up or done something completely stupid. We all have. What you do after you mess up matters more. What matters is how you handle the consequences, how you change, and how you take responsibility to reconcile with God and others. Your sin isn't unique, we all, everyone of us, have sinned. It's what we do with it afterwards that really determines who we are and what we are about.

LOSS 9
LOSING SHAME

> *Romans 8:1-2* <

Therefore, there is now no condemnation for those who are in Christ Jesus, because through Christ Jesus the law of the Spirit of life set me free from the law of sin and death.

I was 18 and I messed up. I did something that I knew I shouldn't have done and I felt terrible about it. For weeks and weeks all I felt was guilt and shame. I thought I was the most terrible person in the world (although now I realize that I hadn't really messed up that badly at all) and I felt as though there was no way that God could love me or use me in the ways I hoped God would.

I was lying on my couch one night, flipping through the channels, and I ran across one of those TV preachers. Now I'm not a TV preacher kind of guy. Maybe you are, and that's cool. I'm not. But I encountered this guy and I paused just long enough to see what he was saying. He was doing that thing where he looks into the camera and says something like, "I know there's someone out there . . . " Well, he said that very thing followed by "dealing with guilt and I know that you believe that there is no way that God can forgive you, but trust me friend, God already has." In some ways, God used this TV preacher to remind me that I didn't have to live a life of guilt. It reminds me of the gospel that I preach all the time: "God's love and grace is bigger than anything we can do, say, or be."

I know your teenage and early adult years can have moments of hidden shame and guilt. It's not wrong to feel badly for what we've done, but never, ever, doubt your standing with God. Your standing with God is always that God loves you, as a beloved child. He will never ease up on that love.

LOSING DIRECTION

> *Jeremiah 1:7-8* <

But the LORD said to me. "Do not say. 'I am only a child.' You must go to everyone I send you to and say whatever I command you. Do not be afraid of them. for I am with you and will rescue you." declares the LORD.

Sometimes our goals and calling are clear. Other times they're muddled and foggy. There are times where we know what we're supposed to do, and other times we're guessing at best. Sometimes the direction is laid out plainly, other times it's a jumbled mess. It's just part of living as flawed human beings.

One thing that frequently causes us to lose direction is that we doubt ourselves and what God calls us to do. We doubt that God will empower us to do it. One of the most common "direction killers" that I hear from people is that they're just not ready or old enough to do what God seems to be putting on their heart. When you read the Bible you see time and time again where God continually uses those who are young to do amazing things. In fact we can look throughout history and see how God has called people who are young to lead great movements that changed our world. Young people have been and can be powerful resources for God to use.

But sometimes when we're young we lose direction because we get distracted. We become distracted with the things that we want more than the things God wants. Now don't get me wrong: these things aren't always in conflict. But we must constantly ask ourselves: where's this desire coming from and how is it affecting the way that God is calling me to live and lead? If God is calling you to it, God is also preparing you for it. This is where our trust in God comes into play. Many times it's not that we've lost our direction, it's that we doubt or are scared of the direction that God is calling us into. I'll leave you with verse 8: "'Do not be afraid of them, for I am with you and will rescue you,' declares the LORD."

GROWING *pg. 247-256*

Are you at a point in your faith where you want to
push yourself some more? Are you at a place where
you want to take your belief to the road and begin to
live it out in new and exciting ways? If so, then this
section is for you. Each day you'll be challenged with
some of Jesus' most famous and challenging words:
the Sermon on the Mount.

WEARY *pg. 257-266*

There are times in our faith journeys where we're just plain tired. It's not that things are going wrong or anything like that. It's just that we're exhausted, and are either getting to a place of giving up or are not far from it. In this section you'll find rest from the onslaught of life, and will discover the comfort that our God gives to the weary.

GROWING

> *Matthew 5:1-2* <

Now when he saw the crowds. he went up on a mountainside and sat down. His disciples came to him. and he began to teach them.

I tend to agree with the Book of Ecclesiastes when it tells us that there are different times for different seasons in our lives. For each of us there are times where we should rest and reflect, time to sit back and take a break. There are other times, however, when we're being called to push, learn, and grow. This set of devotions is for you if you find yourself in the midst of a time of growth. (Or if you find yourself wanting to be in the midst of growth.)

As Christ-followers, one of the most challenging sections of Scripture is, what is often referred to as, the Sermon on the Mount. The Sermon on the Mount is found is Matthew 5-7. Many scholars will say this is Jesus' most important and most profound set of teachings. Some will even say that all of what Jesus taught while on earth can be found in these passages. There's so much in these three chapters that for this section we'll only look at the teachings in chapter 5. These passages could be studied for months at a time so I want you to take it slow and really absorb what each devotion has to say and challenge you with.

This is a time for growth, not for consuming a bunch of devotions over a couple of week period. If you've ever hit a growth spurt you know that it's not always easy. It can throw us off of balance, and can even be painful. Growing in our faith isn't much different. As you let these verses lead you and your life, at points, it'll be hard and might even challenge your faith. You might even experience a few growing pains. Don't be discouraged. This is all a part of growing.

BLESSED

> *Matthew 5:3* <

"Blessed are the poor in spirit, for theirs is the kingdom of heaven."

Read Matthew 5:1-11. Jesus starts off these teachings with an ear catching phrase: "Blessed are the . . ." Talk about a way to get everyone's attention. Jesus starts off what would turn out to be one of His most important sermons telling everyone how to be blessed by God. What they heard was anything but what they were expecting. It was not a three-step sermon on how to have more friends or how to become more financially stable. It was not a "do these five things to get a healthier wealthier you." What Jesus proceeded to teach was completely counterintuitive to what everyone believed made someone blessed.

Jesus' teaching was focused on the poor, the weak, the persecuted, and the mourners. None of these, in Jesus' time or this one, are considered blessed people. Depending on what television preachers you might listen to, some of these people are even considered punished by God. But that's not what Jesus taught. What Jesus taught wasn't very popular. He tells us that the measures of blessing we use aren't the measures of blessing that God uses. Actually, in many cases, it's just the opposite.

This is a major area of growth for us. We live with a foot in two worlds. In one world we're told that blessing and success looks like notoriety, money, possessions, and happiness. In the world that Jesus calls us to, we see a blessed life as a life with pain, sorrow, exclusion, and lowliness. A part of our growth is that we have to align ourselves in the world that Jesus calls us to, not the one our culture calls us to. This is going to involved a major shift in how you think about your life and your life's goals. As the pain of this process sets in, make sure to keep this one thing in the back of your head, "Blessed are the . . ."

SALT

> *Matthew 5:13* <

You are the salt of the earth. But if the salt loses its saltiness, how can it be made salty again? It is no longer good for anything, except to be thrown out and trampled by men.

When you read this verse it might seem completely normal to you, but to me it's perplexing. How can salt lose its saltiness? I've never understood this. Unlike many other foods, salt doesn't become less salty over time or exposure to air. It stays just as salty, right? So I have to ask another question, "what exactly was Jesus getting at here"? I'm a cook. I love to make all sorts of dishes. Cooking is one of my favorite hobbies and a passion of mine. If you do much cooking at all, you'll realize the absolute importance of salt. The amazing thing about salt is that it never plays the starring role in a dish. It does something else all together.

Salt isn't meant to be the focus of any dish. It's always added to enhance the natural flavors of any dish. Its primary purpose is to make whatever it is added to stand out in even more bold and exciting ways. It causes the real flavor to come through in amazing ways. Don't believe me? Add some salt to a lemon. It will become excruciatingly sour and you'll taste the lemon like you've never tasted it before. You can always tell a steak or a burger that has not been seasoned well; it just doesn't have the same deep, meaty flavor. Even chocolate and caramel benefit from the use of salt.

When Jesus calls us to be salt I believe He's calling us to do two things. The first is to remember that we're not the stars of the show. We're not the main dish; we play a support role. The second is that in our support role we're supposed to find the natural goodness in all that we come in contact with and enhance that goodness. That goodness comes from God. We have the opportunity to showcase that goodness to the world. As you grow you will realize more and more that it's not about us. It never was and it never will be.

LIGHT

> *Matthew 5:14-16* <

You are the light of the world. A city on a hill cannot be hidden. Neither do people light a lamp and put it under a bowl. Instead they put it on its stand, and it gives light to everyone in the house. In the same way, let your light shine before men, that they may see your good deeds and praise your Father in heaven.

In the same teaching as salt, Jesus also compares us to light. He uses a couple of different analogies to talk about how we're supposed to be light. The first one is like a city on a hill that, when lit, can't be hidden. The second is that we're like lamps in a house; you don't hide a lamp, because if you do it can no longer serve its purpose. So how do we grow into being lights in our world? How do we understand ourselves as a city on a hill and a lamp in a house?

I think there are two ways to think about this. The first is that a city on a hill stands out as being different from what surrounds it. Think about a city on a hill with nothing surrounding it but the Judean desert that Jesus would've been talking about. It would've stood out in a stark difference to everything that surrounded it. As Christ-followers we too should stand out. How different do you look from those around you? How does your life point to God in ways that other's lives do not? Secondly, a light in a house does a very important job; it dispels darkness. You have to remember that when Jesus was teaching there were no such things as street lamps, light switches, or electricity. A lamp on a dark night was an incredibly important fixture in any home in Jesus' time. We are lights in the world. We're called to drive darkness away. Being lights in the world means that we shine light on and reveal the true nature of all that's around us. We have to be people who show things for what they really are, both good and bad. When we're a light in this world we not only stand out to show others the way of our God, we also tell the darkness it no longer has a place among us.

> *Matthew 5:17* <

Do not think that I have come to abolish the Law or the Prophets; I have not come to abolish them but to fulfill them.

Read Matthew 5:17-20. One thing that separates a maturing Christ-follower from a new one is that the legalism that can sometimes come with being a new Believer has faded; a better understanding of grace will often takes its place. One of the negative side effects of this happening is that while we're learning to not be legalistic, we often can forget that there are still things we need to do and rules that we need to follow. We are still people who must be separated from the rest of the world in how we act, talk, and live our lives. Again, not in a legalistic way, but in a way that shows devotion to the principles and practices of our faith.

Jesus, in His most famous sermon, makes it very clear that we can't slack on doing what's good as well as what we're commanded to do. As you continue to grow in your faith it's imperative that you continue to understand and follow all that we've been told. That's what Jesus was talking about when He said that He wasn't abolishing the Law. The Law was the Old Testament rules that set the Israelites apart as God's people. The Law came from God's character. Jesus was helping us see that while we aren't called to keep all the Law, the standard of God's character is still the guiding force in our life. But it's our motivation that must be kept in check.

We can't be motivated to keep Jesus' commands by thinking that our good behavior earns us favor in God's eyes, or some sort of special place in God's Kingdom. God sees us as righteous because of the work Jesus did on our behalf on the cross. We obey God because of our love for Him and our desire to imitate Him, to be like Him in our world. That's a big difference when compared to obeying God out of legalism. Seek to live as Christ would live if He were you. But do so out of love for Him and for what He's done in your life.

GROWING 6
ANGER

>*Matthew 5:21-22*<

You have heard that it was said to the people long ago, 'Do not murder, and anyone who murders will be subject to judgment.' But I tell you that anyone who is angry with his brother will be subject to judgment. Again, anyone who says to his brother, 'Raca,' is answerable to the Sanhedrin. But anyone who says, 'You fool!' will be in danger of the fire of hell.

Sometimes we get caught up in the idea that as long as we're not doing the really bad stuff that we're ok. We especially feel this way when we see others around us doing really bad stuff. It makes us have a feeling of superiority sometimes, and can cause us to neglect other "smaller" problems in our own life. Jesus knows us. He knows us really well. He knows that we're excellent at rationalizing these sorts of things. So He addresses it head on.

Jesus completely changed the game for those around Him. He took a well known law, "thou shall not murder," and tells His audience that anyone who hates or is deeply angry with someone that they are liable for the same judgment! Ouch. Jesus knows us too well. He knows that there are few who murder but many who hate. For Jesus, both are wrong. He knows how easy it is to hate someone and justify it by thinking to ourselves, "well at least I'm not killing anyone." Jesus reminds us that it's not enough to just do the right actions or to not do the wrong actions. Our minds and intent have to line up with our actions, and that's something far more difficult.

For Jesus it's not good enough to just follow the rules. We also have to embrace the spirit of the rules as well. As you continue to grow you must remember that our faith is a matter of mind, heart, and hands. Your thoughts, feelings, and actions must all reflect the same thing or else you're not aligned with God's desire for our lives. You can't fall into that trap of legalism that tells you as long as you do the right thing you'll be OK. God calls you to so much more that just going through the motions of your faith.

LUST

>*Matthew 5:27-28*<

You have heard that it was said. 'Do not commit adultery.' But I tell you that anyone who looks at a woman lustfully has already committed adultery with her in his heart.

Sex. It's one of the most talked about subjects in church. In fact, we make a very big deal about sex in the modern church. It's interesting though because Jesus didn't really talk about it much at all. Really He only talked about it a few times in the entirety of the four gospels. (Other writers, such as Paul, addressed the issue much more thoroughly.) Jesus did talk about it, well at least one aspect of it, in the Sermon on the Mount. Adultery.

It's interesting though that Jesus really didn't talk about adultery as much as He talked about leveling the playing field for those who committed adultery. Adultery, or cheating on your husband or wife, was a very big deal in the ancient world. For Jews it was such a big deal that you could be punished by death if you were caught. So Jesus starts His teaching on it just like He taught about murder. "You guys know it's against the law to commit adultery. Well, I tell you that anyone who looks at someone else with "those" eyes has done the same thing as the one who has committed the actual act. Let that sink in!" Again, Jesus turned His audience's entire understanding of religion on its head. Jesus made the definition of adultery much more than a literal one. He brought in the spiritual aspect, and in doing so leveled the playing field for sexual purity in general.

As you continue to grow in your faith, I'd encourage you to take this queue from Jesus. Don't jump on the bandwagon where you judge people's sin without acknowledging the sinful tendencies in all of our lives. Learn from Jesus. Learn that those closest to God don't sit in judgment, but should instead stand with mercy. The closer we get to our God, the more we realize how much each of us needs grace, not just the ones at whom it's easiest to point our finger.

PROMISE

> *Matthew 5:33-37* <

Again, you have heard that it was said to the people long ago. 'Do not break your oath, but keep the oaths you have made to the Lord.' But I tell you. Do not swear at all: either by heaven, for it is God's throne; or by the earth, for it is his footstool; or by Jerusalem, for it is the city of the Great King. And do not swear by your head, for you cannot make even one hair white or black. Simply let your 'Yes' be 'Yes,' and your 'No.' 'No'; anything beyond this comes from the evil one.

Have you ever had this conversation: "I will do . . . for you by tomorrow." "Do you promise?" "Yes, I promise that it will be done, I promise." Nothing wrong with that, right? Actually there is. Whenever we have to make a promise our word is being compromised. There are all sorts of things we do in our modern world to make sure that people do what they say they're going to do. We have contracts, lawyers, and recording devices that exist to make sure that no one is going to go against their word and end up making us look like a fool or take something from us. We live in a world where people's word is worth very little. Jesus is telling us in this teaching that we can never be counted among those people.

This isn't a teaching against contracts or promising. It's a teaching about being people who keep our words and do what we say we're going to do! Jesus wants us to be honest, trustworthy people who others respect and trust. The last thing Jesus wants are people representing Him who tell lies one minute and talk about God the next. As you continue to grow make sure that you're someone who is trusted. Don' be sneaky or live a double life. When you say something, make sure it's true and when you commit to do something make sure you do it and do it well. How can you be trusted about your experience with God if you can't be trusted to tell the truth in far less important areas of your life?

GROWING 9
REVENGE

> *Matthew 5:38-39* <

You have heard that it was said. 'Eye for eye. and tooth for tooth.' But I tell you. Do not resist an evil person. If someone strikes you on the right cheek. turn to him the other also.

The law of the land was an eye for an eye. It was a simple law that made very clear what the penalty would be if you were to wrong someone. If my dog killed your cow, then I owed you a cow. If I were to get angry and get in a fight with your brother and knock his tooth out, then I would have to pay with a tooth of my own. This system was both equal and fair. But, as we know from earlier teachings Jesus seems to go against those things that seem very cut and dry.

Jesus took a teaching that had become entrenched in Jewish religious society, and again flipped it on its head. He not only says that this isn't how we should act, but He went further. When someone does wrong to us, we should return their wrong with a right. Jesus tells us very clearly that in order to be a follower of His, we must forgo the desire and the practice of revenge. A lot of times we enter into the thought of revenge believing that it will make us feel better. "If I can just make them feel the way they made me feel, that will show them." But it never does show them.

Jesus continued His counterintuitive teaching here telling us it's not only good to not seek revenge, but to even turn the other cheek. This shows the aggressors that we would rather let them hurt us again than seek vengeance for what they did. As we grow in our faith we must deal with and adopt this central teaching of Jesus. It's a teaching that not only shows the non-violence of Jesus, but also breaks cycles of violence and aggression through our refusal to participate. When the world sees you choose peace over violence and forgiveness over revenge, they'll know that there's something different about you and that difference is the God you serve.

ENEMY

> *Matthew 5:43-48* <

You have heard that it was said, 'Love your neighbor and hate your enemy.' But I tell you: Love your enemies and pray for those who persecute you, that you may be sons of your Father in heaven. He causes his sun to rise on the evil and the good, and sends rain on the righteous and the unrighteous. If you love those who love you, what reward will you get? Are not even the tax collectors doing that? And if you greet only your brothers, what are you doing more than others? Do not even pagans do that? Be perfect, therefore, as your heavenly Father is perfect.

This could possibly be one of the most difficult of Jesus' teachings. Again, Jesus quotes an old standard, "Love your neighbor and hate your enemy." Seems pretty simple right? I mean that's what enemies are for. Except Jesus stops us in our tracks and tells us that if we're going to follow Him and be set apart from the rest of the world, then we must do the unthinkable: we must love our enemy and pray for the one who hurts us.

When this is on a poster or a post card it really sounds nice. When it's put into practice in real life with real enemies whom you really dislike, it can be one of the most difficult things you'll ever do. Jesus is calling us to refuse to dehumanize our enemies. That's something that's so easy to do. But Jesus modeled this for us, didn't He? He asked for forgiveness for those who had hung Him on the cross and left Him to die. Now that's powerful.

As you continue this journey of growth, you have to remember that no matter how badly someone has hurt you, you have to look at him or her the way God does: as a beautiful child of the living God. Like I said this is going to be one of the most difficult things you'll ever do. When you love and pray for those who hate you, you not only refuse to hate them you also refuse to continue arguments and feuds. Each time you choose to love your enemy you choose the way of God and the way that Jesus taught us.

RESTING WHEN WE ARE WEARY

> Genesis 2:1-3 <

Thus the heavens and the earth were completed in all their vast array. By the seventh day God had finished the work he had been doing; so on the seventh day he rested from all his work. And God blessed the seventh day and made it holy, because on it he rested from all the work of creating that he had done.

On the seventh day God rested. I think that is one of the most profound statements in the entire Bible. God rested. First it means that God found it important enough to invent rest. Remember, rest was not something until God said it existed, and on the seventh of creation God decided that it should be. The second thing is that not only did God determine that it was something that should exist, but it's something that He should do as well. So not only does God invent rest, but He chose to rest as well.

Being tired or weary isn't a crime. It's not bad or even lazy. It's good! A lot of our faith is influenced by some of our religious forefathers, the Puritans. With the Puritans came this idea of the Puritan work ethic. While there's a lot of good with this notion of work, there's also a negative. A lot of the times with this idea comes the feeling that we're worth what we do. When you're worth what you do, it can be very easy to spend all of your time trying to prove yourself worthy. This isn't God's plan for you. First your worth has no dependence on what you do. You're worth everything, simply because God made you and called you His own. The second important thing to remember is that this isn't God's plan because God made a day that is simply for rest. If God wanted you to prove yourself by going all out all of the time, then He wouldn't have instituted a day to do nothing.

When you are weary, make sure to rest. Slow down. Take it easy. It's what God wants.

WEARY FROM WRESTLING WITH GOD

> *Genesis 32:24* <

So Jacob was left alone. and a man wrestled with him till daybreak.

Read Genesis 32:1-32. Sometimes our weariness comes because we're struggling with something. It comes because we've been wrestling back and forth with a decision, idea, choice, or direction. I love this story of Jacob wrestling with the messenger from God. Jacob met this stranger late at night and began to wrestle with him. The story says that they wrestled all night until finally before the morning came, Jacob told the messenger that he wouldn't let him go until he was given a blessing. It says that the messenger touched Jacob's hip. From that time on Jacob never walked the same because he had been with God.

Sometimes we're weary because we've been struggling with a problem or situation for so long that it feels like it will never be resolved. I think this story can be applied to problems of all shapes and sizes, but I especially believe it can be understood as our struggle with theology and understanding the work of God in this world. There's a reason why there are so many different denominations in the world; people don't agree about many of the issues about God and the Bible. We have to struggle with our theology, we have to wrestle with it, and ask the hard questions of it. A theology that is easily given to you can also be easily taken away from you. You have to work through your belief, not just adopt what someone tells you. It's too important to just take someone's word for it.

Struggle, wrestle and refuse to let go and before it's all over you'll be different than those around you. They'll know that you've wrestled with your God and have been blessed. This is a weariness that you can be grateful for.

WEARINESS AND BAD HABITS

>*Exodus 32:7-8*<

Then the LORD said to Moses. "Go down. because your people. whom you brought up out of Egypt. have become corrupt. They have been quick to turn away from what I commanded them and have made themselves an idol cast in the shape of a calf. They have bowed down to it and sacrificed to it and have said. 'These are your gods. O Israel. who brought you up out of Egypt.'"

Sometimes we get really tired and in our weariness, we settle for something less than what God wants for us. Take for example the Israelites who were walking through the wilderness. They had just been freed from the Egyptians and were on a quest for the promised land of God. While in the desert they argued, fussed, and some even wondered if the captivity and enslavement they left would have been better than their current freedom. They were tired, hungry, and thirsty. And it showed.

When we're feeling worn out and hopeless we often make some pretty poor choices. God had told the Israelites what they needed to do and to trust God. God didn't say this as a solitary statement. God had backed it up with all of the amazing deeds, and had given the people plenty of reason to trust, but they still questioned. At this point in the story Moses is heading up the Mountain to visit with God and the people became restless. Instead of continuing to trust the God that led them out of captivity they choose to go back to the ways of the world around them. When they were in Egypt many of them probably adopted the practice of worshipping many gods. So they took their gold and they melted it down and formed a golden calf. They reverted to their old ways.

We're a lot like the ancient Israelites. We get tired and then we revert. We go back to those old habits, the ones that were there before we came to faith in Christ. It's important to know the things that we revert to, so that when we are tired we can be doubly aware to stay away from them and continue to look forward to what God is calling us to.

WEARINESS AND LASHING OUT

>Exodus 32:19<

When Moses approached the camp and saw the calf and the dancing, his anger burned and he threw the tablets out of his hands, breaking them to pieces at the foot of the mountain.

Read Exodus 32:15-19. So there's another side to the story of the golden calf. It's the side that happened when Moses came back down the Mountain. One of the most meaningful moments in the history of our faith has just happened, namely, Moses receiving the 10 Commandments. This isn't just a moment where Moses gets a couple of rules on some pieces of rock. This is where God is showing an entire civilization how they'll be different from the rest of the world. It was a moment in history where religions and systems of law trace their founding. This was a big deal. Not only was it a big deal religiously and historically, it was also a big deal because Moses had just spent time with God, a lot of really good quality time with God. So everything is going great, right? Wrong.

Down the mountain the people Moses and God had led out of slavery had decided it was a good idea to stop worshiping God and go back to worshiping the gods of their former slave masters. God got really angry. God was ready to be through with them, but Moses begs God to be patient with them. God agrees. But then Moses walks down the mountain and becomes so angry with what he sees that he takes the stone tablets that God had given him and he throws them down on the ground, breaking them into many pieces.

Sometimes when we've tried and tried and people just don't get it, we become upset. When you're tired you have to be on guard for this type of anger. It can be so easy to feel like the martyr: "Don't you know what all I have done for you? And this is how you repay me?" It's important to remember that when we're tired and lash out, it's not a good thing. Breathe, calm down, and don't lash out at those around you just because you're exhausted. You will create more problems than you will do good.

WEARY FROM CORRECTING OUR MISTAKES

>*Isaiah 40:1-2*<

Comfort. comfort my people. says your God. Speak tenderly to Jerusalem. and proclaim to her that her hard service has been completed. that her sin has been paid for. that she has received from the LORD'S hand double for all her sins.

Have you ever made a really big mistake? Sometimes our mistakes are contained. Other times they're not. What I mean by this is that some of our mistakes can be fixed by a simple "I'm sorry," while other times there are more consequences and more time that has to be spent in order to correct them. The Israelites were dealing with one such mistake. They had gone against God and because of that they were in exile from the land that God had promised them. I'm not saying that God's going to punish us be exiling us to a foreign land, but I do believe there are natural consequences for our actions.

Oftentimes the natural consequences for these kinds of actions come in the form of the long process of healing broken relationships. When we hurt someone close to us, someone we're in relationship with, it can take time, a long time, to restore that relationship. It can be very hard work that takes perseverance and time. Sometimes we can become very tired during this process and can grow weary of the work it takes to reconcile broken relationships. In Isaiah 40 God is speaking to the people of Israel, comforting them and completing the reconciled relationship with them. When you're doing the good work of reconciling your wrongs, or correcting your mistakes, don't grow weary. Know that the work you do is good, and is the basis of the life that Jesus lived. You're righting wrongs and bringing about healing to a world that hurts so badly. Keep it up. God is so pleased with what you're doing.

WEARY IN THE WILDERNESS

> *Matthew 4:11* <

Then the devil left him, and angels came and attended him.

Read Matthew 4:1-11. There are times where we're doing exactly what God has called us to do and we're doing it with all of our heart, soul, mind, and strength. When we're in these times we have energy, strength, and fortitude because we have confidence that God is using us and that we're making a difference in the world. There is one problem: We're still human. We still get tired and we can and still will become weak.

Jesus was doing exactly what God wanted Him to do. He was in the wilderness, fasting and praying before He began his formal ministry. As He was preparing He became tired, weak, and vulnerable. The story says that He was questioned by Satan. The devil began to ask Jesus questions that were meant to test Him. Jesus did not flinch. Although He was weak He stood strong. He was able to stand so strong because He grounded Himself in the truth of God and His presence. Jesus wasn't standing on His strength alone. He rested in His identity and His mission.

There will be times where we're doing exactly what we're supposed to be doing and out of nowhere we'll find ourselves being questioned, tested, and maybe even attacked. When we find ourselves exhausted from working to make this place a little more like heaven, we can lean on a strength other than our own. God calls us and God gives us the ability to do what He has called us to do. Weary in the wilderness is OK because ultimately it's not our strength that we're depending on. Even Jesus leaned on the promises of His Father. If He can so can we.

WEARY WHEN WE ARE NEEDED MOST

> *Matthew 26:36-38* <

Then Jesus went with his disciples to a place called Gethsemane, and he said to them. "Sit here while I go over there and pray." He took Peter and the two sons of Zebedee along with him, and he began to be sorrowful and troubled. Then he said to them. "My soul is overwhelmed with sorrow to the point of death. Stay here and keep watch with me."

I can't help but feel sorry for the disciples in this story. There they were, it'd been a very long day, really a long week to be honest. Tension was high and they'd been going all day, had a late dinner, and now they were in this peaceful garden with Jesus. Jesus had asked them go to here and pray with Him. I bet this seemed like a strange request to them at the time, after a long day, a big meal . . . why go outside of the city walls and pray? But they were good friends, so they went and they sat and they . . . dozed off.

Most of us would do the same thing if we were in the disciples' shoes. They didn't know that this was Jesus' last night on earth. They didn't know how much He needed them. They were just really tired. Let's be honest: being friends with someone going through a hard time can be exhausting. Most of you have probably done it and know just how tough it really can be! But it's in those exhausted moments where we're ready to hang up the phone or drive away when God uses us the most.

It's important to be there for one another through the good and the bad times. Jesus asked His disciples just for one hour. Sometimes those who need us most ask for more, but if we can, with all that we have, we must stand there with them, strong, and ready to be their advocate, their rock, and their friend. Don't fall asleep on your friends. They need you and you need them.

WEARY AND WANTING TO GIVE UP

>*Matthew 26:39*<

Going a little farther, he fell with his face to the ground and prayed. "My Father, if it is possible, may this cup be taken from me. Yet not as I will, but as you will."

Even Jesus became weary. The scene in the later part of Matthew 26 is one of the most compelling and heartbreaking images that we have of the Lord. He's broken, tired, alone, and many believe even scared. Many theologians believe that He knew exactly what He was about to face and that reality was just moments from beginning. So He took is friends, His best friends, and asked them to come and spend some time, a few last moments, in prayer with Him. His prayer? "Please God, if there's another way, lets do that, but if not then I want what you want."

When we're tired and want to give up, I believe we must pray this same prayer. I think it's important to acknowledge that we don't want what we're facing, who would? Jesus didn't either. Pain and painful situations make us want give up and throw in the towel. But that's not what God wants for us. Giving up in these situations, even when we're at our weariest state admits defeat and God isn't a God that is defeated.

The other thing is that you might not be the one going through something that is causing such stress and anxiety. It might be a friend or family member. This message is for them also. Don't give up. Jesus pushed on and took the cup He was given. With that horrible situation He changed everything. Stay strong, struggle through, and believe that your perseverance is not in vain and your commitment doesn't go unnoticed.

WEARY OF BEARING A BURDEN

>2 Corinthians 12:7b<

To keep me from becoming conceited because of these surpassingly great revelations, there was given me a thorn in my flesh, a messenger of Satan, to torment me.

I bet you have that thing. You know what I'm talking about. It's that thing that always seems to keep you from being the person that you really want to be. It's that thing that you're not proud of, maybe embarrassed of, and in some cases you might even be the only one who knows about it. It's different for everyone but in many ways it's very much the same. Paul had something like this too. He writes about it briefly in his letter to the church in Corinth. He calls it his thorn in his flesh. It seems to be a part of the human condition and a part of his life. It's the thing that you can't seem to shake off and seems to keep rearing its head again and again.

Most, if not all of us have these things. For some it can be pride or envy. It can be talking badly about people. It can be anger. Or it can be something that has even deeper consequences like addictions or boundaries with people. No matter what it is, we all struggle with something. I want you to take comfort that you're not alone and in fact you're with pretty much everyone else in the world. We all have a burden, an irritating habit, a hurtful addiction that causes us pain. It causes us to loose focus and ultimately pulls us away from God and what He calls us to do. While it may never go away, it can always be fought. It can always be pushed away and you never have to give in to it. I have several friends who are in Alcoholics Anonymous and one of their understandings of alcoholism is that they'll always be alcoholics, but when they're not drinking they're recovering alcoholics.

Let us each be recovering constantly in whatever it is that nags and pulls at us. Let us fight that good fight and from that weariness and pain, and let us grow stronger and more full of resolve to follow God.

HOPE FOR THE WEARY

>1 Corinthians 9:24-27<

Do you not know that in a race all the runners run, but only one gets the prize? Run in such a way as to get the prize. Everyone who competes in the games goes into strict training. They do it to get a crown that will not last; but we do it to get a crown that will last forever. Therefore I do not run like a man running aimlessly; I do not fight like a man beating the air. No, I beat my body and make it my slave so that after I have preached to others, I myself will not be disqualified for the prize.

There is hope for the weary. There is hope for those who struggle and hope for those who are in pain. There is hope for all who work for good, and there is hope for the least among us. This struggle, battle, painful situation, burden, or test will end. We're called by Paul to run this race and run it well. We're called to run it to win. Whatever it is that you are dealing with, it won't last forever. Whatever you struggle with, there will be a time where you'll struggle no more. There's an end to our race but we must run and strive until that time.

Sometimes when we're in the middle of a situation, it can feel like it's going to last forever. It can feel like it's the worst thing we've ever gone through and that no one else can understand our pain. The truth is that it won't last forever and the fact of it all is that there are others who are going through and have gone through much of what you're dealing with right now. I tell you this not to minimize your struggle, but to give you hope that others have been in your situation and have come out on the other side better than they were before.

So here's your hope: Be strong, because there's someone stronger with you on this journey. Persevere because there's an end. Strive for that end with the promise that it's coming sooner than later.

EXCITED *pg. 269-278*

There are times in our faith where it can just feel boring and mundane. It's OK to admit this. It happens to many people. Sometimes it can just feel like we're going through the motions. If this is you, then take ten days and read through these devotions, where you'll rediscover the exciting nature of your faith and will be challenged with what to do with your newfound excitement.

ANXIOUS *pg. 279-288*

Got a big test coming up? Parents fighting and you've heard whispers of divorce? Scared about the future and have no clue what to do with your life? Don't be afraid. Over the course of these ten days, you'll be comforted and challenged with story after story of God's goodness and faithfulness in times of great anxiety.

EXCITED BECAUSE THE BATTLE IS ALREADY WON

> *John 16:33* <

"I have told you these things, so that in me you may have peace. In this world you will have trouble. But take heart! I have overcome the world."

Life can be really hard. We can get down, feel discouraged, and wonder if we can go on. When you get to this point it's not unwarranted. I can understand why. But there's something that we must remember.

As Christ-followers, we have a promise that God has already overcome this world. We don't have to worry or to sit and wonder. There's nothing that we will experience that our God hasn't promised that we can't overcome. That doesn't mean that it won't be hard, or that we won't suffer. But as we deal with hardships we can do so knowing that it's not in vain. We can hold strong and stay the course because we know that the way in which we've been called is the way of truth and in the end that truth will win out.

So, even when we're in the middle of the storm we can take heart that our God isn't only with us in that moment, but has gone on ahead of us to prepare a way. That should make us more excited than anything else.

EXCITED 2
EXCITED FOR NO MORE PAIN

>*Revelation 21:4*<

He will wipe every tear from their eyes. There will be no more death or mourning or crying or pain, for the old order of things has passed away."

Can you imagine a place where there's no pain, no harm, no murder, and no sickness? Can you imagine a world where everyone is accepted just how he or she is and no one is denied needs? Can you imagine a world where we're not divided along political or religious lines and everyone strives for a common good? No hunger and no thirst, no sadness and no death. That's what we're promised in the last book of the Bible. We're promised that there is a place after this one where love reigns and goodness prevails. We're told that this is the place where Jesus went to prepare for us, and that we will one day all be in this place together. We can be excited for this place.

Although it's a long way away and we can't completely understand it yet, it's a reality and it's coming. While we're here we must not sit and wait for this place. We have a job. We're called to make this place as much like that place as we possibly can. Our job is to end things like hunger and hopelessness, to destroy prejudice and violence and to replace them with hope and love. Jesus told us to strive for this and work for it in all that we do. What are you doing to make this a reality?

EXCITED TO DO MORE THAN YOU EVER THOUGHT POSSIBLE

> *Philippians* 4:13 <

I can do everything through him who gives me strength.

I will never play in the NBA. Seriously, I won't. I'm 5'10, have a decent three pointer, but an infantile vertical. I'm slow and have had three ankle surgeries. So does that make Paul a liar? The verse does say, "I can do all things through Christ who strengthens me," right? So if I can do all things then "all things" should include the NBA. Well, not really.

When we talk about all things in this verse we're not talking about every and any thing. 5'10" Stephen playing in the NBA is not what Paul had in mind. For this reason, it's often one of the most misquoted verses in the Bible. Paul is talking about the ministry that God called him to. He's talking in the previous verses about the lack of physical things he has in order to complete his mission and ministry. Then he reminds the church at Philippi that although he lacks in some things, he has all he needs and can do everything that God has called him to do, simply because God has called him to do it.

NBA, no, but fulfill the mission and ministry God has called me to do, even when it seems way beyond what I feel like I can do on my own? Yes. I can do it because Jesus gives me strength.

EXCITED THAT THINGS WILL WORK OUT

> *Romans 8:28* <

And we know that in all things God works for the good of those who love him, who have been called according to his purpose.

Here's another often misquoted verse. The verse says that "all things work for the good of those who love him." There's a major difference in working out for what we think is good and what God thinks is good. If this verse were about what we think is good, I would imagine we would have a lot more Christians winning the lottery, finding buried treasure in their back yard and becoming celebrities. But that's not what the verse is saying. It's not about the good that we imagine for ourselves, it's about the good that God sees and desires in this world.

Take Paul, the man who wrote these verses for instance. He was killed for his faith. It wasn't pretty. Do you think this is what he would have said is the best thing he could think of for his future? My guess is that it's not. While I don't believe that God caused Paul to be killed for his faith, I do believe that God has this amazing ability to take the worst of situations and create unimaginable good from them.

Your life isn't always going to go the way you imagined it or even want it. But you can find joy and even excitement in the fact that God will make good out of your life, no matter what else happens.

EXCITED THAT GOD IS FOR US

>*Romans 8:31*<

What, then, shall we say in response to this? If God is for us,
who can be against us?

So God is for my school's football team when they play? So God is for our country when we're in a war? So if I rear end someone while driving down the road because I was texting and didn't stop in time? God is for me, right? No. No. No. This verse isn't talking about any of these things or anything similar to them. Unfortunately I've heard too many pep talks and sermons revolving around this verse that try to imply that very thing. So what does it mean?

First we have to start with the word "If." We have to first ask if what we're doing is what God really wants us to do. We can't assume that God is for our pursuits all of the time. In truth there are a lot of times where God isn't for what we're doing. God isn't for us when we hurt others, act in our own interest, or devalue His creation. How can God be for what we're doing when we're going against His commands? If, however, we can say that yes, we're working toward what God is doing in the world and yes, we're making this place more like the Kingdom of heaven, then we can say that, yes, our God is for us. And when God is for us, as Paul writes, we can trust that the goodness of God will win out and that we can be a part of that goodness in all that we do!

EXCITED 6
EXCITED BECAUSE GOD'S LOVE IS FREE

> *Romans 6:23* <

For the wages of sin is death, but the gift of God is eternal life in Christ Jesus our Lord.

It's a pretty daunting idea that there's nothing that we can do to earn God's love.

The inverse is also true: there's nothing we can do to forfeit God's love either.

God has decided, which is His choice to do, that the gift of His love and salvation is something that's free to all. Most of us, especially if we grew up in church, have heard this again and again, and for some this has lost its meaning. But think about it for a minute: God loves you and loves me and the entire world more than we can ever understand, and there's nothing that any of us did to deserve that. There's nothing that any of us can do to make God not love us.

That's one of the most exciting pieces of news I've ever heard. It's incredible the creator of the universe, the beginning and the end, cares enough to make sure that I know how much I'm loved and that His love is eternal. Everything else in our world is conditional, everything but that. That, if nothing else, is something that we can count on and trust in. So, wake up every day, breathe in a deep breath, and know that you have always and will always be a beloved child of the living God.

EXCITED BECAUSE WE ARE ALL EQUAL

> *Galatians 3:28* <

There is neither Jew nor Greek, slave nor free, male nor female, for you are all one in Christ Jesus.

We don't live in a world that's equal or fair. We live in a world that's full of inequality, prejudice, hate, bigotry, corrupt systems, and oppressive discriminatory practices. This isn't right and we should always point these things out and fight them in the name of God. The reason why we know that we should do this is because God doesn't see the things that we see and base our discrimination upon.

Paul made a radical statement for his time in this verse. He writes something that was against governments, family systems, and societal norms when he said that none of these divisive classifications existed in the eyes of God. This alone could have gotten him killed. We can find peace and joy in the face that God never looks at us as less or more than anyone else. Our God, the God who made us all different, not only loves us but loves our differences. How could He not? God is the one who made each of us so very different and amazing! We can not only be excited that God made us unique, but that God loves us because we're so different.

We never have to be ashamed of who we are because in the eyes of our God, we're all equal.

WE SING BECAUSE WE ARE EXCITED

>*Exodus 15:1*<

Then Moses and the Israelites sang this song to the LORD: "I will sing to the LORD, for he is highly exalted. The horse and its rider he has hurled into the sea."

Read Exodus 14:26-15:21. What happens when we're overjoyed? What happens when our emotions can't be contained because something so amazing has happened? Laughter? Shouts of Joy? Tears of Happiness? Spontaneous worship songs?

Wait, what? There's this really neat scene just after the exodus from Egypt. Pharaoh's army has just been swallowed up in the Red Sea and the children of Israel have walked through safely on dry land. And then all of the sudden, they burst out into song. It's interesting because it wasn't an old song that they all knew it was a song about what had just happened. Most historians don't believe that they sang this exact song, but it was written later to commemorate what happened that day.

We have songs in our faith as well. They tell the stories of the Bible, of men and women who experienced God, as well as our current expressions of love, joy, and excitement toward our God. Song can be a powerful tool that brings people together in a common moment under a common banner. Think about being at a Red Sox game and singing Sweet Caroline during the 7th inning stretch at Fenway. Or being at my favorite football team's stadium singing Sweet Home Alabama. It's an incredible experience.

When we worship at church it can be the same way. Unfortunately there are so many times at church where I don't see this happening. I think one of the reasons why this happens less and less is because we don't embody the same experiences together as we once did. Our songs don't reflect our current experiences and don't strike deeply into our hearts. What are your songs? What are the songs that hit a chord inside of you and you can't deny their story, because it's your story too? Let your joy come out in these songs. Let it spring forth from your mouth as they speak of your love for God.

WE GLOW BECAUSE WE ARE EXCITED

>Exodus 34:29<

When Moses came down from Mount Sinai with the two tablets of the Testimony in his hands. he was not aware that his face was radiant because he had spoken with the LORD.

There's just something different about us when we've been with God. You know what I mean. It's after those times where we know that we've been in the presence of our God and we can't deny that something has changed in us. I see this happen all of the time with students who have gone on a mission trip. They come back with some of the most amazing smiles, uplifting words, and inspirational stories. They glow because they've been close to our God.

Read Exodus 34:29-35. I love this story with Moses and how it was undeniable that he had been with his God. The Bible says that his face shined brightly, and he had to keep it veiled because of how radiant it was. Do people notice a difference when you've been with God? Can people tell there's something different about you when you've been deeply impacted by the God who calls you? There should be something different about us. Not that you wear Christian shirts or just listen to Christian music. Something that goes down to your core and affects everything inside and outside of you. It changes your attitude, the way you love, and the way you live.

Are you joyful, patient, peaceful, and kind? Do others trust you and believe what you say? Do you welcome the stranger and take care of people who can't take care of themselves? These are glowing attributes of being in communion with God. How do you shine? What do others notice about you?

WE TELL BECAUSE WE ARE EXCITED

> *John 4:28-30* <

Then. leaving her water jar. the woman went back to the town and said to the people. "Come. see a man who told me everything I ever did. Could this be the Christ?" They came out of the town and made their way toward him.

Read John 4:4-30. When we're excited we can't help but tell. We have to. We can't hold it in. This was the sorry of excitement the first followers of Jesus experienced. Jesus was doing things and telling them things that they knew had to be from God. It was undeniable to these first century Palestinians that God was with this man from Galilee.

The Samarian woman at the well has one of these experiences with Jesus. He told her some hard truths and called her into question. He not only called her out, He called her into His plan for the world and told her that all of the wrong in her life could change in an instant and for good. Jesus told her who she was and more importantly who He was. She had news, news that was too good to keep to herself. So she went and told everyone she could find.

Have we experienced this sort of good news? I would imagine that at some point we've felt this way, and were excited about what God was doing in our lives. My guess is that many of us have gone away from that and are no longer that excited about what God is doing in the world and in our lives. I want to challenge you to go back and see what caused that joy and excitement. What about that message have you forgotten? What has become common place to you? Not only that but what are you seeing God doing now? What is God doing that inspires you where you sit today? Find that, hold on to it, and tell the world about the God who knows you, loves you and wants to change the world.

WHY WE FEAR

> *Philippians 4:6* <

Do not be anxious about anything. but in everything. by prayer and petition. with thanksgiving. present your requests to God.

Anxiety is strong in our society and in our lives. We find ourselves being anxious a lot. Anxiety has one common root: fear. We fear because it's a scary world out there. Let's face it, there's a lot to be afraid of. We live in a world that's saturated with all of the news of the things that we should fear. We fear terrorism, school shootings, strains of flu, diseases, failure, tornados, hurricanes, earthquakes, rejection, random violence, expectation, war, the economy collapsing, and a million other things. Part of the reason we fear is the constant reminders of everything that can harm us.

Media and the news make a lot of money reporting on the sensational and frightful parts of our world. We're often surrounded with an unrelenting chorus of voices calling us to "Beware!" "Caution" and to "Be Afraid." While all of these voices are calling out these warnings we practice a faith that shows God consistently telling us to "fear not." Quite the contrast to the rest of our world, isn't it?

In this section we're going to explore several of the "fear not" verses in the Bible. Today spend some time thinking about what causes you the most anxiety in your life. Think about where these fears come from and when they come the most often.

DON'T FEAR, BE STRONG AND COURAGEOUS

> *Joshua 1:9* <

Have I not commanded you? Be strong and courageous. Do not be terrified; do not be discouraged. for the LORD your God will be with you wherever you go.

The world Joshua lived in was a fearful, fearful place. It was a place with little to no law, and plenty of famine, poverty, violence, and uncertainty. There were plenty of reasons to be anxious and afraid. Not only was the world a very tough place, his people, the Israelites, were a small nomadic tribe searching for a home. They had little resources, few allies, and were certainly the underdogs.

I bet there are a lot of times where you feel like the underdog. I know I do. There are always people that are smarter, stronger, funnier, better looking, more connected, have more money, and just seem to have more luck sometimes! It's easy to become paralyzed when you think about these things especially if you're more of a wallflower and would rather sit and observe than be in the middle of something. I want to help give you courage. First, God loves you just the way you are. Whether you're the quiet wallflower or the center of attention, the richest or the poorest, the strongest or the weakest, God loves you. Each of us have incredible gifts and strengths. We just have to figure out how to let God use those strengths in us. Some of our strengths are evident, others are more difficult to notice and need attention to find where God wants to use them. I think of a writer. No one can just look at her and think to themselves, "man I can't wait to see all of the great poetry and prose she's going to crank out!" Or people do not look at artists and think, "I bet he is crazy good with a brush and pallet!"

I want to encourage you, just because your gifts aren't noticed by others doesn't mean that they're not there. Although you may feel like an underdog in life doesn't mean that you are. Find your calling, your gifting, and your strengths and be strong and courageous!

DON'T FEAR, GOD WANTS TO BLESS MANY THROUGH YOU

> Genesis 26:24 <

That night the LORD appeared to him and said, "I am the God of your father Abraham. Do not be afraid, for I am with you; I will bless you and will increase the number of your descendants for the sake of my servant Abraham."

God doesn't hurt people. God doesn't say that He's going to be for you and then betray you. God wants good in your life and good to come from your life. God doesn't make duds. I talk with youth sometimes who have bought into the lie that God can't do anything through them. This fear brings great anxiety to some of these youth because they want to do God's good work in the world but are afraid that either God has forgotten about them or that God doesn't want to use them. You can't buy into this. God wants to bless the world through you. There are no questions about that. The uncertainty and the fun part is discovering how!

One of the most beautiful aspects of our faith is that God chooses to do His blessing through His people. If God is giving you a heart for those who hurt then you should explore and chase after how God's calling you to be His healing in those lives. If you feel a deep passion for children or even youth, start working in your church to explore and live out that call. If you love numbers and are good at math begin asking God how that can be a ministry for your God.

Don't fear that you can't do what God is calling you to do. You have all that you need, you just need to know how to use it for God's good work in this world.

DON'T FEAR, REMEMBER WHAT GOD HAS DONE

> *Deuteronomy 7:18-19* <

But do not be afraid of them; remember well what the LORD your God did to Pharaoh and to all Egypt. You saw with your own eyes the great trials, the miraculous signs and wonders, the mighty hand and outstretched arm, with which the LORD your God brought you out. The LORD your God will do the same to all the peoples you now fear.

The Jewish faith is a beautiful faith with many inspiring and beautiful components that we as Christians can learn from. One of the most beautiful for me is all of their feast days. One of the primary purposes of the feast days is a way every year to tell the story of how God has been with them so that they'll remember it.

Too often we are forgetful people. We forget where we've seen, experienced, heard, and felt our God. We forget the times where we knew God was near and saw God at work right in front of our eyes. When we forget, we fear. We find ourselves like a ship floating aimlessly at sea. When we have strong memories and remember the work of God in our past, we can no longer float aimlessly wondering what will happen. We have a history with God. We have a relationship and we have a foundation based on love and fidelity from which we know God won't stray.

In the verses above, Moses is taking the time to remind the people of what they're supposed to remember. They were finding themselves questioning where they were going, what they were doing, and if they really could do it. Moses called them to remember God's faithfulness in Egypt and in the wilderness. When we have good memories, when we understand that God has been at work in our past, we can trust much easier that God will be at work in our present and our future. We don't have to fear what is or what will be because we serve a God who we have a long history with. God is faithful.

DON'T FEAR, GOD IS STRONGER

>*Deuteronomy 20:1*<

When you go to war against your enemies and see horses and chariots and an army greater than yours, do not be afraid of them, because the LORD your God, who brought you up out of Egypt, will be with you.

What happens when your enemy is charging? What happens when those who want to see you fail are watching your every move? What happens when absolute catastrophe is inevitable and there's nothing you can do but watch it come crashing towards you? You don't ignore it. You don't run from it. You don't fight. You trust. You act as God has called each of us to act. And, you trust some more.

It's in these times of trials and pain that it's most difficult to hold to our values, trust, and identity as Christ-followers. It's very easy to fall into fear. When we're fearful we don't act as we usually would. We make terrible decisions, decisions that we would never make otherwise. We find ourselves taking on dependencies that we wouldn't otherwise dream of attaching ourselves to. We find ourselves medicating ourselves with unhealthy habits and practices and using these things to cope with the fear that we feel. We do all of these things because we forget. We forget that we serve a God who doesn't take pleasure in the shaming of His people. We serve a God who wants goodness in our world and in your life. Ultimately we serve a God who is stronger than any army that can come against us.

When we focus only on the things or people or situations that we fear, that is all we will ever see. But when we see those things but also see that we serve a God who is the creator even of our enemies our entire perspective changes. It isn't that nothing will ever go wrong; it's just that nothing that goes wrong ever has the final word. God always has the final word, even in death. You don't have to fear, not because your life is going to be perfect, but because there's never a situation beyond what God can see us through.

DON'T FEAR, GOD IS ALREADY AHEAD OF YOU

> *Deuteronomy 31:8* <

The LORD himself goes before you and will be with you; he will never leave you nor forsake you. Do not be afraid; do not be discouraged.

I used to jump off of waterfalls. I know, stupid. Well some of you might not think it was stupid. It was actually a lot of fun! I loved being outdoors, in and near the water, and climbing. I loved the exhilaration of standing at the top of a 40, 50, and even 90 foot waterfall looking over the edge, stomach in knots and feeling once you have committed to the jump, you push off and then . . . you fly. It's stupid, but amazing.

Here is the deal though, it wasn't completely stupid. I never jumped first. I never was the first person to take the plunge. Coward? Maybe. Smart? Definitely. There's something incredibly reassuring when someone goes in front of you or is ahead of you in an unknown situation. Think about it: it's always easier to walk through a haunted house if you're in the middle of your group. It always feels better to take the test if you're in second period instead of the poor souls who took it first period.

In life we always get to go second. God is already ahead of us in our journey. God goes before us and calls us forward in the ways and on paths that He has already treaded. We never have to worry or fear when God calls us. We can always know that He's not sending us into a dark room or down a treacherous path that He hasn't already navigated. Sometimes our journey with God can feel like jumping off of a waterfall or walking into a very scary place not knowing what's lurking around each corner. Even then, don't fear. Know that the road you're walking down already has God's footprints all over it.

DON'T FEAR WHAT OTHERS WILL THINK

> *Matthew 10:26* <

So do not be afraid of them. There is nothing concealed that will not be disclosed,
or hidden that will not be made known.

One thing that causes us the most anxiety and fear in our lives is what others think. What will they think if I do this or that? What will others say if they knew _____? What would happen if they knew or thought this about me? So much of our fear, anxiety, decisions, and actions aren't based on how we want to be known, but on how we don't want to be known. It's funny, everything from how we dress, to the way we talk, to the people we spend time with is, at least in part, determined by what others will think about us. Sometimes we even hide our faith and what we really believe because we are afraid of how others will judge us, talk about us, or even disassociate themselves from us.

Do not be anxious because of what others might say. Jesus, in the Gospel of Matthew, talks about motives and anxiety about how transparent we are as people of faith. At the end of the day here's what matters: You're a child of God. You're loved and accepted by God and everything else is just bonus. Do you get it? What matters is who you are in God's eyes, and that's it! There will always be people who will not like you, be jealous of you, or look down on you. That's reality. But that reality pales in comparison to the reality of our identity as a beloved child of God.

Do others words and thoughts affect us? Sure, that is natural. Should it determine who we are what we should be? Absolutely not. Who we should be is already determined because of the one who made us who we are.

DON'T FEAR, YOU HAVE SOMETHING THEY CANNOT TAKE

> *Matthew 1:20* <

But after he had considered this, an angel of the Lord appeared to him in a dream and said, "Joseph son of David, do not be afraid to take Mary home as your wife, because what is conceived in her is from the Holy Spirit."

My father-in-law was in the Navy. He wasn't your usual Navy guy though. He was more of the trickster, funny, don't take this thing too seriously kind of Navy guy. He said that when drill instructors or higher ups would be in their faces the guys around him would be really fearful. He said he wouldn't because of one simple thing; his birthday. He knew that they could take away his time, his position, rank, etc., but he had one thing they could never take away. His birthday. I always think this is just hilarious and really insightful.

Mary is very similar. When she first found out that she, a teenager, was pregnant with the Son of God, she was really freaked out, and rightfully so. She could have lost everything: her baby, her family, her home, her possessions, her fiancé, and ultimately her life. What Mary didn't realize at that moment was that God was doing something extremely special inside of her, something that couldn't be taken away. You can lose everything in this world and still have what really matters. You can lose all of your possessions, friends, family, and even your life. Even after all of that there's still one thing that remains that really matters.

We talk about the Holy Spirit in a lot of different ways depending on what type of church you go to. One thing I think we all agree on is that the Holy Spirit is God's presence on earth and in each one of us. That presence isn't something that can be taken away. There will be times in your life where you feel like you could lose everything. But remember that even then you still have something, something inside of you, more valuable than gold, that will be with you forever.

DON'T FEAR, GOD HAS BIGGER PLANS

>*Matthew 28:5*<

The angel said to the women, "Do not be afraid, for I know that you are looking for Jesus, who was crucified."

Can you imagine? You've followed this guy for around three years. He was your teacher, friend, mentor, healer . . . your everything. Now He is gone. He is dead, buried, and, as far as it looks at the moment, never coming back. There were a few women who were disciples of Jesus who came to His tomb expecting to find their friend three days dead. Instead a stranger greeted them; a stranger who told them not to be afraid.

What happens when your life falls apart? What happens when everything you believed would be is no more? What happens when everything you planned for your life has now fallen through? What happens? You have to realize that God has bigger plans. There's something bigger than what's happening in you life at that instance. There's a greater good that God's going to accomplish beyond anything you could've ever imagined. It's not that God broke your dreams and hopes and life into a million pieces. God takes the millions of broken pieces in our lives and creates incredible new works of art, things that we could've never imagined before.

God is a God that takes pain and turns it into healing, turns storms into rainbows, and death into beautifully empty tombs of grace. God doesn't leave our lives as closed tombs with death surrounding. God has bigger plans than that. In God, every death is a chance for resurrection.

DON'T FEAR, GO AND TELL

> *Matthew 28:10* <

Then Jesus said to them. "Do not be afraid. Go and tell my brothers to go to Galilee; there they will see me."

We know that anxiety comes from fear. It's an amazing way to end the Gospel of Matthew with Jesus' first post resurrection words being, "Do not be afraid . . . " Because of resurrection, we don't have to fear anything any longer. Once death was defeated there were no more enemies. When we realize this, own this, and make this a part of who we are, everything changes. Everything.

When we find ourselves living post resurrection lives we have a mandate. We must go and tell. We have a story, a miraculous story that must be told again and again. Remember how the Jewish faith depends so much on telling and retelling the story so that they will remember? We too have the call to tell of God's goodness and His movement in our world and our lives.

I can tell you from personal experience our greatest strength in times of fear and anxiety comes from the stories of others who have been through and have come out on the other side with stories of life and resurrection. In my own life I've told the stories of my mom leaving when I was 15, my family completely falling apart, depression, attempted suicide, feelings of abandonment, and how God resurrected each of those situations and allowed beauty to grow from each. Not only did beauty grow from each, but those stories have helped countless others find resurrection and life on the other side. You never know how the stories that are fearful now will turn to stories of hope. Go and tell what God has done.

BUSY *pg. 291–310*

Life is busy. And when it's busy we can often get side-tracked from our devotions. Our routines get messed up because things are just too hectic. It can be difficult to start back sometimes because we have to start up our routine again, or we just feel guilty for missing these times with God. Well fear not!!! In this section you'll find twenty, single word devotions (that's right . . . one word devotions) to help you through this hectic time!

Simply choose a word, read the word, and focus on what thoughts or emotions about God that word triggers in you. Then, carry that thought or feeling with you as you go through your day.

CALM

PEACE

REST

BUSY 4

FOCUS

BUSY 5

PATIENCE

SLEEP

TRUST

AIM

GOAL

ENCOURAGEMENT

THIS TOO SHALL PASS

YOU ARE NOT
WHAT YOU DO

BELOVED

COURAGE

LIVE

BREATHE

TIME

PRIORITY

HOLIDAY TIMES

Remember when we told you in the beginning of the book that (Extra)Ordinary wasn't like any other devotion book you've ever seen? Well, Holiday Times is one of the reasons it's so special.

In this section you'll find what we might call the "normal" holidays you would expect to find devotions for. There's an Advent/Christmas section to help you prepare to celebrate Jesus' birth. And a Lent section where you can prepare to celebrate Easter and Jesus' death and resurrection. But, there are also devotions for holidays such as New Year's Eve, Mother's Day, and Thanksgiving, just to name a few. Oh, and we almost forgot. **There's even a devotion to read on your birthday (pg. 377)!**

Make sure you check back in with the Holiday Times section to help focus on Christ during the holidays.

40

> *Matthew 16:21* <

From that time on Jesus began to explain to his disciples that he must go to Jerusalem and suffer many things at the hands of the elders, chief priests and teachers of the law, and that he must be killed and on the third day be raised to life.

---

40. It's an interesting number in the Bible. We see it crop up often. Some of the most notable are the 40 days in the boat with Noah, the Israelites' 40 years wandering in the desert, and Jesus' 40 days in the wilderness. In each of these situations, we see a time of reflection, testing, and trial. Over the next 40 days, not including Sundays, you will work through some tough images, verses and stories. You will, through this devotional, dive deep into the words of the story of abuse, crucifixion, and death of our Lord. And hopefully, you'll learn something about yourself and about God as a result.

There are many times where this story loses some of its meaning for us because of how many times we've heard it. Over the next 40 days of Lent I want you to focus on each of these words and as you take on this daily journey with Jesus through His death and resurrection. I want you to let it be a point of reflection for you in your life.

We're often encouraged to give up something for Lent. This is always a good thing. This Lent I want to encourage you to deny yourself something that will draw your heart and mind toward Jesus. Only you know what that is. Prayerfully consider what you think God might be telling you to do without.

ASHES

> Genesis 3:19 <

For dust you are and to dust you will return.

Ashes are the beginning of our journey. It's strange to begin a journey with something so simple and dirty as ashes, but they remind us of several things that we have to remember in order to go on this journey. The first is that we're human, and because we're human we will one day die. The Bible says that "it is from dust that we came and it is to dust we will return." We have to remember our own mortality, and that we only have a certain amount of time here. There are only a certain amount of days that we have to do what God is calling us to do. Our time is limited.

The ashes also remind us that the business of the cross is a dirty one. It's dirty for humanity because we're the ones who put Jesus on the cross. We're the ones who took pure beauty and killed it on a Roman torture device. The business of the cross is messy and it gets all of our hands dirty, even God's.

God entered into this relationship with us knowing that it would be dirty. Even in creation it says that God reached down into the dirt and created humanity, then blew the breath of life into it. From day one to the day of the cross, humanity has been a dirty endeavor for God. So as we begin the endeavor of this journey to the cross, we too must get a little dirty. If your church practices ash Wednesday, I encourage you to participate in it. It's an outward symbol that we are doing something together with the rest of the faithful during this Lenten season.

PALMS

> *John 12:13* <

They took palm branches and went out to meet him, shouting, "Hosanna!" "Blessed is he who comes in the name of the Lord!" "Blessed is the King of Israel!"

So, we begin at the beginning. The beginning of Holy Week starts with Palm Sunday. Palm Sunday is the day that the church commemorates Jesus riding into Jerusalem on a donkey. He rode into Jerusalem during a very intense and pivotal time in the history of the world. He rode into an occupied land. The Romans, who were oppressing the Jewish people, occupied the land. He rode in on a donkey as people waved palm branches as He came by. For us this might seem sort of weird, but for a person living in a Roman territory at that time it meant something very special: a king was coming.

As Jesus rode in, the people were calling out "Hosanna," and waving the symbols of worship. It seems incredible that just a few days later they would be waving their fists yelling "crucify him"! But is it really incredible? Are we not guilty of the same things? One day we wave our hands in worship and the next we deny our God through our lives and actions.

It's easy to judge these palm wavers, but in honesty they didn't fully understand who Jesus really was, not the way we do. They didn't know what would happen, what He would mean to history and how He would ultimately change the world. But we do. We know and we still betray Him, waving palms on Sunday and ignoring Him on Monday. Take today and think about how you do this in your life and how you can continue to worship after the crowds have gone.

PASSOVER

> *Matthew 26:17-19* <

On the first day of the Feast of Unleavened Bread, the disciples came to Jesus and asked, "Where do you want us to make preparations for you to eat the Passover?" He replied, "Go into the city to a certain man and tell him, 'The Teacher says: My appointed time is near. I am going to celebrate the Passover with my disciples at your house.'" So the disciples did as Jesus had directed them and prepared the Passover.

While there's debate as to exactly what all Jesus did during His last week before the crucifixion, we do know that He was in Jerusalem for the celebration of the Jewish Passover. In Exodus 12:1-24 we see the original mandate for the Passover as given to Moses and Aaron. This was and is a very important celebration and remembrance for Jewish people. Jesus, being a Jew, was in Jerusalem to celebrate this very important festival.

In Matthew 26:17-19 we see Jesus telling His disciples to go ahead of Him and prepare the Passover feast for Him and the rest of the disciples. This holy feast was to commemorate the Jews fleeing the Egyptians and how the angel of death passed over the Hebrew houses that had lamb's blood wiped across the doorframe.

Christians don't celebrate Passover in the same way as our Jewish brothers and sisters, but we do have much of the same story. We don't have to fear death because of the life, death, and resurrection of Jesus. While we don't have to spread the blood of a lamb over our doors, we do understand the sacrifice of our Lord in much the same way. As we journey deeper into Lent we must know that our freedom from the death sin brings lies in the action of sacrifice. Jesus sacrificed all for us. What are you willing to sacrifice? Who are you willing to sacrifice for?

COMMUNION

> *Luke 22:19* <

And he took bread, gave thanks and broke it, and gave it to them, saying, "This is my body given for you; do this in remembrance of me."

On the night Jesus was betrayed, He was eating supper with His disciples. During the meal Jesus got the attention of the disciples at the table, took the bread that was there, and broke it, saying that this was His body, broken for the salvation of humankind. Then He took the cup of wine, poured it, and told them that this was His blood poured out for the sins of them and for the sins of many. He told them to take and drink, and every time they did this in the future, to remember Him. This one act is the beginning of our long history of communion.

It's a moment in our story where Jesus most clearly tells us what was going to happen to Him and what would happen to us because of it. When we practice communion it's such a beautiful moment where we all come to a common table and eat bread and wine and remember that night where Jesus began His final push towards the cross.

For me, communion is also a time of community between people of faith. It's a time where we serve and are served by each other in this holy meal. Every time we take this meal we should not only remember the meal itself, but what the meal symbolizes for us individually, and for the world. It means that we have hope beyond fear, and that even death itself can't keep the love of God from God's people.

GARDEN

>*Matthew 26:36*<

Then Jesus went with his disciples to a place called Gethsemane. and he said to them. "Sit here while I go over there and pray."

Usually we think of gardens as places full of life and beauty. We usually think of images of small country gardens with corn, beans, and neatly plowed rows. We might also be reminded of English gardens with tall hedges, beautiful flowers, and bright butterflies. This isn't the image of the garden Jesus would journey to.

After Jesus had supper with His disciples, the group went to a garden so that Jesus could pray. This was a garden called the Garden of Gethsemane. This garden was not full of flowers and herbs, but full of ancient olive trees. You can still go to this garden today and see some trees some believe were around near the time of Jesus. On this night a garden, a place usually associated with life and birth, was a place of deep pain, sorrow, and agony. There are times in our life where places that are usually thought of as places of life turn into places of death and sorrow. There are times when our homes are places of hurt, cribs are empty because of tragedy, and supper tables have an untimely empty seat. There are times in our lives where places of nurture turn into places of pain.

Today, remember those places in your life, and in the lives of family and friends, that went from places of joy to places of sorrow. Pray especially today for schools and places of worship where violence has broken out, taking the innocence from an otherwise safe place. Pray that God will turn these gardens back into places where life happens.

PRAYER

> *Matthew 26:39* <

Going a little farther, he fell with his face to the ground and prayed. "My Father, if it is possible, may this cup be taken from me. Yet not as I will, but as you will."

As Jesus began to think about what was going to happen to Him, He retreated, as he often did, to a private place to pray. We don't often get a detailed account of the words that Jesus prayed, but we do have an account of His garden prayer. His prayer in the garden was intense and relatively short. There was not flowery or unnecessary language. As Jesus went to pray He told the three disciples who were with Him that His soul was overwhelmed unto the point of death. Jesus asked them to keep watch with Him. Then He moved away and prayed to God that if there was another way for this to happen, that God would take the cup of suffering away from Him. God did not.

There are some people who are preachers in our world today who will tell you that if you just pray hard enough and just believe enough (and sometimes if you'll just send money enough) that God will grant you the desires of you heart. We know that this isn't true. Jesus, in one of His most vulnerable moments, prayed to God that He would not have to do what He was about to do. Not only did God not let Jesus off the hook, from all we're told, God didn't verbally answer Him at all. We have to remember that God isn't going to answer all of our prayers with a "yes."

Take comfort, when you pray and remain confused or unanswered, that Jesus prayed one of His most desperate prayers and didn't get the response He initially wanted. Our lives of faith aren't always ones that are going to be easy or have all of the answers presented to us. Learn to find comfort with this silence and, as Jesus did, finish with "God, let your will be done."

SLEEP

> *Matthew 26:40-41* <

Then he returned to his disciples and found them sleeping. "Could you men not keep watch with me for one hour?" he asked Peter. "Watch and pray so that you will not fall into temptation. The spirit is willing, but the body is weak."

Have you ever really needed your friends and they completely let you down? Ever been in a situation where you needed someone to vouch for you, take up for you, or just keep you company and you were the only one left? Jesus asked His three closest friends to come to the garden with Him to keep watch and pray. Just a few short feet away, while Jesus prayed desperate prayers for God to take this cup from Him, His disciples nodded off and fell asleep. Not only did they fall asleep, Jesus woke them up three times and each time they dozed back off, leaving Him alone full of pain and sorrow.

There are many times in our lives where our friends will "fall asleep" on us in our most trying times. Don't get me wrong. There will be many times where they are by our side, willing to do whatever it takes. But don't forget that there will be those times where they're nowhere to be found. When this happens know that you're in good company. Even as Jesus was heading to the cross they slept. When we're honest, we know that we too have slept when our friends needed us the most. It could be that we didn't know that they were in this pain, or it could be that we just didn't want to get too involved with such a messy situation. Either way there are times where we're the ones praying in the garden and there are also times where we are the ones sleeping in the garden.

Today pray for those in your school, community, and world who have no friends, those who will stand before the world without any advocates. Pray that God will make you a friend to the friendless.

LENT 9
KISS

>*Matthew 26:48-50*<

Now the betrayer had arranged a signal with them: "The one I kiss is the man: arrest him." Going at once to Jesus. Judas said. "Greetings. Rabbi!" and kissed him. Jesus replied. "Friend. do what you came for." Then the men stepped forward. seized Jesus and arrested him.

The Bible in Matthew 26:48-50 tells the story of Judas' kiss of death. Judas had made a deal with the Jews that he would show them who Jesus was by kissing him on the cheek. A kiss is such an intimate act and can be such a hurtful act when someone does it while at the same time betraying us. There will be people who you're intensely close to who will betray you. There will be people throughout your life who you will trust deeply, who will take that trust, and hurt you with it. This is a horrible thing to think about and it shouldn't cause you to trust others less; most people you meet won't hurt you and will treasure your trust and friendship.

There will be times however, where you'll be betrayed. Maybe you already have. I find it so interesting that Jesus didn't yell at Judas. He didn't strike him or call him names. He only told Judas to do what he has to do. And then Jesus calls him "friend." There is nothing Christian about betrayal, but there's something deeply Christian about how we're called to handle it. We handle it not with anger, resentment, and violence. Instead, through the example of Jesus, we're to handle it with grace, love, and dignity.

Jesus could have done a thousand horrible things to Judas, but instead He chose to call him friend. You can't help it that people will hurt and betray you. You can choose how you will handle it and how you will respond when others do harm.

SILVER

> *Matthew 26:15* <

"What are you willing to give me if I hand him over to you?" So they counted out for him thirty silver coins.

There are those times where others betray us, but there's always the temptation for us to betray our Lord. It's inevitable that as we get older, and as we have more independence, we'll have more and more temptation to face, opportunities to trade faithfulness to our God for faithfulness to the world. Trust me, as you get older there will be more and more things that will pull at you for your attention and affection. There will be tons of opportunities, many of which are good, where you can choose to invest your time, money, and efforts into. As these increase something has to decrease. Often it's our time with God and our faith that takes a second seat.

There will be other times where the deep convictions for the poor, homeless, helpless, and the marginalized will begin to take less of a priority to the things we want to have and to do. The question is not whether you and I will betray Jesus; the real question is what will be our thirty shekels of silver? What will be the thing that breaks our fidelity to Jesus?

Today I want you to spend some time thinking about the things in your life currently, or things you see in your future, that could cause you to turn your back on Jesus. Think about those temptations that dangle in front of you luring your kiss of betrayal to God. It's deeply important to know what these are so that when they come we can recognize them and respond to them in faithful ways.

> *Matthew 26:50-52* <

Jesus replied. "Friend. do what you came for." Then the men stepped forward. seized Jesus and arrested him. With that. one of Jesus' companions reached for his sword. drew it out and struck the servant of the high priest. cutting off his ear. "Put your sword back in its place." Jesus said to him. "for all who draw the sword will die by the sword.

There are things Jesus does in the Gospels that continue to re-amaze me every time I read them. The story in Mathew 26:50-52 is one of those stories. Jesus has just been betrayed. There's a crowd who is with the arresting officers. In that crowd there's a servant of one of the high priests. Peter, being the zealous disciple that he is, draws a sword and begins to attack. He cuts the ear off of the servant of the high priest. This is where it gets interesting.

Think about this: Jesus was in anguish just moment earlier. His disciples had been sleeping while He asked them to pray. Jesus had just been betrayed by one of His friends. And He was in the act of getting arrested. But before we get to what Jesus did, I want to tell you what I would've done. If I were Jesus, life would really stink at that point. I would feel pretty miserable and alone. The last thing I would worry about is someone who's come as a part of a mob ready to arrest and kill me. At this point I would be feeling sorry for myself. But I'm not Jesus. Jesus knelt down, in front of those who would kill Him, picked up the man's ear, and placed it back on his head, effectively healing him. Even on the way to His death, Jesus finds time for someone else.

Today I want you to think about those who you pass each day whose lives would be changed if you would simply make time for them. The Bible doesn't tell us anything else about that man, but I would bet he saw the world in a whole new way simply because Jesus, in the middle of one of the worst moments of His life, took a little time to take care of someone in front of Him.

ROOSTER

> *Luke 22:61-62* <

The Lord turned and looked straight at Peter. Then Peter remembered the word the Lord had spoken to him: "Before the rooster crows today, you will disown me three times." And he went outside and wept bitterly.

Don't you hate it when you do that thing you said you'd never do? I had a professor in college who once told us that the thing we said we'd never do, would be something we'd one day have to admit that we had done. Peter had a conversation with Jesus before He was arrested. In that conversation Jesus told Peter that he would deny Jesus three times before the rooster crowed the next morning. Peter strongly denied these words and told Jesus that he could never do such a thing. Just after Jesus is arrested we see a series of three scenes with Peter in Luke 22:54-62 where Peter does the very thing he swore he'd never do.

In each of the scenes someone recognizes Peter as a close friend of Jesus. Each time Peter denies knowing Jesus. In a very dramatic fashion, just after he denies Jesus the third time, Peter can hear a rooster crowing in the background. What happens when you're Peter and you hear that rooster crow and you've done that thing you swore you'd never do? What happens when you're full of shame, guilt, and sadness at what you've done?

There's a story in John 21:1-19 that follows after the Lenten story. It's a story of Peter, some fish for breakfast by the Sea of Galilee, and a risen Jesus. It's a story of forgiveness, love, and faithfulness. It's a story of grace beyond grace. It's a story that you and I both get to share after we too have done what we said we would never do. Take some time today to read that story and soak in the limitless grace of God.

TRIAL

> Matthew 27:1-2 <

Early in the morning, all the chief priests and the elders of the people came to the decision to put Jesus to death. They bound him, led him away and handed him over to Pilate, the governor.

Life isn't always fair. We're not always fair. Just ask Jesus. You have a person who did nothing but good for the world and the people around Him. You have a person who loved the unlovable, taught about God's goodness and grace, and brought healing to those He met. He was goodness in flesh. So, not only did He not do anything criminal, He was the epitome of goodness in our world. When they arrested Jesus the rulers played a tennis match with His trial. Neither Pilate nor Herod wanted anything to do with His trial. They knew that it was a politically volatile time in the city, tensions were up and Jesus was a well-known figure. They pushed Jesus back and forth between them, neither wanting His blood on their hands. Finally, after several volleys with His life, the task landed on Pilate. Reluctantly he gave into the people and handed over Jesus even though He had done nothing, and more than once had been cleared by the rulers of the land.

There are times in our lives and the lives of others where we will suffer unjustly. There are examples all over our country and world of where people suffer needlessly, having to live lives that are cruelly unfair. Today pray for and think about the people in our world who suffer daily because the life that was prescribed to them is without fairness and hope. Pray for those who live in countries with oppressive governments, victims of genocide and war, are victims of human trafficking, prejudice, unjust laws, and oppressive systems. Pray that your voice will join with the loud cries of injustice lobbying for fairness to all. Let our voices be ones who cry out for God's justice in our world.

CROWD

> *Matthew 27:22-24* <

"What shall I do, then, with Jesus who is called Christ?" Pilate asked. They all answered, "Crucify him!" "Why? What crime has he committed?" asked Pilate. But they shouted all the louder, "Crucify him!"

The crowd chanted "crucify him, crucify him!" Pilate pleaded with them that the man had done nothing wrong. But they insisted and Pilate turned Jesus over to them. Sometimes, actually a lot of times, the "crowd" is just wrong. I want to tell you now that you can't trust something just because it seems popular. I especially believe this in regards to religion and God. I find that the closer I read the Bible and the accounts of people of faith throughout our history, the less I trust the judgment of the many.

Throughout our history of faith it seems that the ones who really made the difference are the ones who went against the religious crowd. Many of them were called extremist and heretics when they were alive, and later they were revered as saints. The prophets were this way: Moses, Noah, John the Baptist, Jesus, Paul, and so on. The list goes on and one. This isn't true with just biblical people either. There are loads of people throughout church history who suffered because they believed God was doing things a different way and called their culture into accountability to follow God's way.

Just as the crowd was wrong on the day Jesus was crucified there are many that are wrong today. A part of your faith is praying and discerning what God is doing in the world. Even if it's unpopular and against what seems normal. There will be times where you know that you must go against the grain and stand up for something that the crowd is for. Enter into these situations and decisions with humility but know that the people who we remember in history are not the ones who followed the crowd. History remembers those who went against the flow for the sake of God and His glory. Does this describe you?

SIMON

> *Matthew 27:32* <

As they were going out, they met a man from Cyrene, named Simon, and they forced him to carry the cross.

One of the most interesting characters in the passion narrative is a man named Simon who was from Cyrene. From what we know, Simon didn't seem to have any real investment in Jesus or His movement. All we really know is that he was passing by and was grabbed and forced into carrying Jesus' cross.

I bet some of you may have a story that feels a little like that. You were perfectly happy with your life and were doing just fine. Then out of nowhere, you were thrown into relationship with Jesus. It might not have felt like a relationship you really wanted to be in either. Carrying a cross isn't something that sounds like a lot of fun. Many of us probably have that story where before we knew it, out of nowhere, we were serving a God we barely knew. That's ok. The Gospel sometimes works that way. God doesn't require a long relationship before He calls us into service.

I find this story very touching. I see someone, although they were forced, carrying a cross that no disciple was even close enough to carry. I will promise you this, there will be times in your life of faith where there are crosses that need to be carried, things that must be done for our God, and none of those who claim to be closest to Jesus will be there to do them. Today pray that where there is something that's difficult to do and requires a lot of time and commitment, that you'll be close enough to our God to pick up the cross that needs to be carried, and that you will be strong enough to carry it.

BARABBAS

> *Mark 15:7, 11* <

A man called Barabbas was in prison with the insurrectionists who had committed murder in the uprising . . . But the chief priests stirred up the crowd to have Pilate release Barabbas instead.

Again, we experience a character in this passion story of Jesus who we don't encounter anywhere else in the Gospels. This is a much more sinister character than the one of Simon of Cyrene. This is a character who has been arrested and convicted as a murderer, and now he's standing beside Jesus in the eyes of the people. For most (if not all) of us this is a no brainer. Of course we would release Jesus and keep Barabbas in custody. So why did the crowd hate Jesus so much that they chose to release a murderer instead of a healer and comforter?

I am not entirely sure why people would have asked for Barabbas. But sometimes when people reveal too much of God and His Kingdom to us it makes us uncomfortable. I think the reason it makes us uncomfortable is because it's like holding up a mirror to ourselves and it reveals our faults, fears, and sins. When this happens it makes us feel badly about ourselves and what we do (and what we don't do). So, many times we'll push away from the one who causes this self examination. I've seen it so many times in youth ministry where youth group members will push away from kids who are really trying to do what's right. It just makes people uncomfortable sometimes.

So instead of gravitating towards the God in each of us sometimes we find ourselves choosing the Barabbas in each other than the Jesus. Ask yourself today: What can you do to reveal God and His ways to others in a way that's so real it might be uncomfortable (in a good way, of course)?

WHIP

> *Matthew 27:26* <

Then he released Barabbas to them. But he had Jesus flogged, and handed him over to be crucified.

It's one thing for the Roman government to kill Jesus. It's an entirely different thing for them to whip, beat, and humiliate Him. But that's what they did. They wanted to make an example out of Jesus and make sure that everyone knew that the government was their only law, and that Tiberius was their only god. The whip was a way to deter any of Jesus' followers from continuing His movement beyond that day. (Though, that didn't work so well, did it?)

Jesus was almost surely beaten with a whip called a "cat of nine tails." This was a special torture device that was a whip consisting of nine long leather whips. Each of these whips had shards of bone and metal so that when they struck victims, they tore into their skin and ripped it. This was a horrific thing to watch, much less experience. This could be a devotion about how our words can be like a whip to people, or it could be a devotion about how Jesus kept His composure and didn't fight back. But that's not what this devotion is about.

I don't want you to try to get any life application from this devotion. I want you to just sit and realize the suffering that Jesus went through. Beaten by soldiers almost beyond recognition, skin ripped into, stripped naked, and made to carry the very thing that would ultimately kill Him. All for what? To purchase life for sinners like you and me. No life application today, just sit and think about His suffering and the price He paid.

CROWN

>*Matthew 27:28-29*<

They stripped him and put a scarlet robe on him. and then twisted together a crown of thorns and set it on his head. They put a staff in his right hand and knelt in front of him and mocked him. "Hail. king of the Jews!" they said.

The soldiers believed Jesus to be a political activist who was trying to raise up a revolution against the Roman government. They believed that He wanted to be a political king, so they made him a crown. The soldiers dressed Jesus up in purple, the color of royalty, and placed a crown made up of thorns on top of His head, pushing it into his scalp. There are times when we make a mockery of Jesus' place as King and Lord as well. Whenever we take on the name of Christ, we're telling the world that we're different. We're telling all who know us that we live by a different set of standards, priorities, and rules. We pledge our allegiance, not to governments or rulers, but to the Father of Jesus, God Himself. When we do this, we place a real crown on his head.

But when we live our lives in rebellion against God, we make another crow of thorns. The reason this happens is because we take on that sacred name saying that we'll represent Christ as the King in all we do. By calling ourselves Christians we're telling the world that our actions and words show the values and mission of the one we serve. When they don't, it makes a mockery of God.

Being faithful, doing what's right, and following the teaching of Jesus isn't just about being a good person. Loads of non-religious people are good people. The reason why we're called to do these things is because we're representing the values and mission of the one with whom we've aligned ourselves. Today, ask yourself who do your values, actions, words, and priorities represent? Is it God or is it yourself?

NAILS

>*Isaiah 53:5*<

But he was pierced for our transgressions. he was crushed for our iniquities: the punishment that brought us peace was upon him. and by his wounds we are healed.

"He was pierced for our transgressions, he was crushed for our iniquities." This is what Isaiah 53 says about the Messiah hundreds of years before Jesus was born. I can't imagine the pain of having nails run through my hands and feet. I can't imagine the pain that Jesus would've experienced. I know the physical pain must have been unbearable, but I think what would've been just as unbearable is the feeling of being trapped, nailed to pieces of wood with no chance of getting away. The nails weren't only the things that were killing Him; they were also the things that were keeping Him from escaping that death.

One of the most terrifying things I think we can face is the feeling of being trapped. There will be times in your life where you'll feel like you're in a trap from which you can't escape, whether it's your fault or because you're a victim of circumstance. The feeling of being trapped can come in so many different areas of life. It can come in relationships. You can feel trapped in a certain identity or way of acting. Some can feel trapped in your city or high school. Sometimes feeling trapped is a matter of perspective, other times it's something that's very real and is a real problem that we must deal with. While we should never feel complacent being trapped in any of our life-circumstances, we can feel a relationship and a close connection with Jesus as He was trapped on the cross that Friday.

Knowing He allowed Himself to be trapped for our benefit? That's something truly powerful. Let that sink in as you go through your day.

FEET

>*Isaiah 52:7*<

How beautiful on the mountains are the feet of those who bring good news.

As I think of Jesus on the cross I can't but help but be drawn to His feet. It's difficult to imagine where all those feet had traveled. I think about the feet of a young Jesus, running and playing with the other children. I think about Him stepping on a rock, or hitting His toe, and His mother Mary holding Him while he cried. I think of Jesus as a teenager, strong and full of life and energy. I think of how He would probably walk though the villages around Galilee talking to those who He passed. I think of Jesus on the shores of the Sea of Galilee, stepping in to the cool water as it washed back and forth on the shore. I think of a Jesus whose feet stepped on the bank of the Jordan as a young man. I see the mud pushing between His toes as He stepped down the banks into the water to begin His ministry. I also see His dry cracked feet walking through the Judean desert for 40 days as He fasted and was tempted. I think about all of the towns and cities that Jesus' feet took Him to. I think of the woman, caught in adultery, kneeling down beside His feet waiting to be stoned by her accusers. I imagine her not daring to look up, only seeing the feet of the one who would save her that day. I think about Mary pouring expensive perfume on Jesus' dirty feet, washing them with her own hair. Finally I think about the feet that would walk through the streets of Jerusalem, caked with blood-soaked mud from His torture. Feet that would hang from a cross, barely able to push up occasionally to grasp at one more breath. These feet that had traveled to so many places, seen so many things and helped so many people. Then these feet become limp. They neither stretch nor push any longer. There is no need for breath now. The feet of our Lord dangle loosely as He's taken down and carried from the cross to a tomb.

It's amazing what all those feet saw. But the most amazing thing about those limp, lifeless feet? Soon, very soon, they would walk again.

CROSS

> *Matthew 27:35-36* <

When they had crucified him, they divided up his clothes by casting lots. And sitting down, they kept watch over him there.

Few symbols in our world are as recognizable as the cross. For some it's a sacred relic, made of precious gems hanging above an altar of a cathedral. For others it's a marketing technique to tell potential patrons that this is a business that's owned by Christians. For some it's decorative. For others it's tattooed on their body. The cross is a symbol that's widely recognized but is not nearly as widely agreed upon.

What really happened on those two pieces of wood that day 2,000 years ago? If we look into the Scriptures, we find an incredible example of love, faith, and peace on that cross. Jesus, in the face of the deepest hatred and violence, didn't fight, didn't spew forth hateful words, didn't raise a rebellion, and didn't harm. In the middle of this horrible death, He not only forgave the thief on the cross beside Him, but also forgave His captors, crucifiers, condemners and His friends who were denying and abandoning Him.

Everything Jesus did while on the cross is completely counterintuitive to what most, if not all of us would've done. I believe so much more happened that day on the cross. But to be amazed and inspired we don't have to look straight to the deeper theological meanings. We can look first to Jesus' actions of non-violence, love, compassion, and grace. When we see the cross, no matter the setting, let it inspire us in the same ways.

FORGIVE

> *Luke 23:34* <

Jesus said. "Father. forgive them. for they do not know what they are doing." And they divided up his clothes by casting lots.

"Father, forgive them, for they know not what they are doing." I'm not sure if there's a more powerful sentence in the entire Bible. In the throws of torture and imminent death, Jesus pronounces forgiveness over His executioners. We look at this story and see Jesus advocating for forgiveness that hasn't been asked for by the ones who have sinned. We see Jesus stepping in and asking forgiveness for them because, as He said, they don't know what they're doing.

I wonder sometimes how often we go astray and we have no clue what we're doing. I wonder how many times we're completely oblivious to our actions of destruction, harm, and pain. When we look at someone with less than loving eyes. When we look at the opposite sex in a way that's less than pure and in their minds they become a little less human. When we say words flippantly, or say nothing at all when someone desperately needs comfort. I wonder how many times we miss the opportunity to hug, to help, to give, and to step in. I wonder just how many of these "for they do not know" sins we commit each day, where we literally have no clue of the damage we care causing.

I hope that Jesus still steps in for us when we are ignorant of the harm we cause. I hope Jesus still feels the same compassion on us when we kill beauty or simply ignore the hurting. I hope that He still advocates for us when we have no clue that we need an advocate. I believe He still does. I pray that our eyes will be more open and our minds more alert so that these passive sins are abolished and in their place we commit deep acts of love. Father, forgive us, for we know not what we do.

BLOOD

>*Colossians 1:19-20*<

For God was pleased to have all his fullness dwell in him. and through him to reconcile to himself all things. whether things on earth or things in heaven. by making peace through his blood. shed on the cross.

Jesus actually bled. We believe, because of the way He was killed, that He bled a lot. While we could talk about the power of that blood and the theological significance of it, we won't. I want to focus on the fact that He bled which meant that He really was a real, living, breathing human. Jesus was a man. He was fully God, but fully human. He was an organism that was covered in flesh, had to breathe air through His nose, drink water and eat food in order to continue to live. He experienced joy, sadness, fear, excitement, and love. He had calluses on hands and feet and was sore after a hard days work. He was real, just like I'm real. He hurt just like you hurt. His blood means so many things but for me, today, it means that He was real.

When we get to the point in our lives where Jesus is real, not just a picture of some guy with flowing hair and hands outstretched, when He's more than a lesson on how to be kind, when He's more than a plastic baby in a manger . . . our world changes. It changes forever. We have to stop studying Him from a distance and begin following Him and following Him closely. We get to stop adding Him to our life and start letting Him become our life.

When we finally get that Jesus was real, we get to start really living the life that He lived and is calling us to live as well. He was real and is real. He is not a metaphor or an idea. He is real and wants to be real in your life too.

LEFT

> *Luke* 23:39 <

One of the criminals who hung there hurled insults at him: "Aren't you the Christ? Save yourself and us!"

Jesus was not the only one on a cross that day. The criminal on the left of Jesus responded to Jesus with insults and mockery. The Gospel of Luke tells us that the man hurled insults at Jesus saying, "aren't you the Messiah? Save yourself and us!" It's interesting because he must have had some knowledge of Jesus to say such a thing. He had some sort of understanding that Jesus was claiming to be Messiah, or at least people were saying that about Him. He knew, but he didn't believe.

Sometimes we think if we can just teach people about who Jesus is, then they will believe and follow Him. This isn't always the case. Just because someone knows who He is doesn't mean that they're going to automatically follow Him, or even want to have anything to do with Him. Sometimes we fool ourselves that a logical interpretation of Jesus' identity is the best method for bringing others to the faith. For so many it's not.

I do wonder why the criminal tried decided to lash out at Jesus. Maybe it was that he'd heard so many things about Him and saw Him dying and felt disappointed that Jesus seemed like nothing more than a common criminal like himself. Who Jesus truly was didn't matter. Ultimately, as far as we know, a man, a thief, died without a glimmer of hope. Pray that your heart would break for those around you who, without Jesus dramatically stepping into their lives, would die apart from Jesus right now. Listen to the Spirit's leading as He guides you to impact their lives for His sake.

RIGHT

>*Luke 23:40-42*<

But the other criminal rebuked him. "Don't you fear God," he said, "since you are under the same sentence? We are punished justly, for we are getting what our deeds deserve. But this man has done nothing wrong." Then he said, "Jesus, remember me when you come into your kingdom."

On the other side of Jesus was another criminal. A man, who like the person on Jesus' left, had been found guilty of a crime and had been placed on a cross to pay the penalty with his life. His final words look very different than the person to the left of Jesus. This criminal seems to have some knowledge of Jesus as well. If nothing else he feels an affinity or sorrow for Him so much so that he chooses, without prompt, to defend Jesus. He tells the other man that they were receiving their just penalty, but Jesus had done nothing. It seems that he not only comes to the aid of Jesus, but has some sort of connection to Him.

If he would've stopped at only defending Jesus, it would have been admirable. He didn't stop there though. He asks/tells Jesus to remember him when Jesus comes into His Kingdom. This is a pretty incredible show of faith on the part of the criminal. Think about it: he was looking at a man who was hanging on a cross, about to die, and from every indication, wasn't about to lead some political revolt where He would be a king. The only thing I can figure out from this is that he did believe that Jesus was the messiah and that death would not be the final word this day.

There will be times where it will feel like God has not proven Himself to us, where there seems to be no evidence from which to draw belief. On these days (and they will come) draw inspiration from this story. Draw inspiration from the hope and belief of the criminal. And finally draw hope from Jesus' response. He told the man that this would not be the last time they talked together. Just next time it will be in a far better place.

PARADISE

> *Luke 23:42-43* <

Then he said. "Jesus. remember me when you come into your kingdom.'" Jesus answered him. "I tell you the truth. today you will be with me in paradise."

Jesus makes a promise to the criminal to His right. It wasn't a promise of wealth, fame, influence, or power. It was a promise of paradise. When I hear the word paradise I can't help but think crystal clear water, beautiful palm trees, white sands, and a hammock with my name on it. I'm not sure this is exactly what Jesus was referring to. We can look at other parts of Scripture and see that when Jesus talks about His Kingdom, it's a place where there's no hunger, no war, no hate, and no thirst. It's a place where lepers are healed and the cripple can walk. In Jesus' paradise we're all complete, have enough, and are ultimately in communion with God. This is an amazing place to look forward to, but there's something else.

Jesus tells us in His prayer, the one we usually call the Lord's Prayer, that we are to cause God's will to be done on earth as it is in paradise. This paradise isn't supposed to just be something that we look forward to, one day. It's a place that we're supposed to bring here on earth. It's a place that we're to work for, strive for, and sacrifice to create here, as much as we possibly can. I don't believe that we will ever rid the world of all disease, hunger, thirst, and war, but we can certainly make a dent. Hate, prejudice, inequality, and systems of oppression will always be a part of the fabric of our societies, but we can work to give them less and less of a voice each day.

When we think of paradise, let's not think of some far off, distant place on either a tropical beach or in an eternal, heavenly place. Let's think about how our town, school, country, and work can look a little better each day.

FINISHED

> *John 19:30* <

When he had received the drink. Jesus said. "It is finished."

"It is finished." When something finishes in our lives sometimes it's a relief. Other times it's devastating. Around the end of the school year students will come by my office and tell me with an excited breath or relief, "I'm finished!" They have accomplished something, another school year, and the beginning of summer. When we think about finishing in this way, it's a joyful experience, the close of the chapter, and an exciting moment in our lives where we're able to move forward into something exciting and new.

Other times when something is finished it can be much more difficult. I've heard people who break up or get a divorce say, "we're just finished . . . we can't go on doing this." There's no excitement, no happiness, and no relief. It's the close of a chapter but not one that was expected and not one that's celebrated. There is sadness and a feeling of loss. While this is very difficult and terribly hard to move past, the finishing of a life can often be so much more agonizing. When someone's life ends it feels so final. I can imagine the disciples in the crowd, Jesus' mother, and His friends all having at least a small glimmer of hope until these words came from His mouth.

When they left his mouth, I can just hear the audible gasp and the leaving of hope from those who loved Him so much. It is finished. Now, death.

DEATH

>*John 19:30*<

With that. he bowed his head and gave up his spirit.

And so it ends.

It's over.

There is nothing any more.

Jesus is dead.

SPEAR

> John 19 : 33-35 <

But when they came to Jesus and found that he was already dead, they did not break his legs. Instead, one of the soldiers pierced Jesus' side with a spear, bringing a sudden flow of blood and water. The man who saw it has given testimony, and his testimony is true. He knows that he tells the truth, and he testifies so that you also may believe.

I know why this was done. I know why it was ordered that a soldier take a spear and stab Jesus in the side. They wanted to make sure He was dead. They wanted to make sure it really was finished. But it just feels cruel. It just feels like one more literal jab in the side of an already horrifying day.

The Bible says that water and blood poured out from Jesus' side. I think if I were in the crowd it would have been just one more unnecessary horrifying act done to such an amazing man that day. When I think of the spear I can't help but think about how there are just some people in our world that can't seem to catch a break. It's bad enough that they're down and have been down for sometime. It seems like when they're down every once in a while someone will come by and give them one more swift kick to make sure they stay down. I bet you know people like that.

Most of us, in a bad time in our lives, will use the saying "when it rains it pours." These people have never known anything but rainy days. The church, we as people of faith, have a call to be with the "least of these" and to care for and love them. So today think about who those people are who are in this perpetual storm of life. Pray that God will make you a healer in their lives and a source of comfort to them in their storm.

DARKNESS

> *Matthew 27:45-46* <

From the sixth hour until the ninth hour darkness came over all the land. About the ninth hour Jesus cried out in a loud voice. "Eloi. Eloi. lama sabachthani?"— which means. "My God. my God. why have you forsaken me?"

It was over. There was nothing left. No hope. No tomorrow.

The Bible says that when Jesus breathed His last breath that darkness covered the land. You'll experience the darkness at some point in your life. It creeps in and across the landscape of your life until it sucks the color from all that you see, and leaves you seeing only grays and monotones where there once was vibrant colors and life. Nothing seems alive in the darkness. It affects everything and makes its presence known everywhere. Dark places are scary. The leave us fearful of what lurks around the next corner and what lays waiting just out of sight that will hurt us and cause us more pain. In the darkness we experience loneliness, anxiety, and depression. It's in the darkness that our ghosts haunt us more fervently, because the darkness is where they are most comfortable. Jesus died and darkness descended over the land.

Darkness in its most literal definition is the absence of light. It is only when light is snuffed out can there be dark. As Jesus exhaled His last breath the light of the world, goodness in flesh, was snuffed out and the dark charged triumphantly in taking everything it could, claiming the world as its own. In those moments, the blackness seemed to overwhelm all.

VEIL

> *Matthew 27:51* <

At that moment the curtain of the temple was torn in two from top to bottom.

In the time when Jesus was alive, the center of the Jew's worship was the Temple in Jerusalem. The Temple was a very special place to the Jews where God's presence dwelled. Inside the innermost part of the temple was a place where the Ark of the Covenant was held called the Holy of Holies. The Holy of Holies was separated from the rest of the Temple by a veil. Since God's presence was understood to dwell behind this curtain, and that it was a place where one priest was only allowed to go once a year, this veil served a very important purpose. Can you imagine what people thought when the veil was split from top to bottom when Jesus died?

Many people have thought and written about what this meant. I love the idea that developed that God was showing the world through this action that God does not desire any separation between those who worship and the God they worship. This intimacy, immediately on the brink of Jesus' death is incredible. Desiring a closer relationship with the very people who murdered His only son is not only a miraculous act of love, but an instant act of grace. God, no matter where you have failed or what you have done, desires that intimate community with you and will tear through any barrier to be with you. Let that sink in as you go through your day.

>*Luke* 23:56<

But they rested on the Sabbath in obedience to the commandment.

Death and darkness have taken over. Uncertainty and fear have been realized. Jesus is gone. And as far as anyone knows, He's not coming back. This was the stark reality of the followers of Jesus the day after He died. Saturday proved that this wasn't a nightmare that they'd wake from. Sometimes in modern Christianity we go straight from the cross on Friday to the empty tomb on Sunday. We completely skip over this holy Saturday. We don't know what happened that day; nothing is written about it. We know it was their sabbath, a day of rest, but I feel certain there was much restlessness that day. Questions had to swirl, "Will they come for us next?" "What are we supposed to do now?" "How can He be gone?" I can imagine these hushed conversations were happening behind closed doors, closed in fear that someone would associate them with the man who was tried and crucified the day before. For the same reason no one could mourn in traditional ways. This was a day of quiet mourning. As it should've been.

Sometimes we find ourselves in a holy Saturday. A day where we realize our nightmares are realities and everything is different now. In these moments it is OK and good to ask questions. It's right to feel confused and even scared. Don't let this overtake you but do know that at some points in your life you'll have more questions than you have answers, and that's OK.

SILENCE

For 33 years the physical incarnation of the living God, Jesus, was walking around, talking, and physically being present here on earth. Now, for the past day and a half, the Word of God had been silent. No teaching, no comforting words, no powerful proclamations of healing and wholeness. Nothing. Silence.

There will be and I'm sure have been silent times in your own life. Times where no matter how hard you try, you just can't seem to hear the God you long so desperately to be engaged by. Fears of abandonment and doubt flood your mind. "What if I made this whole thing up?" "What if the faith I live was just an emotional high?" "What if I was wrong about all of this and I am worshiping a God that does not exist?" Silence can cause you to question everything.

The earth was absent the voice of God. Jesus was dead and the disciples were hiding. When you find yourself in these moments of silence it can be OK to do nothing. If you notice, this isn't the part of the story where the disciples go out into the streets and start telling everyone that it was all a sham. This isn't where they completely abandon their faith and regret the past three years of their lives. Some went home, and others went back to work, but they didn't trash the experience they had. During your times of silence I pray that you'll wait as well.

MARY

> *Matthew 28:1* <

After the Sabbath, at dawn on the first day of the week, Mary Magdalene and the other Mary went to look at the tomb.

Depending on which Gospel account you read you'll see different people who find themselves at the tomb that Sunday morning after Jesus died. Throughout the different accounts one of the common threads is that a group of women went to the tomb that morning. Mary was one of those women. She came. She didn't come expecting reward, but fearing repercussion. She didn't come because she felt obligation, she came based on love. She came expecting to find a tomb with a lifeless body of someone she loved deeply. She was faithful to her love of Him even when there was nothing in it for her. Can we same the same of our love for God and our following Jesus?

Beyond the promise of reward and fear of consequence, would we still follow Jesus? Would we still be faithful to His way if there were nothing in it for us? Would we still follow the way of Jesus if we had no reason other than our commitment to Him? In our culture we're moving to a place where the social reward for following Jesus and being a part of a church is quickly diminishing. We're finding ourselves in a culture that cares less and less about this part of someone's life. As the benefits of being a Christian fades with our faith, involvement, and commitment, will we still go to be with our Lord early in the morning when no one else is watching?

TOMB

> *Matthew 27:58-60* <

Going to Pilate. he asked for Jesus' body. and Pilate ordered that it be given to him. Joseph took the body. wrapped it in a clean linen cloth. and placed it in his own new tomb that he had cut out of the rock. He rolled a big stone in front of the entrance to the tomb and went away.

A tomb is a place where people in the ancient world would place the dead. It was a holding place for things that no longer had life. Jesus was placed in a tomb because He was dead. He was counted as a loss. And was believed to no longer have any possibility of having life again.

What are things in your life that you've placed in a tomb? What are the things that you've counted as loss and are dead to you? Is it a relationship? Is it a hope or a dream that was squashed or squandered? It could even be how you think about your own life. You might feel like your life is all but dead. Maybe you're cruising on auto pilot just waiting for this all to end and be over. There are things in our life that we believe are dead, things we believe have no possibilities or potential, and we've wrapped them up and buried them in tombs. Counted as dead and to never be seen again. This is OK for some things. For others though, even though they may be dead, God might have other plans. Plans that involve rolled away stones and empty tombs.

What part of your life needs resurrecting? Are you willing to turn it over to God so that you can trust Him to bring it back to life?

STONE

> *Mark 16:1-3* <

When the Sabbath was over. Mary Magdalene. Mary the mother of James. and Salome bought spices so that they might go to anoint Jesus' body. Very early on the first day of the week. just after sunrise. they were on their way to the tomb and they asked each other. "Who will roll the stone away from the entrance of the tomb?"

In the book of Mark, as the women walked to the tomb early that morning, Scripture tells us that they talked and asked each other, concerned who would remove the stone for them so that they could get to the body of Jesus to finish preparing His for burial. There was a barrier between them and what was inside the tomb, namely, Jesus.

There are barriers between us and Jesus too. We each have stones between us and our God. For many of us it's something that we do. It could be addictions, apathy, fear, or pride. For others of us there are things that stand between us and Jesus that we didn't put there ourselves. There could be barriers of sexual or physical abuse, abandonment or life situations that we did not choose for ourselves. It could be a number of things, but barriers exist between us and our God and there's nothing we can do ourselves to remove them. It's beyond our power to roll them away.

Notice that although they did not know how they would remove this barrier, the women went anyways. We must do the same. Although we have no clue how we will come closer to our God, we must come believing there will be a way. It is incredible what can happen when we come, seeking, and trusting.

EMPTY

> John 20:6-7 <

Then Simon Peter. who was behind him. arrived and went into the tomb. He saw the strips of linen lying there. as well as the burial cloth that had been around Jesus' head. The cloth was folded up by itself. separate from the linen.

Nothing. Bare. Completely empty besides the bindings that once wrapped His lifeless body. Where is He? What happened? Oh, no. They stole His body.

Sometimes when we're surprised we don't know what to do with the thing we're surprised with. We don't understand all of what has happened and have a difficult time accepting it. Even beyond accepting it, we have a hard time processing it. What happens when we expect things to go a certain way and now everything is completely different than we thought it would be? What happens when the hopelessness that we have felt and are expecting to feel are replaced by questions and the slightest glimmers of hope? What happens when our world, destroyed and left in ashes, begins to reform? This is the scary uncertain beginning of resurrection.

The crazy thing about resurrection is that they never expected it. Mary and the others never saw it coming. We miss resurrection too. We never expect it because whatever is being resurrected was completely dead, no life, no potential, and no hope. No hope that is until that faint glimmer of hope appears out of nowhere. Remember those things that we put in our tombs, those things that are dead and have no chance of being alive again? Yeah, those things are some of the most prime candidates for resurrection.

What tombs in your life is God making empty? What parts of you that were dead is God bringing back to life? You might want to check those tombs again. There might be life stirring inside.

MORNING

> Luke 24:2-3 <

They found the stone rolled away from the tomb, but when they entered, they did not find the body of the Lord Jesus.

You know what morning is don't you? It's the time of the day where darkness ends and light begins. It's interesting. Darkness is at its strongest just before the morning comes. The darkness that enveloped the earth after Jesus was dead was darkest that morning just before the sun rose. But just as the celestial sun rose over the earth and shown its radiant light over everything, the Son of God broke forth over creation that morning expelling darkness and making everything look completely different.

What we have to know is that the night we often encounter in our lives won't last forever. Trust me. There's hope. There's always a tomorrow. There's always a reason to wait out the darkness and look towards the break of day. There will be days where it feels as though the darkness will last forever and there's not hope of a tomorrow. Remember that there's never a time where hope is absent. If the empty tomb that morning tells us anything, it tells us this: as people who believe in resurrection, we can, must, always hope.

With Christ and an empty tomb hope is only one sunrise away.

ANGEL

>Luke 24:4-8<

While they were wondering about this, suddenly two men in clothes that gleamed like lightning stood beside them. In their fright the women bowed down with their faces to the ground, but the men said to them. "Why do you look for the living among the dead? He is not here; he has risen! Remember how he told you, while he was still with you in Galilee: 'The Son of Man must be delivered into the hands of sinful men, be crucified and on the third day be raised again.'" Then they remembered his words.

In the story of the resurrection there are several messengers who interact with the Mary's and the Disciples. The word *angel* when literally translated means messenger. These angels were there at the tomb and were announcing that everything was different. They were announcing to the women that morning that they no longer needed to cry or mourn because the one they believed to be dead was alive and was going to meet them.

We all have angels in our lives, messengers of hope, grace, and love. These people step into our darkest moments, our moments of deepest despair, and announce that death can no longer hold back the forces of goodness and life. For me these people have come in all forms. Some were people who were very close to me and journeyed with me through some of my most difficult times. Others were only in my life for a short time but in those brief moments they spoke words that helped me see empty tombs and life where I only though death existed.

Who are the angels in your life who have spoken hope where hope was lost? Who were your angels at the tomb?

LENT 40
TELL

> *Matthew 28:7* <

Then go quickly and tell his disciples: 'He has risen from the dead and is going ahead of you into Galilee. There you will see him.' Now I have told you.

Go quickly and tell . . .

We're here. It's Easter. We stand in awe at an empty tomb. Death did not win and we now have nothing to fear. Our God is alive and well. But that's not the end of the story. The story continues with us. After the angel told the women that Jesus had risen he showed them His burial clothes and gave them an explicit instructions. "Go quickly and tell the disciples."

We have a job. We have been witness to the amazing power of God in and through the life, teaching, and resurrection of Jesus. We've witnessed how Jesus heals, loves, gives, and refuses to yield to death. We've witnessed the living Christ and now we must go. We must go and tell the world our story. The angel didn't say go and tell the world a bunch of theological ideas or how they are wrong. The angel said to go and tell them that Jesus is no longer in the tomb and that God had raised Him from death to life. We are called to witness to the way Jesus still lives even.

Even more so we are to witness to how those things have changed our lives and how we're examples of resurrection. When we really know and experience the power of a Jesus who did so much, how can we not tell the story of our God? Now, go quickly and tell . . .

ADVENT 1
EXPECTATION

> *Isaiah 9:6* <

For to us a child is born. to us a son is given. and the government will be on his shoulders. And he will be called Wonderful Counselor. Mighty God. Everlasting Father. Prince of Peace.

It's Christmas season! You can just feel it in the air. Everywhere you go you are reminded of that magical day that comes On December 25. Christmas trees, music on the radio, red bows, twinkling lights, not to mention the excitement that comes long with getting out of school for Christmas break. This really is an exciting time of year. Beyond all of the commercials, lights, songs, and shopping there's something that quietly lies at the heart of this exciting season. It's not found in boxes or even in family gatherings around a festive table. It's the story of a young mother, a reluctant father, and a tiny baby that would change the world forever.

As we enter into this holiday season I want to challenge you to rethink your holiday and begin to also celebrate these "holy days." In no way am I suggesting that we shouldn't celebrate with presents, singing jingle bells, or by drinking hot chocolate. Those are all fun and exciting ways to celebrate this wonderful time of year. Instead I want you to make sure you're not simply expecting presents around a tree, or a two-week break from school. Take a moment to mentally rework what all you're expecting. Starting today, look forward to December 25 by expecting the birth of Jesus. Join me on this journey through the story of His birth as we move from simply celebrating holidays, to beginning to celebrate holy days.

ADVENT 2
FEAR

>*Luke 1:29-30*<

Mary was greatly troubled at his words and wondered what kind of greeting this might be. But the angel said to her. "Do not be afraid. Mary. you have found favor with God."

It's unusual to begin such an exciting and festive season with the topic of fear, but remember we're not just thinking about the holidays, but about holy days. This holy season starts with a young teenage girl, engaged and unexpectedly pregnant. Let's just be honest: this isn't how most of us would plan on bringing the Savior of humanity into the world. Not anywhere close! Poor young Mary was terribly scared and I am sure felt terribly alone. It's strange to not only begin the story of Jesus with a pregnant teenager, but also in such a scary time and place. So much of the beginning of the story of Jesus' life was a story of fear.

As we enter into this holiday season, fear is one of the things that can begin to creep in. As school begins to wind down there's a fear of finals and grades coming in. Often there's also a fear of times with family over the holiday as it can be a very difficult time of year as many families are apart and divorced.

I want to encourage you that while there can be many things to fear this time of year, there are so many more things to look forward to. I also want you to know that as you interact with your parents they can often be full of fear. Fear of family dynamics, fear of not making Christmas "big" or meaningful enough, major anxiety about just how busy Christmas is, and so on . . . This alone can be a major stressor on families and can turn these holy days into busy days. So as we enter into this holy season, commit to keep it holy, less busy, and less fearful.

ADVENT 3
ANGEL

>*Luke 1:26-28*<

In the sixth month, God sent the angel Gabriel to Nazareth, a town in Galilee, to a virgin pledged to be married to a man named Joseph, a descendant of David. The virgin's name was Mary. The angel went to her and said, "Greetings, you who are highly favored! The Lord is with you."

There's a central message that we see from angels throughout the Bible: do not be afraid. Angels were messengers with a word from God for people. I think it's interesting that so many of their messages started with or were "do not be afraid." It tells us something about our condition. We are often fearful. It's not just a message of "do not be afraid" but it's also a message that tells us that there are things that are coming that we may not know of yet, but will radically change our lives, and be a source of God's joy in our lives and in the world. Mary was all alone in this world and an angel came to greet her, encourage her, and tell her that she wasn't truly alone.

We all have "angels" in our lives, those people who drop into our lives at just the right moment with a message from God. They're not floating beings with halos and wings; they're just people like you and me who God chooses to speak goodness through. Who are your angels? Who have been those people in your life who help you re-center and know that you're not alone? I have had many and hope to have many more. The other piece of this equation to ask is, "who have you been an angel to"? Some you might know but I bet there are many people who you've been an angel to and you will never find out. I think that's one of the cool parts of how this works.

God does things through us without us even knowing sometimes. During this holiday season, pray that God will use you as an angel to speak hope into a life that needs an encouraging word.

SHAME

> *Matthew 1:19* <

Because Joseph her husband was a righteous man and did not want to expose her to public disgrace. he had in mind to divorce her quietly.

Can you imagine Mary, a teenage girl, pregnant and alone? Maybe you can. Maybe you have or are experiencing that, or maybe you've been in a place in your life where you felt abandoned, scared, and without hope. I imagine that Mary felt shame; while none of this was her fault it was still a shameful place to be in. You might know this feeling as well. Maybe your shame is because of something you did, maybe it's because of something that someone else did to you, or maybe it's do to a life situation where no one is at fault but you still feel ashamed anyways.

There are a couple of things that are important to know about shame. If someone has done something to you that caused you to feel shame, you need to talk to an adult about it. I mean it. Especially if it's some-thing they shouldn't have done, something that has hurt you in some way or another. If it's something that you've done and you feel badly, you need to know that our God is a God that forgives. God forgives and forgives without question or nuance.

Many of us feel shame around this time of year for other reasons though. We feel shame because we might not have as much mon-ey as other families, not get as many presents, deal with separated or dysfunctional families, or that that we're dealing with holiday depression. Each of these things, as well as others, can consume our thoughts and define our actions and moods. When we expe-rience shame, it's important to remember that the mother of our Lord experienced the same thing. But she didn't let it rule her or intimidate her. She listened to God's messenger and found comfort and confidence that she didn't have to be afraid or feel badly. Our God is not a God who delights in shame. Find comfort that God doesn't desire you to feel shame and guilt. These aren't from God.

MALL

> *Galatians 4:4* <

But when the time had fully come. God sent his Son. born of a woman. born under law.

There is the mall and then there is the mall at Christmas time. The mall in and of itself can be a pretty overwhelming place, but when it is Christmas it is a zoo. Everything gets ramped up: the decorations, the number of workers, the displays, and of course the sales. When you walk through the mall at Christmas, everyone is tugging and pulling at you to try to get your attention, and to get you to come into their store and to buy something. It's a constant sensory overload of people wanting things from you. It is a lot like being a teenager nowadays.

When you're in school, there are always things that are competing for your attention, good things, bad things, and things that don't really even matter. Each one pulling and tugging wanting you to pay attention to what it has to say or asking for what it wants. Friends, enemies, frenemies, teachers, coaches, band directors, dance teachers, grades, clubs, and everything in between, pulls and tugs for your attention and your time. You live a life today where more is wanted from you than any other generation. You have so many more opportunities and distractions than generations before you and because of that, you have to learn how to handle them differently than any other generation before you.

When you go to the mall you can't spend money you do not have; there is only so much you have in your pocket. That money is a lot like your time. Although there are tons of things wanting your attention, you only have so much time that you can give them. There are only so many hours in a day. So budget your time well. Only spend it on things that really matter and that really make sense in your life. Remember, not everything that wants your attention, is something that you really need to give your time and attention to.

ADVENT 6

PRESENTS

>1 Corinthians 7:7<

I wish that all men were as I am. But each man has his own gift from God:
one has this gift. another has that.

For some, maybe many, presents or gifts are the main focus of Christmas. I mean, do you blame them? Who doesn't want to receive a gift, out of nowhere, for no reason? You didn't earn it, do anything to deserve it, and may not have even asked for it. It's not only a surprise but a gesture of kindness and love. For many people the giving of gifts is equally as enjoyable. Each of us have gifts that we're called to give. They are a little different than the ones at Christmas. You can't wrap them up and put a bow on them and you can't find them at a store in the mall. They are gifts that live in you.

God has given each and everyone of us different gifts that are given to be share with the world. Think about it: What are you good at? What are the things you really have a passion for and do well? What are the things that live in you that you know or are discovering that you can use for and give to the world? These don't have to just be things that we usually label as being "spiritual." When we do this, we're limiting God. We usually think of these gifts as things like praying, interpreting the Bible, telling others about Jesus, and so on. These are gifts but they are gifts just like being really good at math, being an excellent artist, or having a knack for working with animals.

Whatever God has gifted you with, live into it and know that all gifts that you have can be give to others and the world in God's name. Now go and give your gift to the world.

JOURNEY

> *Luke 2:4* <

So Joseph also went up from the town of Nazareth in Galilee to Judea, to Bethlehem the town of David, because he belonged to the house and line of David.

About a year ago I was in Israel for a pilgrimage (a fancy word for a trip where you go to holy places and seek God through those experiences). While I was in Israel I had the privilege of going on a journey from Nazareth to the town of Bethlehem. This is the same journey that Mary and Joseph took so many years ago, well sort of. I didn't ride a mule or a camel. I rode in a car. I had air conditioning; good thing too because it got to 115 that day. We were able to stop and get supplies as we needed and we were never worried about bandits on the road robbing us or finding somewhere to stay the night. Come to think about it I don't remember worrying about anything on my journey that day. It was relatively uneventful, other than be important parts like visiting the sites, which was amazing. I just imagine Mary and Joseph's journey being much more difficult and having a lot more questions than certainties.

That's the way life is sometimes; you just don't know what the journey will hold. Sometimes it will be full of excitement and promise. Other times, full of fear and uncertainty. No matter where you are in your journey and what type of journey you're on, I want to encourage you that God is with you on that journey. God was with Mary and Joseph and God will be with you. That doesn't mean the journey will be any easier or go as planned. It just means that no matter what happens you will never journey alone.

BETHLEHEM

>Luke 2:5<

He went there to register with Mary, who was pledged to be married to him and was expecting a child.

A lot of times when we think about Bethlehem we think of children's plays and Christmas cards with a perfectly clear night sky and a picturesque wooden stable. Bethlehem was not supposed to happen for Mary and Joseph. For all we know they didn't have many friends in Bethlehem. Bethlehem was foreign. Bethlehem was a detour; it wasn't the destination. Bethlehem wasn't inviting. It proved to be inhospitable. Bethlehem was an accident; it definitely wasn't home. They weren't planning on being there; they had somewhere else they had to be. They had other plans, then Jesus came. When Jesus came, it put Mary and Joseph in a spot they hadn't intended on being in. They had to improvise and do it quickly.

The first Christmas may very well have been nothing like we imagine it to be. I bet a lot of your Christmases are similar in that way. It just doesn't look like the television shows and Christmas cards portray it. It's messy, rarely goes as planned, and can be pretty tough to deal with sometimes. Just like the first Christmas, we set up expectations as to what Christmas is "supposed" to look like. Unfortunately those beautiful ideas are usually not very realistic and we find ourselves feeling disappointed because we subscribe to expectations that are not based in realities but in ideals.

Bethlehem was tough and it was messy, but look what came out of it. Just because your family is a little messed up or things do not go exactly as planned does not mean that Christmas isn't just as meaningful. It can be, and should be. This Christmas lets lower the expectations based on movies and cards and lets set it in grace, peace and hope for imperfect people and families.

ADVENT 9
HOPE

> *Luke 2:6* <

While they were there, the time came for the baby to be born.

Hope is a word that's used a lot around Christmas. "I hope your brother will be able to come home from college this Christmas." "I hope this year will be less busy than the last" "I hope I get everything I asked for from Santa!" Christmas is a season of hope. It's a time where we celebrate the coming of Christ into the world. Through the darkest of situations, in one of the most difficult of times, God brought this light into the world. We know that hope exists because Christ was born.

I do wonder, with how often and in how so many ways the word is used, what hope really means to us today? I think that if we really think about it and the way we use it, it doesn't reflect the kind of hope that God calls us to. Usually when we talk about hope it's something we're not certain will happen or that we really want to happen. When we see hope in the Bible, as people of faith, we get to hope in a different way. We get to hope, believing that God already has given us a promise.

We don't hope aimlessly, simply wanting something. We hope believing that something is already in the works, and that God is already up to something. We hope, not in spite of what might happen, but believing that something better is already happening as we speak.

MANGER

>*Luke 2:7*<

And she gave birth to her firstborn, a son. She wrapped him in cloths and placed him in a manger, because there was no room for them in the inn.

Sometimes our expectations don't match God's. If I'm being honest, I would have never choose to bring the Savior of the World into that world the way God chose to. Here's how I would have gone about it: First, I would've had Jesus born into a family that mattered, someone with influence. If nothing else I would've had Him born to someone that was at least married! Also, let's not have a census that's going to drag them away from friends and family. Let's have them set up at home, nice and happy, so that others can be there to be a part of this monumental event.

This leads me to my next point: No Publicity. What? OK, sure, a star. But there are lots of stars. Why not a giant arrow in the sky with big flashy letters saying "Jesus"? Also, Bethlehem? Why couldn't God have waited until they were a little further down the road in Jerusalem? Jerusalem . . . that's a big place full of important people, not Bethlehem. Then we have the shepherds and wise men. Not exactly the press or dignitaries I would've brought to the table. Well, at least the wise men brought some good gifts. Finally the stable and manger. Nope. Not happening. If it I couldn't find a giant mansion, I'd at least have Jesus born somewhere He didn't have to compete with cows for sleeping quarters.

I say all of this jokingly to make a point: the Son of God, the one who would change everything, lying there in a hay-trough borrowed from feeding animals. A manger . . . Bethlehem . . . My way makes way more sense, to me. But that's why God's ways are different and better than mine. Celebrate this truth today.

STAR

>*Matthew 2:10*<

When they saw the star. they were overjoyed.

A star. There are millions of them in the sky. I remember one night down in Central America, in Panama. There were no artificial lights for miles and miles and the night was crystal clear. I was blown away by the incredible number of stars I could see that night. I've never seen anything like it. But for some reason, this one star stood out from all of the others that night. It made me think of the star in the Christmas story.

There was something about that one star, guiding others to the place where Jesus was born. I often wonder what it looked like. Was it a different shape? Was it brighter than the rest? Something was different. Something made it stand out in the midst of millions of others. The truth is that the star stood out because it had a purpose. Its purpose was to be different. And it was apparently different enough to grab other's attention and direct them to Bethlehem.

There are over 6 billion people in our world. Sometimes I feel like just one among those billions. I bet you do too. The difference is that we have a reason to stand out. We have a reason to shine brighter and be bolder than so many of the others. Jesus told us to be salt and light. We're called to stand out to be different and to show others, through the night, where Jesus is. So many times there are people who shine bright and only bring attention to themselves. We have the opportunity to shine and stand out and then point others to God. For some, the world can be a dark, cold place. What will you do to shine bright and show the way to Jesus?

MAGI

> *Matthew 2:7-8* <

Then Herod called the Magi secretly and found out from them the exact time the star had appeared. He sent them to Bethlehem and said. "Go and make a careful search for the child. As soon as you find him. report to me. so that I too may go and worship him."

The Gospel of Matthew tells us about a group of wise men who came to visit Jesus, worship Him, and give Him gifts. Sometimes these men are referred to as kings, but most scholars believe that they were actually priests of another religion who came to Jesus because they focused on and read the stars. There's something about Christmas that attracts all sorts of people, not just people who call themselves Christians.

At Christmas, especially in the US, it doesn't matter if you have not been to church in the whole year, you will probably find yourself at some sort church around Christmas. Something about the season attracts all sorts of people, not just those who actively follow Christ. Just like the Magi, they come. So my question is, "what will they find when they come"? Sometimes we do everything we can to attract people to Christianity and when they finally come we don't have a lot to show them. We must have a faith that is authentic and real, or else we run the risk of bringing them to a stable with an empty manger.

Who are the Magi in your life? Who are those people who are interested in the faith but are not yet convinced? I bet you have friends like that at school and on your teams. Or maybe at your job. I would also bet that there are even a number of people in your own youth group who aren't quite convinced yet either. So what kind of faith will you show them? Is it a faith that's deeply meaningful, thoughtful, and full of passion? Or will it be a faith that disappoints when they get too close? They are seeking. What will be there when they arrive?

ADVENT 13
SHEPHERDS

>*Luke 2:8-12*<

And there were shepherds living out in the fields nearby, keeping watch over their flocks at night. An angel of the Lord appeared to them, and the glory of the Lord shone around them, and they were terrified. But the angel said to them, "Do not be afraid. I bring you good news of great joy that will be for all the people. Today in the town of David a Savior has been born to you; he is Christ the Lord. This will be a sign to you: You will find a baby wrapped in cloths and lying in a manger."

There was another set of visitors who came to see Jesus as an infant. The Bible says that there were shepherds who were looking after their sheep that night. They were approached by angels and told about Jesus. These shepherds came and they saw what God had promised them, and they left and began to spread the word about what they'd seen. It didn't say that they saw Jesus and learned a ton about Him, and decided a good strategy and then went and spread the word. It just says that they went.

I love the shepherds' enthusiasm. If you noticed it doesn't say that they went and tried to convince people to come and worship this baby, nor does it say that they had it all figured out before they went. It just says that they went and told what they had experienced and what had been told to them about this baby. I want you to think about what you've experienced with God. How has God made Himself known to you and changed you? Secondly, what have others told you about their experience with God? Lastly, who was the last person you told about your experience? I don't mean who's the last person you invited to church. Jesus never tells us that we should invite people to church. He does tell us repeatedly that we should tell people about our experience with Him. There's a difference.

The shepherds wanted others to know what they had experienced. What have you experienced? How can that be helpful to others? What will you tell them about Jesus?

GIFTS

> *Matthew 2:11* <

On coming to the house, they saw the child with his mother Mary, and they bowed down and worshiped him. Then they opened their treasures and presented him with gifts of gold and of incense and of myrrh.

I think that it's such a neat part of the story that the wise men brought gifts to this baby. I picture them laying these really expensive gifts of gold, frankincense, and myrrh around his little manger. It's interesting that those gifts are not really for a baby; they're for other times in a person's life. I bet they didn't know what Jesus would do with them, but they brought them anyways. We're called to do the same thing.

We're called to bring our gifts to Jesus, no matter what they are or what we think Jesus will do with them. Our call is to bring them and commit them to God. Sometimes, in churches, we make the mistake of valuing certain gifts over others. In churches we often will value gifts like leadership, singing, and speaking, to name a few, and this is wrong. Just because you don't do the "up front" stuff doesn't mean that God can't or won't do just as much if not more with your gifts. A lot of times because we value some over others, it keeps away people with less up front gifts. I don't care if you are an incredible writer, or you can fix a car, or you can kick a soccer ball the length of the field, God wants you to bring those gifts and offer them.

No matter what you do, you need to remember that you have the option to do it for God. That doesn't mean that every time you write a fantastic poem that you need to kneel down and do a prayer before you turn it in to the teacher. It just means that when you do these things, you understand them as an act of worship. It also means that through your gifts you try to make the world a better place for people everywhere.

MIRACLE

>*Luke 1:35-37*<

The angel answered. "The Holy Spirit will come upon you. and the power of the Most High will overshadow you. So the holy one to be born will be called the Son of God. Even Elizabeth your relative is going to have a child in her old age. and she who was said to be barren is in her sixth month. For nothing is impossible with God."

Miracles are things that we rarely talk about outside of the Bible. While it's a common word in our language, we don't usually speak of them literally but figuratively. "It's a miracle we got to school on time after you took an hour long shower," or "It's a miracle that our team is still in the playoffs after that loss." We use the word but usually with no real consequence other than it being that something happened against significant odds. Most modern people don't believe that if someone touches a blind person's eyes that they'll be healed. That's just not something we talk about as modern people, even modern people who believe in God. So what do we do as modern people of faith the idea of miracles?

First, we have to believe that God still works miracles even though we don't often see them. The world is a big place. How can we know what God is or isn't doing all over the world right now? Second, I don't automatically think that miracles are only the sensational kind of miracles we see in Scripture. When I think of a miracle I think of how God chooses to work in our world in unexpected and beautiful ways. When I see reconciliation between races, it's miraculous. When I see love resurrected from betrayal, it's miraculous. When someone comes out of depression and into health, it's miraculous. It does not have to be flashy to be a miracle.

Where are you seeing miracles in your life? When have you experienced God in ways where beautiful things are made and love prevails? Start looking for the miraculous in your world and I promise you'll find that they're happening all around you. You may have just never noticed.

FAMILY

> *Joshua 24:15* <

But if serving the LORD seems undesirable to you, then choose for yourselves this day whom you will serve, whether the gods your forefathers served beyond the River, or the gods of the Amorites, in whose land you are living. But as for me and my household, we will serve the LORD.

So, I bet that most of you wouldn't say that your family is completely normal. Right? I mean, let's face it, we're all just a little (if not a lot) weird. We all have our quirks, strange habits, and imperfections that keep us from being the Brady Bunch. Few times is this more evident than at Christmas time. The stress, tension, and hectic pace of Christmas bring out some very interesting moments in a family. Here's the good news: there's no such thing as normal, especially when it comes to families. Now, don't get me wrong: there are some families that make it look "normal," but when it comes down to it we all have our problems. So did Jesus and his family.

Think about it. Mary was probably a teenager. There was some pretty serious scandal around the pregnancy. Joseph was seeing angels. They had the baby while on a really rough journey and ended up, according to at least one story, fleeing to Egypt. Yep, they had some issues. Joseph is really not even mentioned after the birth of Jesus, whereas Mary is throughout the life of Jesus. It couldn't have been easy. They also had a blended family. We know that Jesus had siblings, and we also know that Joseph was not Jesus' biological dad. See? It wasn't perfect by any means. But it worked.

What about your family? What makes you different? Blended? Divorced? Still together but a little crazy? A brother or sister who is a little wild? During this holiday season, make sure to not let that get you down. All of our families are a little crazy, even Jesus' family. When you really think about it, that's what normal family looks like. Enjoy your normal family this Christmas!

TREE

> *Psalm 145:13* <

The LORD is faithful to all his promises and loving toward all he has made.

So the first thing about a Christmas tree is that it is totally not in the Bible. I mean, it would've been cool if the shepherds would've brought a little shrub from the desert and had the wise men decorated it with gems. That would be cool if that was how we got our Christmas tree tradition. But it's not. There are several origin stories for the Christmas tree, but the most probable is that they originated in Germany in the 1500's. So why does it matter? Well, for me it matters because it's a place where we gather. If your home is like mine, my wife, my three kids and I go and we pick out a tree together, which is a big deal of course. We then take it in, untie it, put it in the holder and together we decorate it.

Our Christmas tree doesn't have a lot of fancy decorations that we bought at a store. It's covered by hand made decorations and decorations that were ours when we were kids and have been passed down. As we take each decoration out of the box there is a story that comes with each. My first Christmas. My wife's ornament from when she was born. One that my great grandmother, who died when I was a baby, gave me (it is my favorite). And so on. Our kids have special ornaments too. They have ornaments that they made, and some that have their pictures from when they were babies. We hang them, decorate the tree, and then finally light the entire thing.

Why is a tree important? Because it is a place to share stories, old memories, and make new memories with family that will be shared for lifetimes. It doesn't have to be a tree, but it's so important to share stories with each other, as family, and friends. What are your traditions that bring you closer to your family?

STOCKINGS

>*Psalm 136:1*<

Give thanks to the LORD. for he is good. His love endures forever. Give thanks to the God of gods. His love endures forever. Give thanks to the Lord of lords: His love endures forever.

Again, stockings are definitely not in the Bible. But that's OK! Not all traditions have to be. The original story behind hanging stockings was that the socks, also known as stockings, were hung by the fireplace to dry out after being soaked from walking around outside in the snow. Then when Santa Clause came, these stockings were filled with fruit and nuts and if someone were really lucky, a small toy. There were not stacks of presents around a tree. There were no boxes on top of boxes of lavish gifts. It was only some fruit, nuts, and maybe a trinket of sorts.

When I look at our stockings I can't help but be reminded that no matter what we "get" for Christmas, we should be so thankful. Sometimes people get wrapped up in trying to get the perfect presents or making sure that a certain dollar amount is spent. Some people even will become depressed or upset when they don't get what they want. Stockings remind me that most of us already have everything we need anyways. It's incredible just how much we all have, and how much we don't need.

This is not a devotion to make you feel badly about what you have, but to help you feel grateful and content with what you don't have. So as you hang your stockings by the chimney with care, make sure you also hang them with gratitude and thanksgiving for all we have.

FAMILY CHRISTMAS 1

>Luke 2:1-3<

In those days Caesar Augustus issued a decree that a census should be taken of the entire Roman world. (This was the first census that took place while Quirinius was governor of Syria.) And everyone went to his own town to register.

On this Christmas Eve, ask if your family can sit together and read the Christmas story together. Most know the version that is in Luke 2:1-21. Read this together, maybe even different members of the family reading different parts.

When you finish, ask what everyone's favorite part was and why. Then go and do something fun together, make some hot chocolate, or wassail. Watch a Christmas movie, or play a board game.

Whatever you do, just make sure to do it together.

FAMILY CHRISTMAS 2

>*Luke 2:13-14*<

Suddenly a great company of the heavenly host appeared with the angel, praising God and saying, "Glory to God in the highest, and on earth peace to men on whom his favor rests."

It's Christmas morning. There's so much anticipation and excitement. Your parents are probably pretty tired so if you can, help them out and be patient. Before you all open your presents, take a moment together and each person answer this one question about each person in the room:

I'm thankful to God for you because . . .

This is a great way to start your day in a way that's not focused around presents, but the gift that God has given you as a family. The gifts that truly matter.

Merry Christmas!!!!

CHRISTMAS EVE

>Luke 2:1-5<

In those days Caesar Augustus issued a decree that a census should be taken of the entire Roman world. (This was the first census that took place while Quirinius was governor of Syria.) And everyone went to his own town to register. So Joseph also went up from the town of Nazareth in Galilee to Judea, to Bethlehem the town of David, because he belonged to the house and line of David. He went there to register with Mary, who was pledged to be married to him and was expecting a child.

You may have a younger brother or sister that you can remember when they were born. You might remember some excitement and some anxiety as your parents waited for this new little baby to come into the world. As a parent of three kids I can't describe to you how incredible and how nerve wracking it is leading up to your child being born. In a day with modern medicine, technology, cars, and hospitals we have it pretty easy when it comes to having babies.

In the days of Mary and Joseph it wasn't anywhere near as pleasant. It was also not too pleasant that they were on the road, away from home, with nowhere to stay. It had to be completely crazy for this man and especially his young bride. I couldn't imagine just how anxious they were as they waited on God to send His only son into the world through Mary.

Sometimes we find ourselves waiting on God to come into our situations. We wait nervously, trusting that God has a plan and will do what He needs to do. But it can be so nerve wracking, full of fear, and anxiety. As people of faith, we have faith in God that He will not leave us out to dry, but sometimes waiting drives us crazy. When I'm in these situations I can't help but think of Mary and Joseph on that night so long ago. Waiting. Waiting and waiting some more. They just had to wait on what God was going to do. In the midst of a very scary time in history, and a very scary part of the world, all they could do is wait on the miracle that God was going to perform in their lives. On this Christmas eve, I encourage you, even as you wait for the amazingly fun day that tomorrow will bring, think about how Mary and Joseph and how they waited on the work that God would do in their world.

CHRISTMAS DAY

>*Luke 2:6-7*<

While they were there, the time came for the baby to be born, and she gave birth to her firstborn, a son. She wrapped him in cloths and placed him in a manger, because there was no room for them in the inn.

Read Luke 2:6-21. It's a beautiful day. Today is one of the two most holy days of the Christian year. Today is a day to celebrate, be with friends and family, and remember the day that our Lord was born into this world. I will not write a long devotion today because there are a lot of things you should be doing other than reading my words. But I will challenge you with this: Read the nativity story. Take your time and read it slowly. Don't rush but read each word taking it in and imagining the story playing out in front of you. Be grateful for what happened and know that God still births miracles into our world today.

Even in the most uncertain of places God is still doing amazing work. Read the story again. Go and be with the people you love and the people who love you. Celebrate, laugh, smile, take a nap, and know that our God love us so much that He sent His son into this pretty crazy world to live, to love, and to show us a better way. Go and live that better way today.

NEW YEARS EVE

>*Ecclesiastes 3:11*<

He has made everything beautiful in its time. He has also set eternity in the hearts of men; yet they cannot fathom what God has done from beginning to end.

So here we sit. Another year has gone by and we look at the dawn of a new beginning. As you look back at the past year what do you see? Do you see pain or joy? Do you see helpfulness or the need for help? Do you see things you're proud of or things you wish you didn't have to remember? If we're being honest we can probably answer each of these questions with a yes.

There's no such thing as a perfect year and there's no such thing as a year that had no goodness in it. I love this verse in Ecclesiastes 3. It helps give us perspective and a long view that, in time, God can make everything beautiful. I want you to think about the things in this past year that don't seem beautiful. Things that are ugly, embarrassing, and maybe even scary. Look at them and give them over to God, asking God to make all things beautiful. I also want you to think about your accomplishments, the things you are proud of, and the things that make you swell with joy. Give those over to God and ask God to make them beautiful too.

After, you have looked back, look forward. Look forward to what God is going to do in your life next year. Look forward to how God will use even the bad things that will happen next year for beauty in the world. Today you stand at a crossroads. It's a line in the sand where you have the opportunity to reflect and think about what God has done, but you also get to look forward to what God is going to do. Pray for God's beauty in your life and to make your life a thing of beauty for all of those who you meet in this coming year.

NEW YEARS DAY

>2 Corinthians 5:17<

Therefore, if anyone is in Christ, he is a new creation: the old has gone, the new has come!

New Years is an amazing time. It's a time of hope, excitement, and possibilities! It's a time of year where we believe that anything is possible. We have renewed confidence in ourselves that we can do what we set our minds to and be a different person. Sometimes we think about this in how we eat, or exercise, or even spiritual matters like reading our Bibles, praying, or doing good in the world. No matter what it is we feel like, we can be a new creation because it's a new year.

Sadly so many of our New Year's resolutions fall by the wayside and we find ourselves falling into old patters and relearning old habits. I want to encourage you before that time comes that if you're a Christ-follower (which you probably are if you're reading this) you're already a new creation. God has changed us in a way that's significant and that matters. The change that God does in us is a real and permanent change. While diets and resolutions are really good things, we have to remember that they are both things that we are choosing to try to do. The difference in this and becoming a new creation the way Paul describes it is that something is being done to us. We're being changed, not changing ourselves.

So this New Year's pray that God will continue to change you, mold you, shape you, and develop you into that creation that He is calling you to be. Keep on working on the resolutions; they're good! But remember whether you keep them or not, there's a good work being done inside you by God all of the time.

YOUR BIRTHDAY

>*Numbers 6:24-26*<

The LORD bless you and keep you; the LORD make his face shine upon you and be gracious to you; the LORD turn his face toward you and give you peace.

Congratulations!!! You were born!!! Not only that, you were born today!!! Well, not really today as in this day, but this day several years ago . . . But it's still exciting! You were given the greatest gift anyone could ever ask for. You were given the gift of life. This is a gift that has incredible potential and incredible possibilities. Because you were born, you can love, you can breathe, you can give people high fives, you can cry, you can hug, you can throw a ball, you can watch a movie, you can write a poem, you can watch a tree wave in the wind, you can smell the rain, you can hear a baby cry, you can eat lunch, you can love and be loved, you can feel the sun warm your skin and the cold give you goose bumps . . . There's so MUCH you can do. You can sing aloud, you can fall asleep on a warm afternoon, and you can wake up to a new and exciting day, all because you were born.

You have these things and so many more to look forward to. My prayer for you on this, your birthday, is that you will really live. So much so that when the day comes where you will live no more, you can look back at your life and smile at the wondrous things you experienced and did in the name of God. I want you to live a life that you feel and that others feel the effects of. Live today. And know that today is a gift, not only to you but to everyone who knows you. Finally read the blessing from Numbers and let it be a blessing to you on this amazing day where God gave the world the gift of you. Happy Birthday!

MLK DAY

> *Mark 6:4* <

Jesus said to them. "Only in his hometown. among his relatives and in his own house is a prophet without honor."

Usually when we talk about prophets, we think of people in the Old Testament who would preach the fiery message of God to others and hope for their repentance. We think of names like Elijah, Amos, Jonah, Micah, Zachariah, Isaiah, Ezekiel, and Jeremiah. We usually don't think of the prophet Martin.

Martin Luther King, Jr. was a modern day prophet. He, like the other prophets saw the world as it was, and then God gave him a vision of how it could be. Not only did God give him a vision, God gave him a fire that could not be quenched until his work was done. Dr. King drew his inspiration from many of these prophets, quoting them often in his sermons and speeches. But just as Jesus said, it's very difficult for a prophet to be respected in his own land. Being a prophet for God isn't easy; your life is always on the line, and sometimes it's with your life that you pay the ultimate cost. Dr. King looked at the world and believed that God had a different plan for it and he told the world that plan. Some despised him, while others cheered him on. One man even despised this message of hope and equality so much that he killed this amazing man of God.

On this day that celebrates his birthday, it's important to remember that God doesn't only call prophets to see the world as it could be and work for that change. God calls you and I to do that too. Do not let the memories of these incredible prophets become faded visions lost in statues and paintings. Let their prophetic spirit come alive in you. Go and speak truth in love and help this world take one step closer to the reality that God envisions for us all.

VALENTINES DAY

>1 Corinthians 13:4-7<

Love is patient. love is kind. It does not envy. it does not boast. it is not proud. It is not rude. it is not self-seeking. it is not easily angered. it keeps no record of wrongs. Love does not delight in evil but rejoices with the truth. It always protects. always trusts. always hopes. always perseveres.

In case you didn't know, or have never been to a wedding, the 13th chapter of 1 Corinthians is the "love chapter." If you're reading this on February 14th, you're probably being inundated with all sorts of sappy, red heart shaped advertisements and gift ideas that are supposed to symbolize love. There is nothing wrong with this. But love is a little more complicated than chocolates, flowers, and a pretty card.

It's important for us to know that in Greek, the language the New Testament was originally written in, there are actually four words that are all used to talk about love. We only have one. This section of verses does something special for us. Instead of trying to get us to understand each of the four different kinds of love and their nuances, it gives us a list of attributes of love. This is love that's for family, for friends, for a significant other, and even a special God-type love. As you read each of these attributes I want you to ask yourself, "How do I love in this way?" Then, "How have I seen and felt others love me in this way?" Take your time, write these observations down. Where you find yourself having a difficult time answering, mark that one to work harder on. Were you find yourself having the answers come easily mark that one too because it is obvious that aspect of love comes naturally to you.

ST. PATRICK'S DAY

>*Matthew 5:44*<

But I tell you: Love your enemies
and pray for those who persecute you.

Behind all of the funny leprechaun hats, four leaf clovers, and pots of gold there was a real man named Patrick who did some pretty amazing things in God's name. When he was only 16 he was kidnapped by some Irish raiders from his home in Britain (yep, he wasn't Irish).

By most accounts Patrick was held as a prisoner in Ireland for more than six years. During those lonely six years he became a Christian and began to follow God. After six years he escaped his Irish captors and returned to Britain. While in Britain he had a revelation that he was supposed to go back to Ireland, back to the ones who kidnapped him and took six years of his life away, and show them who God was. Can you believe it?

Just after Patrick was able to escape their captivity he returned to them. He really understood what Jesus was talking about when He said to pray for and love your enemies. Not only did he pray for them, but he wanted them to understand and come into God's love so badly that he went back to the country of his imprisonment to teach his captors. So after all of the parties and silly outfits we can really remember and be challenged by Jesus' teaching as lived out by this amazing man, St. Patrick.

EARTH DAY

> *Genesis 1:28* <

God blessed them and said to them. "Be fruitful and increase in number; fill the earth and subdue it. Rule over the fish of the sea and the birds of the air and over every living creature that moves on the ground."

Sometimes people try to say that Earth Day is some sort of hippie, "go hug a tree" sort of holiday that has nothing to do with our faith. I couldn't disagree more. Let me explain.

When we read the very first chapter in our Bible we're given the job of taking care of creation. We're called to make sure that it's taken care of and protected. In the creation account, we see God giving the job to humanity to be caretakers of something that He crafted and created. In our history many people of faith have been against taking care of the environment. Some will say that the world is in a downward spiral that we are to store up our treasures in heaven. They'll say that the world is broken and irreparable. This is simply not Biblical or Christian. There is a deep bond between creation and humanity, so deep that we don't exist outside of creation; we're a part of it. The Bible says that we came from dust and we will return to dust. To not take care of this earth, that God gave us to protect, is to go against one of the very earliest commandments.

It matters what we do to the earth and how we treat it not just because we depend on it for survival (kind of a big deal), but because God is depending on us to take care of it as well. When you advocate for the environment, you're advocating for the very things that God molded and shaped and breathed the breath of life into. If God were to hand you a precious handmade gift and told you that one of your job was to take care of it, what you would do? Yeah, me too: guard it with my life. Yep, that gift is creation. Taking care of it is an act of worship and obedience. That's a pretty big deal if you ask me.

NATIONAL DAY OF PRAYER

> *Matthew 7:12* <

So in everything, do to others what you would have them do to you, for this sums up the Law and the Prophets.

The National Day of Prayer is a very interesting day. It's always the first Thursday in May and has been in law since 1952. For so many of us who are reading this devotional, our thoughts probably shift directly to it being a uniquely Christian day that found its way into our law. We would be wrong though. The National Day of Prayer is a day where all people of faith are called upon to pray for our nation, world, and one another. This might offend some people. Yet, when I think about it, I can't help but feel inspired. Yes, our religion differs from other religions like Judaism, Hinduism, Islam and Buddhism. Unfortunately those differences have led to many wars and many terrible things done in the name of God (from us too). The National Day of Prayer reminds me that, while we're different in many ways, we can all work together for the things we have in common. We can work together for peace, taking care of those who cannot care for themselves, hunger, poverty, and goodness. Those are things that each of our religions share in common.

We also share prayer. So when you pray on this National Day of Prayer remember that there are others praying too. Others who are like you and others who are different than you. Just as you each pray on this day, remember that there are other things you can do together that are good for this world as well.

MOTHERS DAY

> *Isaiah 66:13* <

As a mother comforts her child. so will I comfort you: and you will be comforted over Jerusalem.

So often we refer to God as our Father, and for good reason. Jesus referred to God as father almost exclusively. While there are many references to God as Father, and while "Father" is the way God is most commonly projected in Scripture, you may be surprised to know that there are also many verses that show God with mother-like attributes. Isaiah 66:3 is one of those verses.

When we think of God we often think of a strong, father figure who protects us with His strength. In this image of God we see a God who comforts and nurtures us like a mother. For some, this is very helpful imagery as so much of the love that they've experienced is the love of their mother. On this Mothers day take time, if you're in relationship with your mother or if you have other mother figures in your life, to make sure to thank her for how she's nurtured you, taken care of you, and shown you a different side of God's love. Mothers can be incredible people. They carry us, birth us, cradle, and feed us. They nurture us, encourage us, and shape us into the people we are today.

For me personally, this is a tough holiday. My mother left me and my family when I was 14. It's tough in many ways but in other ways I find myself incredibly grateful. I'm grateful for those people in my life who've been like mothers to me. There are several women who have taken that role for me and I've seen God through then their nurture and their love. Find these women and honor them today.

PENTECOST

>*Acts 2:1-12*<

When the day of Pentecost came, they were all together in one place. Suddenly a sound like the blowing of a violent wind came from heaven and filled the whole house where they were sitting. They saw what seemed to be tongues of fire that separated and came to rest on each of them. All of them were filled with the Holy Spirit and began to speak in other tongues as the Spirit enabled them.

Pentecost is one of the most misunderstood Christian holy days. Many Christians are not even aware that there is such a holiday. Pentecost, in most churches, is celebrated 50 days after Easter. For this reason Pentecost falls on different Sundays each year. This church holy day commemorates what happened in Acts 2 with the coming of the Holy Spirit.

When we hear the word Pentecost many images might come to mind, one of which is the image of speaking in tongues. It's been interpreted in a variety of ways over the years. When we look at what happened at Pentecost we see one thing for sure. God's message to the Jew's through the life of Jesus became a global message to all people on the earth. The reason why they spoke in different tongues is because there was so many different languages represented there that day. God wanted the world to hear God's message, a message of love and acceptance for all people and a desire for everyone to come to God.

When we celebrate Pentecost we aren't only celebrating the coming of God's Spirit among us, we're also celebrating this incredible moment where God tells the world that His love is for everyone. No matter how different. No matter the color of their skin, their language, or their nationality. God doesn't see those things. God only sees His creation through the eyes of love. Today as you celebrate Pentecost, remember how God loves people who are just like you and are very different than you, and everywhere in between. Let this love challenge you to do the same.

FATHERS DAY

> *Matthew 3:17* <

And a voice from heaven said. "This is my Son. whom I love;
with him I am well pleased."

Today is a special day for dads everywhere. It's a day where they're honored for helping you learn to ride a bike, throwing the ball with you, holding you tightly while telling you it'll be alright after you fall or had your feelings hurt. Today is a day we tell dad's thank you for just being dad. I know that there are many who will read these words who don't have a good or existing relationship with their dad, and I'm sure that this day is difficult for you. Just as we tried to understand the role of mother in a different way, so must we understand the role of our fathers.

We have a very interesting relationship with Jesus and His father; not Joseph but His Father in heaven. Jesus talked with Him and the Father proclaimed to those at this baptism that this was His son and He was really proud of Him When this happens with our fathers it makes us feel really good. For those of us who don't have fathers in our lives these images can be very painful. No matter what our relationship with our earthly father we can know that we do have a Father in heaven who loves us, celebrates us, and wants to love us with all of his being.

As we enter into this Fathers Day make sure to thank those around you who are either your father or have acted as a father figure to you. Tell them thank you for showing you the love of God and taking care of you. It's also a good day to think about and reflect on your relationship with your Father who is in heaven.

REMEMBERING 9/11

>Luke 6:27-28<

But I tell you who hear me: Love your enemies, do good to those who hate you, bless those who curse you, pray for those who mistreat you.

Read Luke 6:27-36. Today is a complicated day for people who call themselves Christians. Today is a day where we, as people of faith, can stand in stark contrast with our culture. We have the opportunity to not simply forget but to forgive, and in some cases ask forgiveness.

We're a people whose identity rests most wholly in a doctrine of grace, a doctrine that we espouse which has no limits and casts the burden of sin as far as the East is from the West. Yet, we choose to proclaim loudly that we will never forget, implying that we will never forgive. When we do this, these battle cries quickly become the epitaphs on the tombs we put ourselves in. We chain ourselves to anger and bitterness, we hold tightly to these emotions like a teddy bear in the darkness of night, believing if we close our eyes and hold on tight enough that surely the monsters will stop haunting us and it will never happen again.

As people of faith, as followers of the Prince of Peace, our call is not to cling to the security blankets of angst and anger but to step forth into the light, knowing that we must forgive because we're people who have experienced forgiveness. But, as people of faith our reaction and our action can't be defined or propagated out of anger and pain. We must live from a greater cause and call.

Let our battle cry be one that looks forward and not backward, that grows from love and goodness and banishes hate and prejudice. Let our call be one of peace and reconciliation. May we be people who shape a world that is broken, scared and full of anger, and let us not be conformed to these vices, for we are Christ-followers. We follow and trust our Savior who purchased our life with His blood. Let us not forget what our nation lost. But let us also not forget who we are.

HALLOWEEN

> *John 11:14* <

So then he told them plainly, "Lazarus is dead."

Usually when we think of Halloween we're reminded of Jack-O-Lanterns, scary costumes, and way too much candy! There is actually a reason why those costumes are so scary. Halloween is actually a Christian holiday that commemorates and remembers those who have passed away and are no longer with us. Its real name is All Hallows Eve. It's called this because it's the night before All Saints Day. It's celebrated many different ways throughout the world, most recognizably in Mexico and other Spanish speaking countries where the celebrations are actually held at the graves of their loved ones.

Sometimes our American version of faith is all about the good, happy, and joyful things of the faith. We often shy away from those things that are especially painful, like death. Halloween is an opportunity for you, with much of the rest of the world, to remember and celebrate the lives of those who have gone on before you and are not with us now. It's a time to honor those who made a difference in our lives and showed us love and care. It is a time to remember, mourn, and be thankful for those who we no longer have here on earth with us. It might be a grandparent, an older person in the church, a parent or even a friend who died entirely too early.

This is a day, one day in the year, where we can look back at the lives of those people, be thankful for them and for us to also remember that we too will one day pass away. For me it's also a reminder that I must live this life in such a way that those who I leave behind will have fond thoughts and memories about me that they can share and remember.

ALL SAINTS DAY

> *Hebrews 12:1* <

Therefore, since we are surrounded by such a great cloud of witnesses, let us throw off everything that hinders and the sin that so easily entangles, and let us run with perseverance the race marked out for us.

There are times when I'm down and wonder if I'll ever make a difference in the world with the way I practice my faith. I often wonder if it's ever really worth it and I begin to question if I'm the only one who ever thinks these things. I also find myself during these times looking for inspiration. There are just times where I want to see how this life has been lived and has played out for others. All Saints Day, observed each year on November 1, is an opportunity to look back at the saints of our faith and celebrate their lives.

All Saints Day is a time to look back at saints of old as well as modern saints, remember them, and be inspired by them. I love this verse in Hebrews 12; it talks about being surrounded by a great cloud of witnesses. I often think of saints of our faith in this way. I see a cloud of them, those who have inspired me, trudged the grounds of faith before me, and devoted their whole lives to the way of Jesus. I see this cloud surrounding other people of faith and inspiring them and encouraging them to continue on with their work and journey.

A saint in your life might be that Sunday school teacher who helped show you faith in a different way, a youth minister, or a grandparent who always took the time to show you the love of our God. I hope, no matter who your saints are, you will take time on this day and remember those who have gone on before you, and have made a difference in your life and in the life of our faith.

THANKSGIVING

>*Colossians 3:17*<

And whatever you do, whether in word or deed, do it all in the name of the Lord Jesus, giving thanks to God the Father through him.

Thanksgiving is such a cool holiday. Sometimes we forget what Thanksgiving really is because we become so preoccupied with turkeys, stuffing, and the beginning of Christmas shopping that we often overlook what a remarkable holiday we have. Thanksgiving can be traced back to 1621 in Plymouth, MA. It was originally a celebration of a good harvest and the thankfulness of our earliest colonizers. Later, in 1863 during some of the bloodiest days of the Civil War, President Abraham Lincoln declared it a national holiday to be celebrated by all of the states. I think these two situations are very interesting and tell us a lot about how and when we are supposed to be thankful.

In the first instance, we see people who've had a very difficult time settling a new land who feel like they're finally catching a break with a very good harvest. They want to show their thankfulness for these blessings and good fortune with the harvest. In the other instance we find the scene much more dire. It was 1863 and a new nation was fighting one of its bloodiest wars, a war within its own borders against its own people. It was one of the scariest times in our country's history. In the middle of this incredibly fearful and scary time, our president, Abraham Lincoln, declared that the country should pause and be thankful for everything we have together.

So on this Thanksgiving Day I want you to pause and be thankful. Whether it's a great day full of blessing or a day that's in the middle of a terrible period of your live, you are blessed. Just like the writer says in Colossians, "In whatever you do, give thanks to the Lord."

LONGEST NIGHT OF THE YEAR

> *John 1:5* <

The light shines in the darkness. but the darkness has not understood it.

Every year, on December 21, also known as winter solstice, the Western Hemisphere experiences the longest night of the year. That night in North America will last 14 hours and 28 minutes. For most of us that's no big deal other than it will get dark really early and stay dark until we wake up the next morning. It's a completely different story for those in our country who are homeless.

Nights are very difficult times for the homeless. It's a scary, dark, and cold time they have to endure full of uncertainty and fear. The longest night of the year is also in the middle of December which can also make it one of the coldest night of the year. For those who sleep underneath overpasses, in parks, and in the back alleys of our cities and towns, this can be one of the most trying nights of each year. The Gospel of John reminds us that we're people of light not of darkness. We are to be people who run off the darkness with the light of God through Jesus. Now I don't believe that God is calling us to try to change the natural cycle of the earth and the planets on this night. I do believe that we can be bearers of light on this and other very dark and cold nights for our brothers and sisters on the streets. We can be the bearers of light with warm blankets, hot food, conversation, and shelter.

We have the opportunity on this longest night of the year, not only to comfort those who are in need, but to also raise awareness that they are there, hurting and suffering in our midst. Be bearers of light, a light that the darkness cannot overcome, on this longest night of the year.